BULLIES

HOW THE LEFT'S CULTURE OF FEAR AND INTIMIDATION SILENCES AMERICANS

BEN SHAPIRO

THRESHOLD EDITIONS
New York London Toronto Sydney New Delhi

Threshold Editions
A Division of Simon & Schuster, Inc.
1230 Avenue of the Americas
New York, NY 10020

First Threshold Editions hardcover edition January 2013

Designed by Claudia Martinez

Manufactured in the United States of America

10 9 8 7 6 5 4 3 2 1

Library of Congress Cataloging-in-Publication Data

Shapiro, Ben.
Bullies : how the left's culture of fear and intimidation silences America / Ben Shapiro.
p. cm.
Summary: "From the editor-at-large of Breitbart.com comes a galvanizing and alarming look at the strategy of leftist thuggery to silence their opponents"—Provided by publisher.
1. Threat (Psychology)—United States. 2. Intimidation—United States. 3. Bullying—United States. 4. Liberalism—United States. 5. Right and left (Political science)—United States. I. Title.
BF575.T45S53 2013
320.51'30973—dc23
2012030633

ISBN 978-1-4767-0999-4
ISBN 978-1-4767-1001-3 (ebook)

TO MY FRIEND AND MENTOR, THE IRREPLACEABLE
ANDREW BREITBART

CONTENTS

BULLIES

★

INTRODUCTION

★

On March 10, 2011, President Barack Obama led a White House conference on a crisis plaguing America: the crisis of bullying.

In the middle of the greatest economic collapse since the Great Depression, with American soldiers involved in two wars overseas, with Iran on the brink of nuclear weapons development, the White House was focused, laserlike, on kids getting thrown into lockers.

There had been no measurable uptick in school bullying across America. In fact, by all available statistics, bullying is down across the board, with young Americans demonstrating particular tolerance for those of different backgrounds. All Americans, virtually without exception, hate bullies.[1] But President Obama felt the necessity to call leaders across America together to decry bullying.

"Bullying isn't a problem that makes headlines every day," the president said, his sonorous baritone trembling with emotion. "But every day it touches the lives of young people all across this country. . . . And that's why we're here today. If there's one goal of this conference, it's to dispel the myth that bullying is just a harmless rite of passage or an inevitable part of growing up. It's not."[2]

Obama didn't stop there. He appeared on Cartoon Network to preface a documentary on bullying, solemnly intoning, "I care about this issue deeply, not just as the president, but as a dad. . . . We've all got more to do. Everyone has to take action against bullying."[3] He launched a website under the auspices of the Department of Health and Human Services, StopBullying.gov—because God knows that HHS shouldn't be utilizing its resources on, say, fighting cancer. Obama even cut videos on behalf of anti-bullying groups like the It Gets Better campaign.

So, what prompted President Obama's sudden recognition, two years after taking office, that bullying was an issue worth tackling? Jonathan Capehart, an Obama administration ally at the *Washington Post*, asked White House senior advisor and Obama mentor Valerie Jarrett exactly that question the day of the White House conference. Taking on bullying, Jarrett admitted, was part of the president's "Winning the Future" campaign strategy. In fact, the goal was to recruit all Americans as part of Obama's anti-bullying campaign: "The purpose here is to engage people in that conversation and to give it the spotlight of the White House so that perhaps people who've been ignoring this issue or weren't aware of it—we can capture their attention. . . . Everybody in the community has a role to play. Not just parents and students."[4]

What could a childless eighty-year-old shut-in from Hoboken, for example, do about bullying? Obama and Jarrett never made that clear. What they did make clear, however, was that bullying—not just school bullying—was something that had to be fought. Americans had to take up the challenge. America had to become an anti-bullying country.

This was a weird pitch, to say the least. After all, America has the greatest anti-bullying record of any country in human history. America *hates* bullies. Over the course of the twentieth century,

America defeated Nazism and communism abroad, Jim Crow and sexism at home. Why would Americans—Americans, of all people on earth—need a remedial course in anti-bullying?

We didn't. We just needed a bit of Obama reeducation.

The strategy here was simple. Obama and his friends in the media and on the organized left picked the one thing all Americans can agree on: bullying. They strategically placed President Obama at the head of the anti-bullying cause. Then came the brilliant gambit: they appropriated bullying to apply only to anything remotely conservative.

The Tea Party? A bunch of bullies. Religious people? Bullies. Global warming unbelievers, defense hawks, venture capitalists, fans of voter identification or traditional marriage, opponents of affirmative action, right-to-work advocates, supporters of Israel, haters of *Glee*? Bullies. Those who dislike President Obama? They were the biggest bullies of all. Liberalism and anti-bullying, it turned out, were—miracle of miracles!—one and the same.

Their twisted logic was deceptively easy. Liberals claim that they are all about protecting victim classes from bullies. Conservatives oppose liberals. Therefore, by definition, conservatives must be bullies. And bullies must be stopped.

This was the Obama campaign's entire reelection strategy. Everyone is against bullying; unite Americans behind Obama on bullying; then redefine bullying to include everything that Obama and the left oppose. Voilà! A unified coalition against bullying becomes a unified coalition against conservatism. Leftists, by definition, become anti-bullying pugilists standing up for the little guy; right-wingers, by definition, become bullies who ought to be punched in the mouth.

The Obama embrace of the anti-bullying cause, and the subsequent linguistic trick of conflating anti-bullying with anti-conservatism, is the single best bully tactic in the history of American politics. The liberal anti-bullying campaign justifies every leftist thug tactic they've ever embraced.

It's not a new tactic. Victims hold a cherished place in the liberal heart. With victimhood comes moral power, and the power to extort the supposed victimizers. Liberals have always claimed to be fighting bullies. The only difference is that now the president of the United States openly conflates opposing his agenda with bullying.

To that end, President Obama routinely plays the victim. He's told us—even as he plays the race card—that people treat him differently because he has a "funny name" and because if he had a son, he'd look like Trayvon Martin. He trots out race flaks like 9/11 truther Touré to suggest that white people—the same white people who idiotically voted him into office—have been turned violent by the rise of a successful black man. He's got Tom Hanks narrating a campaign video in which he suggests that Obama's failures are due to this naïve, beautiful waif of a man facing down the harsh realities of scum-sucking Republicans who oppose Glorious Change. No wonder Obama looks like he's lost weight. He's been lugging that gigantic cross around for the last four years.

But, says the Obama campaign, there is a way to end Obama's victimization. Vote for him. And destroy anybody who opposes him.

See, that's the dirty little secret: buried beneath all of the left's supposed hatred for bullying is a passionate *love* for bullying—the use of power to force those who disagree to shut up, back down, or face crushing consequences up to and including loss of reputation, career destruction, and even death.

The left's anti-bullying stance is an enormous lie. It is a purposeful lie. It is a lie designed to disguise the fact that leftists are the greatest group of bullies in American history.

The day before Andrew Breitbart died, he was obsessing, as he often did, about Media Matters for America, the George Soros–funded, Obama-connected think tank dedicated to pressuring its opponents into silence. Andrew had recently dictated a column to me in which he ripped the founder of Media Matters, former conservative turncoat David Brock. Media Matters, Andrew wrote, was a mechanism to promote a "special brand of David Brock career-enhancing blindly self-motivated political assassinations."

Brock and company, Andrew would point out again and again, were the worst kind of bullies.

And Andrew hated bullies.

In fact, he hated them so much that he'd go around the office shouting it from the rafters. Literally.

The Breitbart offices had recently been relocated in a bizarre 1990s-style dot-com-bust warehouse. It was a storage garage with no light, a giant green screen that doubled as a home for the Ping-Pong table (Andrew played while chatting on his cell phone), a group of chairs apparently hijacked from the set of *Austin Powers*, and a balcony that lined the walls and looked down on the common area below. Andrew would sit up top; the rest of the editorial team had desks up top, too, but we'd often sit below in group formation.

And every so often, we'd hear him shout at random: "I hate these people!"

Andrew had a very clear picture of himself. He wasn't a philosopher. He wasn't an academic. He was a fighter. "A lot of what has happened to me," he once told me, "is less because of what I know what it is that needs to be protected, than that I've fundamentally figured out what the left wants to destroy." And what they wanted to destroy, more than anything, was American freedom. America, Andrew said, was about one simple message: "Follow your individual dreams, hopes, and aspirations. America provides all men, all women, of all religions, the opportunity to pursue life, liberty, and happiness. That's about as sexy a selling point to a nation as I can possibly imagine."

The reason Andrew hated the left is that he recognized what they were trying to do. They were trying to separate Americans from one another by pitting "victims" against "bullies." "The left has created a false order that separates people away from *e pluribus unum*, one from many, where we have our language and our culture, our Constitution in common," he explained. "And it has separated us into these artificial sections and then pitted them against one another. And it's achieved all that by portraying one side of the aisle as motivated by base, nasty faults like racism and sexism and greed."

The left, Andrew knew, has rammed large chunks of its radical socialist agenda down Americans' throats, and they've done so with one simple tactic: bullying.

One of Andrew's earliest experiences with this phenomenon came long before he became a conservative.

Andrew barely graduated from Tulane University, where he indulged in every vice imaginable. When Andrew got back to Los Angeles from Tulane, he decided to get a job and become a productive citizen. He began working at a "very liberal, hipster place in Venice called Hal's." It was Andrew's favorite restaurant—and Andrew fit right in. He was a self-described "brain-dead liberal." But there was one guy who worked there who would make Andrew's life miserable—an African-American fellow I'll call Will. Will used to target Andrew and accuse him of racism at every possible turn—despite the fact that Andrew had, at Tulane, been the sole sponsor of the first black pledge in the history of his fraternity.

Andrew recalled being stunned by Will's hostility. "I thought, 'But you don't understand, Will. I'm a liberal Jew. I'm for you, baby!' But there was no hoop [I could jump through], nothing I could say to him that didn't reinforce his hatred of me. I thought my newfound liberalism was a badge that granted me absolution. And I kept playing it."

It didn't work. And soon enough, the Andrew Breitbart we all came to know and love came to the forefront. The jaw-jutting, take-on-the-world Andrew Breitbart who wouldn't take crap from anyone, especially bullies.

"Finally," Andrew told me, "I started to taunt him. I finally got my first taste of going against the politically correct grain . . . I started punching back. I started mocking him. . . . That was one of the first moments it occurred to me: these liberals are bullies."

And, Andrew said with a grin, "I realized how fun it is to call out these intellectual bullies."

It was this task that got Andrew up in the morning. It's the fight he sought. It's the fight in which he reveled.

Andrew's fight really had two components. The first was exposing the fact that the left is filled with bullies. Andrew planned gambit after gambit intended to draw them into the open. That's why he helped build the *Huffington Post*. "The goal," he said, "was to expose the left for how crazy they were." In that he succeeded beyond his wildest dreams.

But Andrew's favorite tool, of course, was Twitter, where hateful leftists spewed enough bile at him to melt through six feet of titanium. Andrew was the father of the now-famous Twitter tactic: retweeting the hate. He loved to show the world what nasty people resided on the supposed kind and tolerant left. As he tweeted the week he died, "My fave leftist H8 tweets are ones that drip with desire to inflict emotional pain. The desperation is deliciously palpable."

Andrew made the left insane. And he knew it. They accused him of cocaine use, alcoholism, homosexuality (he got particular joy from that label, since he never considered it an insult as the left apparently did). He tweeted two days before he died, "For all my alleged drinking, coking & homosexualizing, I've managed the time to get really under the skin of organized left."

There was no question about that. Bullies can't deal with those who stand up to them.

I knew that Andrew hated bullies from the day I met him. Back in 2001, Andrew, hanging out in Westwood, picked up a copy of the UCLA *Daily Bruin*. I was a columnist for the *Bruin* at the time—actually, their token conservative columnist. The column was well read around campus, mainly because it was the only column in the paper that provided a different opinion from the politically correct bull that pervaded the rest of the pages.

Andrew saw my column and emailed me. The email went something like this: "Hey, my name's Andrew, and I work with Matt Drudge. I'd love to get together."

And that's how, at age seventeen, I found myself sitting across from an anonymous webmaster, listening to him unravel the mysteries of the leftist universe. And first and foremost on Andrew's mind was bullying. Political correctness, Andrew said, was a form of bullying. And he was overjoyed to see somebody hitting the bullies back.

We were friends from then on. We talked regularly as I went through UCLA, got a syndicated column with Creators Syndicate, and wrote my first books; he came over to my parents' house for dinner with his beautiful family; we chatted frequently as I went through Harvard Law. When he wrote his book, I had the tremendous honor of giving him comments. By the time he hired me in February 2012 to be editor-at-large of Breitbart News, we'd known each other for more than a decade. He termed it "the longest flirtation in political history."

I started work formally with Andrew the day before his famed speech at the Conservative Political Action Conference, better known as CPAC, in which he told President Obama that we'd be vetting him. I watched him stalk out to the Occupy bullies and tell them to stop raping people.

Three weeks later, he was gone.

On the morning after Andrew died, I went into the office early and sat a couple of desks down from his. He'd left his computer on, and it pinged every few seconds as his emails began to come in.

Later, we went through the emails. We also went through the tweets. And, not surprisingly, a huge swath of them were unbelievably hateful.

"It is very hard to have sympathy for an evil person like Andrew Breitbart!" wrote one tweeter. "I am done being NICE."

"America truly lost an a—h—. I'm sure Satan will treat him good."

"Ya reap what ya sow #breitbart."

"L.A. Coroner confirms Andrew Breitbart will lie no more."

All day, the hate flowed in. The leftist bullies came out of the woodwork to celebrate his death. Andrew's wife, Suzie, received a Hallmark card telling her how happy the anonymous writer was that Andrew was dead.

"Even in death," tweeted Michelle Malkin, "@andrewbreitbart exposes the rabid Left's intolerance."

The worst of the worst offenders was Matt Taibbi of *Rolling Stone*. Before Andrew's body was cold, he put up a long column titled "Death of a Douche":

> So Andrew Breitbart is dead. Here's what I have to say to that, and I'm sure Breitbart himself would have respected this reaction: *Good!* F—him. I couldn't be happier that he's dead. . . . Good riddance, c—s—er. Don't let the door hit you on the way out.

Andrew despised Taibbi, and with good reason—Taibbi was a shock troop for what Andrew called the Democrat-Media Complex. But Andrew would have been perfectly happy to see Taibbi do what he did. Andrew drew the hatred of the left like a zapper does moths.

Then he zapped them.

Which is precisely what happened to Taibbi. His Wikipedia page was hacked and rewritten. Hilariously, Taibbi failed to understand that Andrew wasn't just about exposing the hate, he was about fighting it.

And the right must understand that, too. Conservatives have allowed liberals to win the culture war because we're generally civil people. When the left says we're uncivil, we tend to shy away from the fight rather than, as Andrew put it, walking toward the fire.

That's a huge mistake. A century of civility has bought us a century of liberalism. We're not the thugs here. They are.

Bullying is the left's go-to tactic. It has become a way of life for them. Leftists think and act like protofascists. Control is the key. And control through fear, threat of force, and rhetorical intimidation is the modus operandi.

Now, we're not talking about legislation here. All legislation is inherently coercive: it forces somebody to do something. That's not bullying, because it takes form via a consent process—we vote for the clowns who put our laws into place.

When we talk about political bullying, we're talking about the bullying of private citizens by government actors, media heavies, Hollywood, and organizational allies outside of government. *That* sort of bullying creates a climate of fear among Americans, forcing them to abandon cherished principles, back nasty causes, or shut up entirely. And the left relies on that sort of bullying to the exclusion of all other tactics.

Barack Obama is a Chicago thug who threatened during 2008, "If they bring a knife to the fight, we bring a gun." Obama surrounded himself with the worst sort of hatchet men. Guys like Rahm Emanuel, who sent dead fish to political opponents and reportedly accosted unfriendly congressmen naked in the House showers. People like Van Jones, who suggested that the Bush administration "may indeed have deliberately allowed 9/11 to happen," and who later founded an Obama-associated group called ColorOfChange, designed to destroy Obama's political opponents. Folks like Robert Gibbs, who said that Obama would have to put his foot on the neck of British Petroleum. During the 2012 campaign, Obama ratcheted it up—as one aide reported, Obama was "putting the bully in bully pulpit."[5]

And he opened the White House to other bullies. Andrew Sullivan, the former gay conservative journalist turned radical leftist, suggested that Sarah Palin didn't give birth to her own child, Trig—and for that, Sullivan earned a White House invitation to a state dinner with Great Britain. Louis C.K.—the monotone comedian most famous for his despicably vulgar tweets, which we will thankfully not confront until later—went to the

White House, too, and visited with White House speechwriter Jonathan Favreau. Joy Behar of *The View* also got to visit the White House—well after she had called Nevada U.S. Senate candidate Sharron Angle a "b—," of course. Obama accepted $1 million from once-humorous jester dwarf Bill Maher, who called Sarah Palin a "c—t." Meanwhile, Obama's media allies granted all of these establishment left figures the patina of "objectivity" and legitimacy.

It's not just Obama and friends of Obama, either. The bullies pervade the left. They come in all shapes and sizes. They're a diverse crowd. They're black and white and Hispanic and Asian and Jewish and Christian. They're environmentalists and socialists and pacifists and feminists. But they all share an ideology. And they all share a love for grinding their opponents under their heel with absolute lies.

They ooze from every green nook and every red cranny. Anti-American bullies portray America as a force for evil in the world, a great maw of global nastiness, chewing up subject populations (usually "brown" and "yellow") on behalf of their corporate overlords. They are, like Senator Dick Durbin (D-IL), believers that the American military is filled with Pol Pot knockoffs and Hitler and Stalin fans; they think, like John Kerry (D-MA), that the military is filled with morons who just couldn't make it in life and instead ended up in the deserts of Iraq. They label America a terrorist nation.

Race bullies like Al Sharpton help incite riots ending in murder, trumpet charges against innocent district attorneys, or threaten civil disobedience to small towns in Florida; groups like the Nation of Islam and the New Black Panthers stand outside polling places with billy clubs, all with the approval of leftist power players like the Eric Holder Department of Justice. Immigration bullies send death threats to Arizona governor Jan Brewer for enforcing the border, or compare Arizona to the Third Reich.

Class bullies like the Occupy Wall Street Neanderthals fling poop and urine while chanting incoherently at the behest of their union paymasters; government redistributionist bullies like Obama threaten corporations with "the pitchforks" should the corporations fail to give Obama and his cronies what they want.

Feminist bullies call pro-life women traitors to the female gender for not supporting the liberal agenda. Gay activist bullies are perhaps the most vicious of all, destroying careers, outing enemies, and insisting that schoolchildren be indoctrinated with homosexual history.

Environmentalist bullies like Obama science czar John Holdren pen books suggesting forced abortion and mandatory sterilization as potential solutions to planetary overcrowding. Secular bullies follow President Obama's lead, ripping religious folks as Dark Age morons, "bitter clingers" who think God is important only because they're racist and ignorant. Anti-Israel bullies like M. J. "Alfred" Rosenberg of Media Matters label pro-Israel Jews "Israel Firsters," mirroring the worst attributes of white supremacist rhetoric; others, like Stephen Walt and John Mearsheimer, write books talking about how the Jews control government with their dirty Hebe money.

The bullying strategy couldn't work without a complex public relations, governmental, and astroturfed strategy. And that's precisely what the left has constructed.

The old-school strategy for the left was easy: use the government to bully your opponents. President Clinton used the FBI and Department of Justice as his personal enemy-fighting force, unleashing them on Republican opponents.

Obama has done this, too. During the 2008 campaign, Obama minions famously went after Joe the Plumber, digging up his tax records illegally after he had the temerity to ask Obama about his tax policy. During the 2012 campaign, Obama ratcheted up such tactics. Even as Obama played the victim, asking his supporters to "get Barack's back"—normally, that's the job of the Secret Service—he targeted private citizens for destruction simply because they opposed him.

But all of this is old hat. It's out in the open, and it's easy to spot and fight.

So the left has gotten more sophisticated. Where Clinton used the levers of government to target his opponents directly, Obama's strategy is more subtle: he coordinates with his extragovernmental allies to launch devastating attacks on political enemies.

It begins inside the White House and the Democratic Party, where anti-conservative strategies are hatched. The White House begins putting out its talking points via groups like the Center for American Progress and David Brock's Media Matters. Those groups put in phone calls and emails to their allies in the mainstream media—people like Ben Smith at BuzzFeed, the crew at MSNBC, Greg Sargent and E. J. Dionne at the *Washington Post*, Sam Stein and Nico Pitney at *Huffington Post*, and Brian Stelter at the *New York Times*, among others.

That's the media strategy. And that's why you'll hear a Greek chorus chanting mantras in unison: "War on women!" "Racial profiling!" "The 1 percent!" Zubin Mehta couldn't conduct the media any better than the Democratic Party does.

But the media isn't enough: liberals need public support. Or at least the appearance of public support. That's where Media Matters and its allies in unions across the country play a crucial role. These groups work with other Obama allies to boycott advertisers who have the temerity to spend their money on shows Obama doesn't like. So far, this strategy has resulted in massive astroturfed attacks on Don Imus, Lou Dobbs, Glenn Beck, Rush Limbaugh, Susan G. Komen for the Cure, and the American Legislative Exchange Council. And it won't stop there. Businesses are Alinskyed—targeted, isolated, destroyed. It doesn't matter that the businesses have nothing to do with politics. If they're spending money on Rush, they have to be smacked around. Individuals, too, are destroyed—if they're backing efforts like Proposition 8 in California, their restaurants should be boycotted, their jobs should be stripped from them. They should be bullied into submission.

Finally, there's the government itself. With the media supposedly creating public outcry—and with Media Matters and friends building fake public outcry to match the media's propagandizing—the perfect loop has been created. Now there's supposed support for legislation. Bring on the Lily Ledbetter Act, or whatever the latest trial lawyer giveaway is. Knock down the "stand your ground" laws. Destroy state voter ID laws. Or whatever the hot cause of the moment is.

It's a wonderful strategy. And it works, so long as the American people remain silent.

Incredibly, for the past few decades, the American people have remained silent. That's because they're scared of the left. And rightly so.

This isn't to say there aren't bullies on the right, people who want to shut up their political opponents. Of course there are. But as a practical matter, bullying requires power—and when it comes to politics, all the centers of power are inherently geared toward the left. The government is one center of power; its power grows as its size grows. Because the left believes that government growth is the end goal of all politics, the left tends to utilize the government as a coercive tool far more than the right does. The press is a second center of power; the press is massively biased toward the left. The same holds true of Hollywood. The education system in America is a fourth center of power, and it too skews left, both for reasons of government funding and for ideological reasons. The heretofore undiscovered fifth center of power in American politics is nonprofit organizations, which have been utilized to great effect by both sides—but in which only leftist nonprofits receive significant government support, and therefore have a tremendous advantage.

Power derives from institutions. The right thinks individually; the left thinks institutionally. And so the left wields more power, and therefore has far more opportunity to bully.

As an ideological matter, too, the left has far more of a tendency to bully than the right. This plain fact makes the left insanely uncomfortable—hence their pathetic attempts to categorize the National Socialist (Nazi) Party in Germany as a right-wing party, and even to brand Castro, Mao, and Stalin as right-wing authoritarians. But it is leftism that insists that collective needs trump individual needs, that freedom be subjected to societal dictates, and that rights spring not from nature or God, but from the state. It is a left-wing point of view that says that to make an omelet, you have to bully a few eggs.

The left likes to bully, and it's good at it. The predictable outcome has been the incredible rise of the American left in a country that leans to the right.

Domestically, the left has been able to bully Americans into accepting abortion-on-demand as somehow mandated by emanations, penumbras, and Casper the Friendly Ghost in the Constitution. The left has forced Americans into accepting the radical redefinition of economic freedom to encompass government control over how you flush your toilet; unwed motherhood as equal in moral quality and outcome to traditional family structure; the complete removal of religion from public life, and its replacement with vulgarity; rejection of a color-blind society in favor of reverse racism; the creation of a massive social safety net that provides safety for the lazy and a net for the productive. The list goes on and on.

America was a nation built on the notion that nobody should be bullied by the government. That's what freedom means. Now the left has convinced Americans that they're bullies if they *oppose* the increasing encroachment of government. We're bullies if we want to control our own fate. We're victims if we don't get to control how other people live their lives.

When it comes to foreign policy, the left has completely reversed notions of American goodness. America has destroyed more bullies than every other nation in the history of mankind combined. We started as a rebel nation against the bully and tyrant King George III; we continued to fight the good fight against slavery; we took down the Kaiser and Hitler; we brought down the

Soviet Union and Saddam Hussein and the Taliban; we prevented the domination of South Korea and, if the left had allowed for it, would have prevented the domination of Vietnam by bullies.

And yet the left has convinced the world—and many Americans—that America is the world's biggest bully. Patriotism, they say, is bullying; dissent, they say, is patriotism. When America was struck on September 11, 2001, leftists like Professor Ward Churchill described the victims as the "technocratic corps at the very heart of America's global financial empire . . . little Eichmanns." We were the bad guys. We deserved it, because we are global bullies, and bullies deserve chickens coming home to roost, in the words of Jeremiah Wright.

Like any good bullies, these ones deserve an enormous punch in the face. But you're considered a bully if you suggest that hating America might be mildly unpatriotic. And you're considered a flag-waver if you're a flag-burner.

This is the world the left has bequeathed to us. It is filled with lies; it says that truth is thuggish, and obfuscation of truth a required element of civility. It says that moral clarity is nasty and uncouth, and moral relativism morally preferable. It reverses bullies and victims, emboldening the world's true bullies in the process.

That promise the founders made to us—what Andrew called the sexiest selling point in human history—has been turned into the mark of Cain by the left.

"I hate these people," Andrew said. He exposed them. And he fought them.

"I see exactly what is going on here," Andrew said to me about two years before he died. "It is my unfortunate burden to take my understanding of what these people are, what their tactics are, and to start trying to form an army to destroy them."

Now we must pick up Andrew's torch. We must expose the bullies. And we must stand up to them.

1.

★

INSTITUTIONAL BULLIES

For decades, the biggest problem for conservatives—and the biggest advantage for liberals—has been the fact that conservatives think individually, while liberals think institutionally. Think about politics in terms of religious outreach. Conservatives are like Jehovah's Witnesses, going door to door, trying to convince people of the truth of their teachings. Liberals are like radical Muslims, toppling governments and installing shariah law, then forcibly converting enormous masses of the population.

That's why all the major instruments of political persuasion are in the hands of liberals. And it's also why liberalism, though almost invariably based on pernicious and dangerous misinterpretation at best, and outright falsehood at worst, has been ascendant in America for the last hundred years.

Look at every major bully move by the left over the past few decades and you'll be able to spot the coordination between the left's instruments. The politicians and regulators work with the unions; the unions work with the journalists; the journalists work with the Hollywood clique; the Hollywood clique works with the leftist charitable foundations; the leftist charitable foundations work with the university professors; the university professors work with the judges. And all of them work with each other.

There is only one way to make an institution *conservativerein.* It has to be purged.

Now, in America, we generally don't look fondly on Soviet-style purges, complete with gulags and hastily dug graves. And so the American left has stayed away from that sort of thing. The left *has* taken advantage, however, of the American freedom to employ and work with whom you choose. The left doesn't do anything illegal in preventing their ideological opponents from working. They just do something tremendously immoral—and unbelievably hypocritical, considering that they want private religious schools to have to employ transvestites who show up one day wearing a feather boa and a tutu.

To understand just how the system of bullying works, we need to explore how the left took over the institutions that enable that bullying—and we have to take a look at how the current system works.

MEDIA BULLIES

On April 18, 2006, police arrested Duke University lacrosse players Reade Seligmann and Collin Finnerty for the alleged rape and kidnapping of stripper Crystal Mangum. Mangum had falsely accused three white lacrosse players of raping her at a March party; the entire 2006 Duke lacrosse season was ultimately canceled.

The media couldn't get enough of the case. They quickly turned it into an example of white-on-black racism, brutal exploitation in the mold of pre–Civil War slavery. Amanda Marcotte, a feminist bully blogger, attacked CNN for not immediately condemning the accused: "Can't a few white boys sexually assault a black woman anymore without people getting all wound up about it? So unfair." A few months later, Marcotte was hired by the John Edwards presidential campaign as an official blogger.[1] (As it turned out, there was actually a better shot that John Edwards had had sex with Crystal Mangum than that the Duke lacrosse players had.)

Marcotte may have been the loudest of the bunch, but she certainly wasn't the only journalist preternaturally eager to beat Duke lacrosse with a stripper pole. *USA Today* tracked down a Duke graduate student to complain, "I'm still afraid that the people involved will just get a slap on the wrist. Because of Duke's culture of privilege and superiority, they'll get away with it." That same reporter also lauded Duke students for distributing a flyer that "looked like a wanted poster: 40 faces of young men, smiling smugly for the camera. . . . These men are wanted on the Duke campus." Janet Reitman of *Rolling Stone* "reported" on Duke's "retro view of rape."[2] Reitman did not report on the strippers' retro view of perjury.

Nancy Grace of CNN led the disgraceful posse looking to string up the Duke defendants sans evidence. On June 9, 2006, Grace interviewed a local North Carolina reporter, who expressed the widespread sentiment that the case was falling apart already. Grace quickly whipped a Hitler mustache out of her back pocket and stapled it to the guy's upper lip: "Well I'm glad you have already decided the outcome of the case, based on all of the defense filings. Why don't we just all move to Nazi Germany, where we don't have a justice system and a jury of one's peers? What about it, Joe Lawless?"[3]

The *New York Times*, too, worked to keep the case alive, even as it began to crumble. Duff Wilson and Jonathan Glater penned a piece in August 2006 stating, "By disclosing pieces of evidence favorable to the defendants, the defense has created an image of a case heading for the rocks. But an examination of the entire 1,850 pages of evidence gathered by the prosecution in the four months after the accusation yields a more ambiguous picture. It shows that while there are big weaknesses in Mr. Nifong's case, there is also a body of evidence to support his decision to take the matter to a jury."[4]

Except that there wasn't a body of evidence to support it. As it turned out, the stripper accuser had told a second dancer at the lacrosse party to "put marks on me" to fake injury after the party; Nifong admitted he hadn't talked to the alleged victim as late as October. DNA tests showed no DNA from the supposed rapists. Seligmann, it turned out, had a solid alibi. Nifong, who was running for reelection as he was pursuing the case, ended up dropping it and resigning his job. But not before the *Times* ran more than one hundred pieces on the case.[5]

Even after the Duke lacrosse rape case fell apart, the liberal media wouldn't let it go. "As students of Duke University or other elite institutions, these young men will get on with their privileged lives," wrote Terry Moran of ABCNews.com. "They are very differently situated in life from, say, the young women of the Rutgers University women's basketball team."[6] The Rutgers basketball team had indeed been foolishly and nastily slandered as "nappy-headed hos" by radio host Don Imus, generating national headlines. But the Duke lacrosse team had been accused of a brutal lynch raping, which could have resulted in long prison sentences—and at the very least, would follow them the rest of their lives. But Terry Moran was comparing the two. Somehow, this didn't pass the smell test.

In the aftermath of the Duke lacrosse fiasco, those in the media held their noses and admitted culpability. "It was too delicious a story," said former *New York Times* public editor Daniel Okrent. "It conformed too well to too many preconceived notions of too many in the press: white over black, rich over poor, athletes over non-athletes, men over women, educated over non-educated. Wow. That's a package of sins that really fit the preconceptions of a lot of us."[7]

This was the crux of the matter. It wasn't that the media was fooled. They have the same reasoning skills as the rest of us—and it was clear within days of the Duke lacrosse allegations that the case was somewhere between the Loch Ness Monster and Bigfoot on the truth scale. So why didn't they catch on to the fact that all of this was less credible than Paris Hilton swearing chastity? Because they *wanted* it to be true. They *needed* it to be true. They had an agenda. And they were going to ensure that the story played out the way they wanted it to. The facts were irrelevant.

In the case of the Duke lacrosse faux rape, there was no real coordination between the media and other leftist power institutions. But often, that isn't the case. In situations of national importance, there is clear and convincing evidence of collusion between the leftist media and leftist politicians, interest groups, and other power brokers. And the media is the tip of that spear. They're the new IRS, sicced by the organized Democratic infrastructure to destroy anyone who dares defy them. While the much-derided blogosphere breaks virtually every big story these days—Weinergate, Rathergate, Trayvon Martin—the mainstream media lag behind. And snipes. Tina Brown of *Newsweek*, a formerly great publication recently sold for the bargain-basement price of one dollar, suggests that those in the blogosphere aren't "real journalists."

And she's right. She's right because all the real journalists are Democratic Party hacks.

In March 2009, *Politico*—a publication that used to play at objectivity, but has become an obviously key cog in the left-wing media—revealed the existence of "an off-the-record online meeting space called JournoList." The list was formed by Ezra Klein, a blogger for the far-left *American Prospect*—and who later became a columnist for the *Washington Post*. "Basically," he told Politico, "it's just a list where journalists and policy wonks can discuss issues freely." Which journalists? Eric Alterman of the *Nation;* Jeffrey Toobin of CNN and the *New Yorker;* Paul Krugman of the *New*

York Times; writers from the *Huffington Post, Politico, Newsweek*. The list went on and on.

And they sure did coordinate. In April 2008, journalists suddenly began ripping ABC's Democratic presidential debate coverage—particularly the focus on Barack Obama's longtime mentor and pastor Jeremiah Wright. It seemed like a grassroots phenomenon. Not quite. *Politico* reported, "POLITICO contacted nearly three dozen current JList members for this story. The majority either declined to comment or didn't respond to interview requests—and then returned to JList to post items on why they wouldn't be talking to POLITICO about what goes on there." But, said Toobin, "No one's pushing an agenda."[8]

Right.

In June 2009, Andrew Breitbart offered one hundred thousand dollars for a full emporium of all the JournoList emails. Nobody at JournoList took him up on the offer, though Ben Smith, then of *Politico*, played defense for JournoList: "This is a classic case in which secrecy produces wild imaginings. There aren't many good conspiracies involving 400 people, some of them ideologues, some columnists, some mainstream media types like me who enjoyed access to that conversation, as I sometimes enjoy access to private conservative conversations at venues like New York's off-record conservative Monday Meeting."[9] (Ben Smith, it's worth noting, minimizes left-wing scandal so often that John Nolte, one of my Breitbart News colleagues, has coined a term for the tactic: Ben-Smithing.) The point, of course, wasn't that every email in the JournoList chain was solid gold. The point was that these reporters were coordinating messages. Left-wing messages.

Klein, who organized the list, admitted it. "The membership would range from nonpartisan to liberal, center to left. I didn't like that rule, but I thought it necessary. . . . What I didn't expect was that a member of the list, or someone given access by a member of the list, would trawl through the archives to assemble a dossier of quotes from one particular member and then release them to an interested media outlet to embarrass him. But that's what happened to David Weigel."[10]

Weigel was, at the time, a *Washington Post* reporter. His job there was to report on conservatives.

You can guess what happened next.

On JournoList, it turned out, Weigel had been putting out one rabidly anti-conservative email after another. When Rush Limbaugh had chest pains, Weigel wrote, "I hope he fails. . . . Too soon?" Weigel wrote that conservatives used the media to "violently, angrily divide America," mainly because they were racists protecting "white privilege." And, of course, he went after the daddy of all right-wing influence wielders, Matt Drudge: "It's really a disgrace that an amoral shut-in like Drudge maintains the influence he does on the news cycle while gay-baiting, lying, and flubbing facts to this degree." As for Sarah Palin: "Let's move the f—on already." And on James O'Keefe, the man who broke ACORN, after O'Keefe's run-in with Louisiana authorities: "He's either going to get a radio talk show or start a prison ministry. That's was [*sic*] successful conservative ratf—ers do for their second acts."[11] Weigel had to step down from his job at the *Post*—and promptly began reporting for *Slate*. Had Weigel been a conservative masquerading at objectivity and unmasked politically, he would have found himself demonized by the mainstream media. But Weigel undoubtedly will at some point find himself serving in a Democratic administration. Then, after that, he can moderate presidential debates. After all, if it worked for George "the Keebler Elf" Stephanopoulos . . .

Now, none of this is to argue that conservative journalists don't talk among themselves and with people on their side of the political aisle. Of course they do. But they also don't hide behind the façade of objectivity. Michelle Malkin is conservative. So is Sean Hannity. Bill O'Reilly is a populist. Rush Limbaugh's a conservative. Conservative journalists are opinion journalists—and that doesn't stop them from breaking stories. In fact, it's that nonobjectivity that makes them more honest than the supposedly above-it-all crowd at the *New York Times*, which secretly shills for the Obama administration.

But the left-wing journalistic establishment, which actively fights to keep right-wingers out, as Bernard Goldberg of CBS News pointed out in his book *Bias*, still pretends that they're not biased. And that means that as their profit margins shrink, they call for aid from government. For the same reason that the government supports National Public Radio, they suggest, the government ought to support them.

Not surprisingly, President Obama thinks this is a great idea. "I haven't seen detailed proposals yet, but I'll be happy to look at them," he said of prospective bills that would grant tax breaks to failing newspapers to turn nonprofit. "I am concerned that if the direction of the news is all blogosphere, all opinions, with no serious fact-checking," said Obama, "no serious attempts to put stories into context, that what you will end up getting is people shouting at each other across the void but not a lot of mutual understanding."[12]

Or you might get a variety of voices that report the news from different angles. You could even call it something creative . . . like the "blogosphere," or something. You might end the hegemony of a Democratic journalistic establishment dedicated to upholding liberalism at all costs. And God knows, the media couldn't allow that—the left couldn't deal with the loss of control of viewpoint. The kind of control they had on the JournoList. And most of all, Obama couldn't allow that. If he did, what would happen to him, and the movement that stands behind him?

NONPROFIT BULLIES

In 2004, perverse former conservative David Brock, a highly paranoid alleged drug devotee, founded Media Matters for America. It was an offshoot of the John Podesta–run Center for American Progress (CAP). Podesta, of course, was the former chief of staff to

President Clinton, and CAP was a liberal nonprofit designed to act as an outlet for leftist politicians and viewpoints. CAP originally granted office space to Media Matters; Hillary Clinton advised it, and one of her closest confidants received some $200,000 to help out.[13] Clinton even explained, "I only wish that we had this active and fighting blogosphere about 15 years ago because we have certainly suffered over the last years from a real imbalance in the political world in our country. But we are righting that balance—or lefting that balance—not sure which, and we are certainly better prepared and more focused on taking our arguments and making them effective and disseminating them widely and really putting together a network in the blogosphere in a lot of the new progressive infrastructure—institutions that I helped to start and support like Media Matters and Center for American Progress. We're beginning to match what I had said for years was the advantage of the other side."[14]

The goal of Media Matters was simple: play defense for liberal politicians. And do it by attacking mercilessly all right-wing points of view.

Media Matters' bias is so obvious that even wild leftists like NBC's Chuck Todd, who has a shrine to President Obama complete with lubricants and scented candles, can't deal with them. Back in 2007, he pointed out that Media Matters was shilling for its erstwhile ally, Hillary, with a list of don'ts suggested for debate moderators. "Their 'don'ts' read more like facetious attacks on Edwards and Obama—right out of the oppo shop of either the RNC or, say, opponents of Edwards and Obama. By repeating these things, isn't Media Matters doing Clinton or other opponents of Edwards and Obama a favor?"[15] Or, as David Folkenflik of NPR put it, "They're looking at every dangling participle, every dependent clause, every semicolon, every quotation—to see if there's some way it unfairly frames a cause, a party, a candidate, that they may have some feelings for."[16]

It didn't matter. The left loved it. As the *New York Times* reported, producers for *The Daily Show* with Jon Stewart and *The Colbert Report* coordinate regularly with Media Matters. James Carville, master Democrat strategist, says, "It was always kind of a dream, that we needed something like that."[17]

The funding flowed in, especially from leftist bullies like George Soros and the Tides Foundation. By November 2008, the organization—which, remember, provided no actual services other than Alinskyite distortion of conservative words—had grown to more than one hundred employees and $8 million in budget. While its longtime boss, Eric Burns, insisted that the organization had "leveled the playing field and maybe given Barack Obama a fair shake," he said, "I'm not the Obama campaign. We're an independent organization not beholden to anybody. . . . It's bigger than any one candidate, it's bigger than any one election."[18]

This is Media Matters' favorite line. They constantly say they're not coordinating with President Obama. That's a lie.

As it turns out, Media Matters is in the back pocket of the Obama administration—and acts as their go-between for other media outlets. When Brock wasn't too busy reportedly indulging in illicit substances,[19] he raised $50,000 for Obama. What's more shocking is that Brock's organization coordinates on a weekly basis with the White House. They were planning to spend some $20 million in 2012 to help Obama. Anita Dunn, a high-ranking Obama administration member, used to visit the Media Matters headquarters regularly.

And they scored hit after hit against Obama enemy after Obama enemy. As the *Daily Caller* reported, they worked with other groups like ColorOfChange, Van Jones's nonprofit, to organize astroturfed campaigns against figures like Glenn Beck and Lou Dobbs.

But just as importantly, they were funneling White House talking points to media outlets, which were willingly taking them. "In '08 it became pretty apparent MSNBC was going left," one source told the *Caller*. "They were using our research to write their stories." Media Matters staffers apparently called MSNBC president Phil Griffin regularly. They were also in touch with Greg Sargent of the *Washington Post; Daily Kos;* Sam Stein and Nico Pitney of *Huffington Post;* Jim Rainey at the *Los Angeles Times;* Eugene Robinson and E. J. Dionne at the *Washington Post;* and Brian Stelter at the *New York Times*. And, of course, Ben Smith. If a reporter didn't work with Media Matters and published something Media Matters didn't like, they'd get smacked by thousands of emails inundating them for bias.[20]

How close was the coordination between Media Matters and the White House? So close that Alan Dershowitz, no ardent right-winger, suggested that he'd support President Obama only if he disassociated from Media Matters. Why? Media Matters' senior foreign policy reporter, M. J. Rosenberg, was a massive anti-Semite who routinely used the white supremacist phrase "Israel Firsters" when describing pro-Israel Jews.[21]

Within a few weeks, Rosenberg had stepped down at Media Matters. Rosenberg himself spelled out the rationale for his resignation: "The reason for this step is that it disturbed me greatly to see an organization to which I am devoted facing possible harm because of my critical writings about Israel. I have no doubt that the crowd that opposes any and all criticism of Israeli government policies will continue to turn its guns on Media Matters if I am associated with it. I could not live with myself if that happened—not only because I care deeply about the organization and my colleagues, but also because Media Matters does such important work confronting the lies that emanate from the far right and especially Fox News."[22]

In other words, President Obama told Media Matters to toss Rosenberg under the bus. Rosenberg would still be able to use Media Matters resources, of course.

Now, all of this would be fine and dandy, except for one small problem: Media Matters is a charitable nonprofit organization. One element of that status: organizations can't "attempt to influence legislation as a substantial part of its activities" or "participate in any campaign activity for or against political candidates." In particular, Media Matters is distinguished from its conservative counterparts by the fact that it actually engages in partisan training for Democratic campaigns—like the "Progressive Talent Initiative"—and the fact that it's covertly coordinating with the White House regularly.[23]

It's entirely possible that Media Matters isn't violating its nonprofit status. But the 501(c)3 world has come to be dominated by liberal organizations that bully the living hell out of their opponents in a way no conservative organization does or would. Leading boycotts against Rush Limbaugh, Glenn Beck, Don Imus, and Lou Dobbs? Par for the course for Media Matters, Center for American Progress, and the myriad other leftist surrogates set up by Democratic Party hacks. The use of such organizations to bully conservatives into silence is just the latest tool in the liberal arsenal. They want fewer voices, not more. And they'll work with their political allies to achieve their fascistic vision of politics.

UNIVERSITY BULLIES

There is no less tolerant place on the planet than the faculty lounges of America's major universities. Not only is dissent not tolerated, it's not even acknowledged to exist. Every poll of college faculty ever taken has shown an unhinged imbalance between conservatives and liberals on campuses. A recent 2012 poll showed that for every conservative professor, there were at least three liberals. And a full third openly admitted that ideology entered the classroom.[24] Older polls show a full 72 percent of American university and college faculty identifying as liberal, with just 15 percent conservative. At top universities, that statistic is 87 percent to 13 percent.[25]

Big government is worshipped on campus. While 60 percent of professors said that Ronald Reagan wasn't one of America's top ten presidents, a full 54 percent of professors, polled in 2012, thought that Franklin Roosevelt was America's best president ever—they must have missed those eight long years of the Great Depression prior to the start of World War II. If it weren't for FDR, the Great Depression would have been a lot less Great, and a lot less Depressed. But according to college professors, FDR is God.[26] If there were a God, that is. College professors are significantly less religious than the general public. Over half of professors say they never or rarely go to religious services; just 31 percent say they go to religious services regularly.[27]

Anti-Americanism runs rampant on college campuses. In fact, America's campuses are the only places where these ne'er-do-wells can find a job that doesn't involve a mop and a pail. Who else would employ former Palestine Liberation Organization spokesman and Obama bestie Rashid Khalidi? Or pay a rapping racialist who preaches communist theory upward of six figures to travel around the country lamenting the fate of poor blacks, as Cornel West does? Or keep fake Native Americans who believe that the victims of September 11 were "little Eichmanns" employed, as University of Colorado did with Ward Churchill? Or pick up the tab on terrorist professor Sami Al-Arian, who supported Hamas financially? The list of unmentionably bad employees goes on and on. And all of them are employed by the universities.

The question isn't why universities see fit to hand over six-figure salaries to unrepentant former terrorists Bernardine Dohrn and Bill Ayers. The question is why there's nobody on the other side of the aisle. And the answer is simple: in order to become a professor, you need other professors to oversee your Ph.D. studies. You can't hope to butt up against the liberal infrastructure and win. Conservatives are automatically weeded out of the system. Try getting a Ph.D. with a thesis about how FDR's policies destroyed America's fiscal health for the next century. Then get ready to distribute résumés to local fast-food joints.

So how did colleges become so liberal? Back in the 1940s and 1950s, colleges weren't nearly as liberal as they are now. But in the 1960s, college faculty decided it was easier to appease rampaging leftist students than to deal with them. They came to an agreement with the wildebeests: stop taking over the buildings and locking the doors, and we'll start teaching you about how America sucks. The professorial strategy on America's college campuses was the same as the management style there: surrender. Even as idiot smelly hippies rioted and brought the National Guard down upon them, America's leading leftist intellectual lights enabled them. "The present generation of young people in our universities are the best informed, the most intelligent and the most idealistic this country has ever known," said Professor Archibald Cox of Harvard Law School, my alma mater. That same year, 1968, there were well over two hundred demonstrations at American universities. It was students who led the violence at the Democratic National Convention that same year. No wonder Professor Louis Kampf of the Massachusetts Institute of Technology admitted, "[T]he young go into the profession with dread, the old can scarcely wait for retirement, and those of the middle years yearn for sabbaticals."[28]

Do colleges have an impact on the kids who attend them? You bet they do. Even though you thought you were ignoring your professor and chatting up the hot blonde in the back of your Philosophy 101 course, chances are that you had to take a final in that course. And chances are that if you wanted to do well in that final, citing Ayn Rand probably wasn't the best strategy. There's a reason studies show that people skew more liberal the longer they're in school. As of 2010, just 25 percent of people who graduated from high school supported same-sex marriage; for college graduates, that was 39 percent; for master's students, that was 46 percent.

And students don't get smarter over the same period—surveys also show that college seniors know just as little about basic civics as college freshmen do.[29] However, they do know infinitely more about where to find free condoms, and what environmentalist lines work best on idealistic leftist coeds (hint: the answer is "I work with dolphins").

The level of intolerance on college campuses for traditionally conservative thinking is astonishing. Religious people find themselves under assault from professors and administrations that despise their thinking. And meanwhile, those professors and administrators get paid substantial sums to generate white papers on behalf of liberal politicians. Want to be quoted in the *New York Times* about how evil George W. Bush is? Just grab a job at a top university. After all, the media's always looking for someone they can tag an "expert."

That's why Barack Obama and his cronies are constantly seeking to put more people into the college system. In his 2012 State of the Union address, he referred to kids going to college as an element of the "basic American promise." In February 2009, he said to a joint session of Congress, "Tonight, I ask every American to commit to at least one year or more of higher education or career training . . . every American will need to get more than a high school diploma." And in September 2011, he said, "Not only do you have to graduate from high school, but you're going to have to continue education after you leave. You have to not only graduate, but you've got to keep going after you graduate." And in May 2011: "I want every child . . . in America ready to graduate, ready to go to college. . . ."[30]

To that end, Obama has pushed for government to increase subsidization of student loan rates, making it less expensive for your kid to get that crucial degree in Lesbian Dance Theory. And, not coincidentally, for your kid to imbibe the liberalism that has poisoned the body politic at the universities.

HOLLYWOOD BULLIES

Hollywood is a liberal industry, and everybody knows it. Hollywood is full of bullies, and everybody knows it. Only in Hollywood are bullies like Harvey Weinstein—who reportedly is one of the nastiest people in Hollywood, a man who once headlocked and dragged *New York Observer* reporter Andrew Goldman out of an event, threatened to "beat the s—" out of director Julie Taymor's dinner companion, and told Democratic politico Terry McAuliffe "You motherf—er! I'll rip your balls off!"[31]—able to hypocritically produce movies like *Bully*. And then, of course, bully the ratings board to change the rating from R to PG-13.

Bullying in Hollywood is ubiquitous. It's ubiquitous from people like Barbra Streisand, who thinks it's ideological fascism to replace Robert Scheer with Jonah Goldberg in the pages of the *Los Angeles Times*[32] but demands that members of the servant class elevate her bed a specific number of degrees in hotels and recarpet her bedroom.[33] Mariah Carey requires an attendant to discard her gum.[34] Michael Moore demands an enormous hock of ham, a beanbag filled with Jell-O, and a whoopee cushion with George W. Bush's face. Okay, that last example isn't real. But the other ones are.

Nobody treats people worse than the biggest stars in Hollywood. Personally, they're bullies.

But ideologically, they're even bigger bullies. These stars all live in beautiful homes off Sunset Boulevard, ensconced behind walls of leaves and enormous staffs of personal attendants. They walk into bars in New York City, leave them looking like outtakes from a Bosnian documentary, and never get prosecuted. They get married, divorced, married, divorced again, married, go to drug rehab, get divorced, get married . . . and then finally announce they're gay, to the applause of the mainstream media. It's a great life.

Hollywood routinely discriminates against people who refuse to be bullied, as many top-level Hollywood executives, writers, and producers admitted to me. If you're a conservative in Hollywood, you stay underground for fear of firing. If you happen to have voted for California's Proposition 8, upholding traditional marriage, you keep that buried behind NSA-level security—the moment your peers find you out, you're out of a job. As Nicholas Meyer, director of *The Day After*, as well as writer of *Star Trek II*, *IV*, and *VI*, told me when asked about discrimination in Hollywood, "Well, I hope so." Or as Vin DiBona, producer of *MacGyver* and *America's Funniest Home Videos*, explained to me, "I think it's probably accurate [that there's anti-conservative discrimination] and I'm happy about it actually. . . . If the accusation is there, I'm okay with it."

The point? Only liberal content will be produced if liberals can bully conservatives out of the industry.

The Hollywood crowd engages with the political and media crowd on a regular basis, crafting narrative for the left. It's no surprise that President Obama and his regulatory friends have gone out of their way to focus on issues near and dear to Hollywood. They're his palace guard, bullying on his behalf—and doing it to tremendous effect.

CONCLUSION

All of these bullies act as a phalanx, targeting their opposition for destruction. And their bullying works. It works so well, in fact, that even the most untouchable people and institutions feel the wrath of their thuggishness.

Take, for example, Obamacare.

Now, for years, the media and Hollywood had coordinated to attack the American health-care system. Movies like *John Q* suggested that America's health-care system was massively discriminatory and required vigilante justice to set it straight. Every television show seemed to focus on some poor sap who lost his house because Grandma needed dialysis. The media, meanwhile, covered every bankruptcy, every sob story, from every person who developed a disease and didn't get proper insurance. This isn't to say that America's health system is perfect—it isn't. But by the time Barack Obama came to office, many Americans were under the impression that the American health-care system was worse than Zimbabwe's.

Rather than recognizing the fact that America's life-expectancy rate after cancer diagnosis was the best on the planet, rather than seeing that America's surgeons set the global standard, rather than understanding that America is the global leader in research and development in the medical field—and most of all, rather than spotting the obvious truth that overregulation and oversuing of the medical industry had set up a thicket of red tape, raising costs and lowering quality of care—the media and Hollywood portrayed America's health system as a paragon of failure. Not only that, they suggested that that failure was due to capitalism, not the forest of legal nonsense set up by well-meaning politicians (and politicians who'd been paid off).

By the time Obama took office, the ground was prepped.

Obama promptly created a faux groundswell in favor of complete overhaul of the health-care system in America. Nobody demanded it. In fact, most Americans wanted Obama focused on the economy. Mitt Romney ripped Obama for his failure to focus: "When you have an enterprise in trouble," he said, "the Number One rule is this: Focus, focus, focus."[35] Even the leftist media wondered what Obama was doing. "President Obama's goal of remaking the health care system was always going to be difficult to reach," lamented the *New York Times* in March 2009. "But as he prepares to begin a campaign for universal coverage this week, the ailing economy has complicated his task."[36]

But with the help of his friends—with the help of the folks at places like Center for American Progress, and his friends in the media, and his friends in Hollywood—Obama did what he wanted to do. He bullied the Tea Party; he suggested they were racist; he tore apart the insurance companies, denouncing them as greedy. He rammed his health-care plan down the throat of Americans. And Americans did what they wanted to do: they booted Nancy Pelosi and the Democrats from their perches of power in Congress in response.

That's when the most shocking bullying of all began.

See, there was one little problem with President Obama's health-care plan: it was blatantly unconstitutional. The Constitution of the United States does not allow the federal government to force people to buy health insurance, as Obamacare mandated. Certain specific taxes were okay under the Constitution, but this wasn't one of them.

And the Supreme Court majority knew it.

That majority was composed of five justices: Justice Alito, Justice Scalia, Justice Thomas, Chief Justice Roberts, and the supposed swing voter, Justice Kennedy. All five of those justices were expected to vote to strike down the so-called Obamacare individual mandate; they were expected to strike down the law as a whole. They were expected to strike it down because it was one of the worst violations of individual liberty in American history—the federal government was claiming the authority to punish you for failing to buy something they wanted you to buy.

Instead, in a shocking turn of events, Chief Justice John Roberts, an appointee of President George W. Bush, voted with the liberals on the court to uphold Obamacare in its entirety. This was no surprise to me—I'd opposed Roberts's nomination all the way back in 2005.[37] But it was a surprise to virtually everyone else, mainly because Roberts had clearly signaled during oral arguments that he was against the Obamacare mandate. Now he ruled that the mandate wasn't actually a mandate; it was a tax. As a tax, said Roberts, it was constitutional; as a mandate, it wasn't. Therefore, it was constitutional.

This was, to put it bluntly, the worst kind of bullcrap ever put on Supreme Court paper.

As it turned out, Chief Justice Roberts had switched his vote. He didn't switch his vote because he suddenly discovered a new legal theory that knocked his socks off. He did it because of external pressure. As CBS News observed, approvingly, "Roberts pays attention to media coverage. As chief justice, he is keenly aware of his leadership role on the court, and he also is sensitive to how the court is perceived by the public. There were countless news articles in May warning of damage to the court—and to Roberts' reputation—if the court were to strike down the mandate."[38] President Obama himself led the bullying charge, stating in early April 2012 that if the Supreme Court saw fit to overturn his signature legislation, it would be "unprecedented." "Ultimately I am confident that the Supreme Court will not take what would be an unprecedented, extraordinary step of overturning a law that was passed by a strong majority of a democratically elected Congress," he blathered, his ears quivering with rage.[39]

And Roberts caved.

Now, the Supreme Court of the United States is supposed to be free of politics. That's why these legalistic doofuses in silly-looking robes get a lifetime appointment and a free supply of arrogance to go with it. They're not supposed to be susceptible to bullying—upholding the Constitution is supposed to be a bully-free job.

Clearly, it wasn't.

And the American people paid the price.

The American people continue to pay the price exacted by the liberal bullies each and every day. Conservatives in particular face the mighty wrath of the leftist thugs—and they typically back down. That's why America is on the verge of moral and economic bankruptcy, racial chaos, and loss of confidence in herself. The bullies are winning. And they won't stop until we punch back.

2.

ANTI-PATRIOTIC BULLIES

On January 27, 2009, the very same week that President Obama entered office, he granted an interview to Al Arabiya, the pan-Arab news channel that routinely spouts the Saudi royal line. It was Obama's first formal interview as president of the United States. Presumably, either *The View* was booked that day, or Obama wanted to reach out to heretofore American enemies and present them with the philosophy of his newly minted administration.

It was the latter. The Obama administration actively reached out to Al Arabiya to procure the interview. Hisham Melhem, Obama's interviewer and an Arabist polemicist, made Obama feel right at home, explaining to him that his wife and daughter were Obama fans. Obama, ever humble, puffed up like a blowfish.

And Melhem got just what he wanted: a pandering interview in which the president of the United States threw his country under the bus. As *Time* reported, "Melhem, long a vocal critic of U.S.

Middle East policy, says he was touched by Obama's conciliatory tone and references to his Muslim roots." The interview, said Melhem, "was [Obama's] way of saying, 'There is a new wind coming from Washington.'"[1]

It was unclear whether this new wind was coming from Obama's head, or from his posterior.

"My job to the Muslim world," said the president, "is to communicate that the Americans are not your enemy. We sometimes make mistakes. We have not been perfect. But if you look at the track record, as you say, America was not born as a colonial power, and that the same respect and partnership that America had with the Muslim world as recently as 20 or 30 years ago, there's no reason why we can't restore that." In other words, the problem in the Middle East is America.[2]

As it turned out, Obama didn't just think America was the problem in the Middle East. He thought we were the problem in Europe, Asia, Africa, and the undiscovered islands of the Philippines. And he determined to visit them all to let them know just how sorry we were.

This vital mission would involve going on bended knee to countries around the world, spitting on the records of past American presidents, and disgracing the American warriors who had spilled their blood to secure American freedom. After all, he had to do *something* to justify that Nobel Peace Prize.

So after his stop in Cairo, Obama headed over to Istanbul, Turkey. He didn't discuss the looming threat of Islamism there, or the problem of Iranian nuclear development. Instead, he focused on American slavery. "The United States is still working through some of our own darker periods in our history," he blathered. "Our country still struggles with the legacies of slavery and segregation, the past treatment of Native Americans." What this had to do with Turkey was anyone's guess. Perhaps Obama just heard Turkey and thought Thanksgiving.[3] Or perhaps he was trying to strategically overlook the fact that Turkey was already moving in opposition to America's ally, Israel.

We hadn't just been a "colonial power" in the Middle East, Obama said. We had rammed our views down the throats of our allies in Europe—we'd been "arrogant," failing "to appreciate Europe's leading role in the world," as Obama told the French.[4] This was unfair. Americans *do* recognize Europe's leading role in two world wars and the rise of European communism, as well as the creation of Euro Disney.

But wait, there was more!

In South America, America had made "promises of partnership" and then broken them, been "disengaged," and "sought to dictate our terms." America, Obama pledged in Trinidad and Tobago, would "be willing to acknowledge past errors where those errors have been made."[5] Errors by Hugo Chavez? No big deal—Obama was too busy laughing and joking with the fat dictator to talk about such trivial matters. Chavez couldn't have been more pleased. The only downside for Chavez was that his gift to Obama—an anti-American tract by Eduardo Galeano titled *Open Veins of Latin America: Five Centuries of the Pillage of a Continent*—was probably already in Obama's Kindle.[6] As Obama said, it "was a nice gesture to give me a book. I'm a reader."[7] He's lucky Chavez didn't give him a land mine. Word is Obama's a fan of machines.

These were just the apologies abroad. At home, Obama apologized for going "off course" in the war on terror, the errors of the CIA,[8] and the internment of terrorists at Guantanamo Bay.[9] About the only American thing Obama didn't apologize for was American cheese. And it's only a matter of time before he and Michael Bloomberg team up to ban it for fat content.

After all of that breast-beating, Obama undoubtedly felt better. Confession is good for the soul. Unfortunately, Obama wasn't confessing his own sins—he was confessing America's collective sins. Or, more accurately, he was confessing America's non-sins to the rest of the world in an attempt to seize the mantle of World Citizen, distancing himself from American parochialism in the process.

Obama himself admitted as much back in 2007, when asked about American exceptionalism—the notion that America is an exceptional place, different and better in its foundational ideas from other countries. Sure, he acknowledged, America has some terrific ideas embodied in its Constitution and law—although they're imperfect. But that doesn't mean that America is exceptional enough to dictate its values to others. Rather, America is exceptional in the same way other countries are exceptional. In the words of Obama's apparent foreign policy spokesperson, Barney the Dinosaur: we are special; everyone is special in his or her own way. "I believe in American exceptionalism," said then-senator Obama, "just as I suspect that the Brits believe in British exceptionalism and the Greeks believe in Greek exceptionalism." Perhaps we're slightly more special than other countries; perhaps not. In any case, America has to "compromise."[10]

Compromise. It always sounds so nice. But the consequences of American compromise are slightly less pleasant for the rest of the world. As it turns out, it's bad for both America and for the globe when America slashes her military budget, as Obama seeks to do—it incentivizes nasty regimes to engage in aggression (see China, North Korea, the Viet Cong, Iran, the old Soviet Union, the Nazis). It's a problem when the United States unilaterally disarms itself of nuclear weapons, while simultaneously failing to develop missile defense. It's a *bad thing* when the anti-American, Nazi-allied, terrorist-supporting Muslim Brotherhood is emboldened in Egypt (Obama's director of national intelligence, James Clapper, hilariously termed the Brotherhood a "largely secular" organization "which has eschewed violence"), and when American ally Hosni Mubarak is overthrown with tacit American support. The world suffers when America hits a "reset button" with Russia that involves her selling Eastern Europe down the river. Millions prepare for decades more in chains when the president of the United States bows to the dictators of Saudi Arabia and China. When America actively undercuts a democratic coup in Honduras, supports an Islamist coup in Libya, tries to push the population of the Falkland Islands into the hands of the dysfunctional Argentinian government, and leaves the Iranian mullahs to slaughter their citizens in the streets—these are all bad things.

When America sublimates her international interests—when we put the United Nations or Vladimir Putin in charge of foreign policy—that's a net negative for the globe.

But for the left, and for President Obama, it's a grand triumph.

In this, Obama is the apotheosis of the 1960s generation. Since that tumultuous time of three-way sex in the mud at Woodstock and violent race riots in America's biggest cities, the left has seen America as a force for ill in the world, a neocolonialist power bent on world domination, strong-arming peaceful and/or democratic nations into embracing our favored policies. Obama's perspective is different in tone from that of Jeremiah Wright; Obama isn't nearly as strident, and he's far cleverer than Wright in presenting his anti-Americanism. But at its root, Obama's philosophy is still Wright's: it's a "God damn America," "US of KKKA," "America's chickens are coming home to roost" perspective. Contrary to popular media belief, you don't sit in the pews of your spiritual mentor for two decades without imbibing a few of his ideas—even if your name *is* Barack Obama.

President Obama may pose with the incoming coffins of our corpsmen at Dover Air Force Base,[11] but it's clear that he sees our "corpse men" as a "photo op" (his words) rather than a group of heroes never to be exploited for political gain. After all, when Obama isn't there to monitor them, our troops are busy "air-raiding villages and killing civilians."[12]

President Obama may speak in front of the Vietnam Veterans Memorial and talk about how veterans were "sometimes blamed for the misdeeds of a few . . . sometimes denigrated when you should have been celebrated,"[13] but he has no problem associating with Bill Ayers, who bombed the Pentagon during the Vietnam War, proclaiming that he wanted to see a "U.S. defeat." It also hasn't stopped Obama from taking donations from "Hanoi" Jane Fonda, who famously went to North Vietnam and labeled our soldiers "war criminals," or Senator John F. Kerry (D-MA), who suggested that our soldiers had routinely "raped, cut off ears, cut off heads," etc. Kerry, in fact, is widely considered Obama's foreign policy surrogate.[14]

President Obama may mimic the patriotic words of the founding fathers but he sees the Constitution as a deeply problematic document. He blames America for global inequality—hence his constant focus on the percentage of world resources Americans consume versus the percentage of the world population we represent. And he blames "the powerful" who maintain this inequality for both domestic crime and international terrorism.[15] Growth of American power can only mean more of both.

This perspective certainly doesn't serve American interests. In fact, it coincides with the interests of Al Qaeda, who also want to see American power wane. So do the communist Chinese. And the power-mad Putin regime. And countless other nasty characters around the world, most of whom can be found in the UN scenes of *Team America*.

But American interests are not paramount to the left. Quite the opposite: anti-American interests are paramount to the left, and to President Obama as their chosen representative. As Douglas Feith, undersecretary of defense for policy under President George W. Bush, said, Obama is "undertaking a radical reformulation of 70 years of American foreign policy. At least since the U.S. entered World War II, there has been a view of the United States as a leading power, a democratic power, a country that acts boldly in its own interests. I think President Obama does not believe that's the role America should play in the world. . . . Essentially, the President wants to cut America down to size—he would say make America a better citizen of the world. But what he is talking about is moving America away from a position of leadership."[16]

If you think America should not play the leading role in the world, you are not a patriot. It's that simple. Patriotism doesn't require that you believe that American history is free of mistakes. That would be frivolous and nonsensical. It *does* require, however, that you recognize that America's founding ideology is the greatest single governing ideology in the history of mankind; that America's military has been the greatest fighting force for freedom in world history; that America does not require apologizing for, but fighting for.

The left has disowned this perspective for decades.

Only the left sees terms like *flag-waver*, *jingoist*, and *super-patriot* as insults. Patriotism, in their view, is bad.

They don't believe this, because they're globalists. It's not as easy as that. Globalism is not anti-patriotism. Going back millennia, both Socrates and Diogenes claimed they were "citizens of the world." But you can be a citizen of the world without disowning America. Citizens all over the world wish their countries were more like America. When Ronald Reagan said that the United States remains the "last best hope for a mankind plagued by tyranny and deprivation," he wasn't being jingoistic. He was being a good global citizen and a good patriot.

The left is filled, however, with self-professed good global citizens and bad patriots. Or rather, anti-patriots. Anti-patriotism means something more than belief in the brotherhood of man. It means an active dislike for America, and American power.

The left is anti-patriotic. What's more, they bully all those who dare disagree. They've twisted the American education system to teach generations of Americans that their country is a planetary scourge, second only to global warming in the pantheon of great moral evils. Anti-patriotic bullies slander their opponents as jingoistic boobs in thrall to the military-industrial complex, racists who want to kill brown and yellow people. They say we're terrorists, and actual terrorists are freedom fighters, as Michael Moore famously spluttered between bites of bacon burger.

Worst of all, the anti-patriotic bullies redefine patriotism to fit their own agenda. Traditional patriotism, it turns out, is bullying; true patriotism is leftist dissent. This leads to the logical conundrum pointed out by John O'Sullivan of the *National Review:* "Dissent is the highest form of patriotism. Treason is the highest form of dissent. Therefore treason is the highest form of patriotism."[17]

But to the left, treason *is* the highest form of patriotism. No one was more gleeful than the left when Private Bradley Manning leaked a bevy of classified military documents to Julian Assange of WikiLeaks—they saw Manning's activity as a form of patriotism rather than treachery. Kevin Zeese of the *Huffington Post* said that Manning's actions showed "the true meaning of patriotism." Glenn Greenwald of Salon.com wrote, "Manning clearly believed that he was a whistle-blower acting with the noblest of motives, and probably was exactly that . . . [a] national hero." At the *Nation*, Chase Madar called Manning a "patriot"; Manning, according to Madar, "brought these wrongdoings to light out of a profound sense of duty to his country, as a citizen and a soldier, and his patriotism cost him dearly." Andrew Sullivan of the *Atlantic*—he is one of President Obama's favorite bloggers—decried Manning's placement in solitary confinement, calling it "prisoner abuse." Michael Bérubé of *Dissent* magazine labeled Manning a "patriotic whistleblower." The city of Berkeley, California, actually discussed a resolution that would have called Manning "an American hero" and noted "the good that has been done."[18] Of course, the city of Berkeley actually thinks that marijuana cultivation is a charming hobby and that Nancy Pelosi is a brilliant woman. So we have to take their opinion with a grain of salt.

But the point remains: If traditional traitors are newfound patriots, then traditional patriots are newfound traitors. And they must be stopped at all costs.

And that is precisely what the left seeks to do.

WHEN LIBERALS WERE *PATRIOTIC* BULLIES

Ironically enough, before leftist anti-patriotic bullying, there was leftist *patriotic* bullying. It was fun for modern leftists to suggest that George W. Bush wanted to send them all to the gulag for opposing the war in Iraq, but it wasn't any truer than Tim Geithner's tax returns. Nobody got arrested for opposing President Bush. In fact, anti–Iraq War "patriots" like Cindy Sheehan were lionized by the mainstream media, granted "absolute . . . moral authority" by deep thinkers like Maureen Dowd of the *New York Times*.[19] It was only when Sheehan stopped paying her taxes that the left decided she no longer deserved papal infallibility.

But historically, the same hasn't been true for liberal presidents. When they believed something was unpatriotic, they became the world's biggest bullies. President Woodrow Wilson was the leader of the early-twentieth-century progressive movement, the basic underpinning for today's liberalism. He campaigned for reelection in 1916 on the promise to keep America out of World War I. When he failed to do so, public outcry reached massive proportions. So Wilson did what leftists always want to do: he locked up his critics in jail and threw away the key. Wilson forced a Sedition Act through Congress that prohibited "uttering, printing, writing, or publishing any disloyal, profane, scurrilous, or abusive language about the United States government or the military." The government was granted the power to prevent distribution of any publications that didn't meet Wilsonian standards. What violated those standards? As Jonah Goldberg reports in his book *Liberal Fascism*, Postmaster General Albert Sidney Burleson explained that such standards were violated when anyone "begins to say that this Government got in the war wrong, that it is in it for the wrong purposes, or anything that will impugn the motives of the Government for going into the war. They cannot say that this Government is the tool of Wall Street or the munitions-makers. . . . There can be no campaign against conscription and the Draft Law."

Overall, tens of thousands were arrested by the Justice Department under the Sedition Act. "Obey the law: keep your mouth shut," read one letter to the German community from the Wilson administration (the same letter should be sent today to all of Gloria Allred's clients). "A Hollywood producer," Goldberg reports, "received a ten-year stint in jail for making a film that depicted British troops committing atrocities *during the American Revolution*."[20]

If George W. Bush had been as much of a bully as Woodrow Wilson, then Michael Moore, Oliver Stone, Barack Obama, the entire newsroom at MSNBC, and most college professors would have found themselves in San Quentin pretty quickly.

During the Great Depression, FDR bullied Americans who disagreed with him in similar fashion. Hugh "Iron Pants" Johnson led the charge on FDR's National Recovery Administration, the civilian regime charged with healing the economy; he said Americans who bucked FDR deserved a "sock in the nose."

Products were labeled with the Blue Eagle—a piece of symbolism designed to show that people were in compliance with FDR's regulations. In what could aptly be termed a war on women, Johnson said, "It is women in homes—and not soldiers in uniform—who will this time save our country. They will go over the top to as great a victory as the Argonne. It is zero hour for housewives. Their battle cry is 'Buy now under the Blue Eagle!'" As Goldberg writes, FDR "questioned the patriotism of anybody who opposed his economic programs, never mind the war itself."[21] FDR, never hesitant to question the patriotism of his opponents, was more than happy to use bully tactics against them, too.

THE ANTI-PATRIOTIC LEFT RISES

It was in the 1960s, however, that liberal patriotic bullying turned to liberal anti-patriotic bullying. With the rise of the anticolonialist left, America shifted from global good guy to global bad guy in the minds of liberals. John F. Kennedy's assassination opened the door to the Marxist left's view of America as global colonizer, a raping, pillaging force intent on world domination for capitalist gain. Where once the left under Wilson had jailed those who protested that war was waged for Wall Street or weapons manufacturers, now the left claimed that war *was* waged for the military-industrial complex. Where once dissent had been considered unpatriotic, now it was supremely patriotic.

In fact, only traditional patriotism was now unpatriotic.

The backlash against patriotism itself started in the aftermath of World War II. Post–World War II literature was replete with it. Irwin Shaw's 1948 bestseller, *The Young Lions*, described patriotism as a pastime "for the rich."[22] In James Jones's 1961 bestseller, *The Thin Red Line*, the shirt of a dead soldier became "some forever windless flag symbolic of the darker, nether side of patriotism."[23] This strain had been building since World War I, when it had been a strong but minority viewpoint, with authors like John Dos Passos and Elliot Paul making the case against nationalism. It carried forward and grew during the Korean War. Leftist favorites like World War II bombardier Howard Zinn summed up the philosophy well decades later: "Is not nationalism—that devotion to a flag, an anthem, a boundary so fierce it engenders mass murder—one of the great evils of our time, along with racism, along with religious hatred? . . . We need to refute the idea that our nation is different from, morally superior to, the other imperial powers of world history. We need to assert our allegiance to the human race, and not to any one nation."[24]

But there was one tiny problem: American patriotism *is* unique.

If nationalism was the obstacle to world peace, *American* nationalism was the solution. American patriotism had a solid basis: we had saved Europe twice, resisted the lure of fascism at home, ended slavery, and moved toward perfecting the union in terms of race and sex. All in all, America had a lot to be proud of.

But not for long. The left decided to rewrite history. American patriotism had to be debunked. And so revisionist historians began portraying America as a nasty place, a colonialist land dedicated to the wiping out of brown and yellow peoples. The Founders were a bunch of rich white oligarchs intent on protecting their property. Abraham Lincoln fought the Civil War for economic rather than moral reasons. World War I was about competing colonial powers beating the snot out of one another. World War II—well, that was about mashing up Europe to make new markets for American capitalism.

After JFK's assassination, the left ran off the rails. They were no longer proud of their country. In fact, true patriots were *ashamed* of their country.

In 1962, the initial founders of the radical left group Students for a Democratic Society (SDS) met in Port Huron, Michigan, to draft what would become a defining leftist statement about America. Their perspective was clear: America was a lie.

In typical leftist fashion, they made themselves feel good by pleading mea culpa for their own wealth. "We are people of this generation, bred in at least modest comfort, housed now in universities, looking uncomfortably to the world we inherit." But they weren't grateful for this—they were ashamed of it.

"Freedom and equality for each individual," the statement continued, "government of, by, and for the people—these American values we found good, principles by which we could live as men. Many of us began maturing in complacency." But that complacency was shattered by the leftist reality that America was rotten to the core: "As we grew, however, our comfort was penetrated by events too troubling to dismiss." America, said the Port Huron statement, was racist, militaristic, materialistic, classist, sexist, and nasty. The only thing worse than America was finding half a worm in your apple.

But while America—and most nations—were evil, people collectively were tons of fun. Men, said the statement, were "infinitely precious and possessed of unfulfilled capacities for reason, freedom, and love."

The statement was infinitely precious. It was also infinitely long, running a behemoth twenty-five thousand words (the entire Constitution of the United States runs only 4,440 words). Since everyone who wrote it was likely smoking dope, it undoubtedly made lots of sense at the time. It was mental masturbation of the highest order.

But it was mental masturbation that brought mental venereal disease.

The Port Huron statement was the launch of the great anti-patriotic bullying campaign. The statement beats patriotism half to death. It rips "super-patriotic groups" that represent "ultra-conservatism" (specifically citing Senator Barry Goldwater) and calls such super-patriotic movements a "disgrace [to] the United States." It complains about anticommunists who are "patriotically willing to do anything to achieve 'total victory.'" It blames patriotism for the "boondoggling, belligerence, and privilege of military and economic elites."

With a philosophy like that, it's no wonder that the anti-patriotic crowd felt the moral necessity to bully patriots. And they found their critical cause in the Vietnam War.

While SDS had been launched prior to the escalation of action in Vietnam, the Vietnam War quickly took on all the characteristics that the new anti-patriotic left hated: flag-waving citizens backing their boys to prevent the takeover of communism in a far-flung nation. The Vietnam War was bad because flags were bad, American judgmentalism was bad, white people were bad, and soldiers were bad. There were plenty of good reasons to oppose the Vietnam War—and the left skipped right past all of them in search of a blowtorch to wield against American nationalism. The sentiment was spelled out best by leftist Vietnam vet Oliver Stone in *Platoon*. As neophyte Chris Taylor (Charlie Sheen) and saintlike Sergeant Elias (Willem Dafoe) sit under the stars discussing the war, Elias tells Taylor that America will lose the war. "Come on!" says Taylor. "You really think so? Us?" "We've been kicking other people's asses for so long, I figured it's time we got ours kicked," Elias replies. America, the bully, was going to get what was coming to her.

Vietnam is precisely the sort of war that liberal patriots like Woodrow Wilson and FDR would have embraced—it was dedicated to helping those who couldn't help themselves fight for freedom against overbearing tyranny. And it couldn't even be perceived as American imperialism, since there were no oil or territorial interests. But the anti-patriotic left *hated* the Vietnam War. Remembering their catechism that patriotism was rooted in capitalistic self-interest and exploitation of Third World peoples, the left quickly decided that the Vietnam War was immoral and racist, even though white Americans were dying in the thousands largely on behalf of nonwhite Vietnamese a world away.

But to the left, the war wasn't just immoral. It was unpatriotic, because it was patriotic. And thus citizens who supported it had to be fought, tooth and nail. The left didn't just want America out of Vietnam. They wanted America to lose.

Thus the SDS eventually embraced violence against normal patriotic citizens. In 1969, the Weathermen faction of the SDS, headed by flag-haters like Bill Ayers and his future wife, Bernardine Dohrn, led the "Days of Rage" protests in Chicago. The slogan of the event: "bring the war home." John Jacobs, one of the leaders of the protests, spelled out its goals clearly: "Weathermen would shove the war down their dumb, fascist throats and show them, while we were at it, how much better we were than them, both tactically and strategically, as a people. In an all-out civil war over Vietnam and other fascist U.S. imperialism, we were going to bring the war home. 'Turn the imperalists' war into a civil war,' in Lenin's words. And we were going to kick ass."[25] In preparation for the "Days of Rage," the Weathermen met with representatives of North Vietnam in Cuba to train them in tactics. The North Vietnamese promptly asked them to start a war on U.S. soil. The Weathermen would be only too happy to oblige.[26]

The Weathermen eventually became the Weathermen Underground, bombing police stations, the Pentagon, the homes of private citizens—all while decrying America. "We're against everything that's 'good and decent' in honky America," said Jacobs. "We will burn and loot and destroy. We are the incubation of your mother's nightmare." In 1969 and 1970, the Weathermen and their allies were responsible for approximately 250 attacks.[27]

It wasn't just the Weathermen. Students across America engaged in acts of bullying, spitting on, cursing, and abusing soldiers returning from Vietnam; radical leftists, enraged by the traditional liberal patriotism of presidential candidate Hubert Humphrey, rioted at the Democratic National Convention in Chicago in 1968. John Kerry, returning from the Vietnam War, made himself famous by using the floor of Congress as a propaganda tool against soldiers in Vietnam, testifying comtroversially: "They told the stories at times they had personally raped, cut off ears, cut off heads, taped wires from portable telephones to human genitals and turned up the power, cut off limbs, blown up bodies, randomly shot at civilians, razed villages in fashion reminiscent of Genghis Khan, shot cattle and dogs for fun, poisoned food stocks, and generally ravaged the countryside of South Vietnam in addition to the normal ravage of war, and the normal and very particular ravaging which is done by the applied bombing power of this country."[28]

America was evil. Patriotism was a symptom of that evil.

ESTABLISHMENT ANTI-PATRIOTISM

Today, the anti-patriotic bullying of the left has softened dramatically. The anti-military fervor of the left dried up after the Vietnam War; the anti-patriotic bullying went into hiding with the rise of Ronald Reagan. But it is present, both in ideology and in practice.

It is cleverly hidden. After the left's atrocities during the Vietnam War era, the left has recognized that its open radicalism simply won't fly with regard to the military—America loves its soldiers too much. Loyalty to the military is perhaps the one area where the left has been unable to cow Americans into submission.

And so the left has abandoned open anti-military language. Instead, they wrap themselves in the flag while pushing the most anti-patriotic views imaginable.

Thus, in June 2008, then-senator Barack Obama spoke of patriotism in glowing terms: "For me, as for most Americans, patriotism starts as a gut instinct, a loyalty and love for country rooted in my earliest memories. . . . As I got older, that gut instinct—that America is the greatest country on earth—would survive my growing awareness of our nation's imperfections." Patriotism, said Obama, "is always more than just loyalty to a place on a map or a certain kind of people. Instead, it is also loyalty to America's ideals—ideals for which anyone can sacrifice, or defend, or give their last full measure of devotion." And Obama didn't stop there. As it turned out, the members of the military were now sacrosanct again, too—especially our Vietnam veterans. Vietnam, said Obama, was "one of the most painful chapters in our history. Most particularly, how we treated our troops who served there. . . . Patriots can support a war. Patriots can oppose a war. And whatever our view, let us always stand united in support of our troops, who we placed in harm's way."[29]

Obama hit all the right notes.

Yet it didn't ring true.

Obama's political allies are the same folks who spit on the troops as they arrived back home from Vietnam. They are the same folks who see America as an imperialistic evildoer on the world stage.

In ideology, the radicals of yesteryear have become today's establishment. The pathetic Port Huron statement is now considered a classic American document—even though it's actually a classic anti-American document. The *New York Times* quoted historian Michael Kazin calling the document "the most ambitious, the most specific and the most eloquent manifesto in the history of the American left."[30]

On its fiftieth anniversary, SDS cofounder and statement drafter Tom Hayden—now a former state senator in California—wrote an op-ed for the *Los Angeles Times* in which he called the signing of the document a "holy moment."[31] Hayden, along with then-wife Jane Fonda, had traveled routinely to Hanoi during the Vietnam War, giving the Viet Cong advice about how to defeat the United States and labeling American POWs in Vietnam "liars." But now he was a mainstream political figure.

And he hadn't changed a bit. After 9/11, Hayden in familiar language accused George W. Bush of patriotic treason: "[T]hey are playing patriot games with the nation's future," he scoffed. More importantly, he bullied American soldiers who were fighting in Iraq. "The strategy," he said, "must be to deny the U.S. occupation funding, political standing, sufficient troops, and alliances necessary to their strategy for dominance."[32]

During the 2008 race, Hayden named Obama his ideological successor. "Is Barack the one we have been waiting for? Or is it the other way around? Are we the people we have been waiting for? Barack Obama is giving voice and space to an awakening beyond his wildest expectations," he wrote.[33]

The same held true of figures like Bill Ayers, now a respected educator in Chicago and confidant of President Barack Obama. On September 11, 2001, the *New York Times* printed an interview with Ayers in which Ayers doubled down on his Weathermen-era terrorism. He ripped the Vietnam War soldiers, including war hero and former Democratic senator Bob Kerrey. The interview was especially ill-timed, given that Ayers was pictured stomping on an American flag, as Americans leaped from the flaming World Trade Center.[34] But President Obama still attended a July 4, 2005, barbecue at Ayers's house. What better way to celebrate Independence Day than by munching a hamburger and waving a flag with a domestic terrorist and flag-burner?

There is a difference between Obama and the Haydens and Ayerses of the world, however. Obama's left is Anti-Patriotism 2.0. The Hayden/Ayers strategy was to attack not just soldiers as war criminals but also civilians as xenophobic pigs. Predictably enough, that alienated both soldiers and civilians, and drove them closer together.

The Obama strategy is more clever. It's to bully both soldiers and civilians into silence. Soldiers will be undercut on the battlefields abroad while being lauded as heroes at home; civilians will be told that true support of the troops lies in abandoning patriotism (and its corollary, militarism) so the troops can come home.

This isn't lunch-money bullying. It's psychological warfare.

And it works.

MULTICULTURAL BULLIES

Civilians have to be convinced, first and foremost, that it would be wrong to stand up for traditional patriotic values. Such values cause conflict. Instead, the left tells Americans that they should embrace a more positive notion: multiculturalism. Multiculturalism puts a happy face on flag-burning—it suggests that all cultures are equal, so those who wave our own flags are a bunch of Hitler-wannabes without the funny mustache. Greek patriotism is the same as American patriotism. Any slight differences can probably be ironed out via diplomacy, the United Nations General Assembly, and unilateral disarmament.

The battle for international multiculturalism starts at home.

In that battle, symbols matter.

It's not rare these days for leftists to crack down on patriotic symbolism out of "respect" for other cultures. Never mind that those other cultures wouldn't have a place to plant their roots without the soil of American values—American values are patriarchal. If that cabby from Pakistan is insulted by your flag pin, you'd best take it off. If the Pakistani cabby wants to play headache-inducing music with ululating banshees, however, you'd best sit back and shut up. In fact, double your tip, you colonialist rube.

In Denair, California, a thirteen-year-old boy was forced to remove an American flag from the back of his bicycle by his school; the school said that the flag had raised "racial tensions." The school district superintendent explained the prevailing leftist thought: "Our Hispanic, you know, kids will, you know, bring their Mexican flags and they'll display it, and then of course the kids would do the American flag situation, and it does cause kind of a racial tension which we don't really want. We want them to appreciate the cultures."[35] The school later retracted its order, explaining that it wasn't really responsible for the anti-flag action—in reality, the student had been *threatened* by other students for having an American flag on school grounds. That's actually more of an indictment of leftism than anything else: the notion that flag-wavers have to back down thanks to coddled anti-American thugs.[36]

California is a state just insane enough to elect Governor Jerry Brown—twice. Brown's main policy proposal these days is a $68 billion high-speed rail from heavily populated Northern California through barren Central California. In California, this is perceived as "visionary." So it's no surprise that the largest spate of anti-flag activities spring from there. In May 2010, at Live Oak High School, in the town of Morgan Hill, several students were thrown off school grounds after they wore shirts with American flags on them, then refused to remove them at administration behest. What was the school administration's problem? The students had the temerity to wear the flags on Cinco de Mayo, a Mexican holiday. So while the administration allowed students to parade around in body-painted Mexican flags, students who wanted to wear the star-spangled banner were told to go home. When an offended parent asked the assistant principal about the ban, the principal spat back, "Not today. We need to give them [celebrants of Cinco de Mayo] their day today."[37] The students, with the help of the Thomas More Law Center, sued the school . . . and lost. The possibility that the students would be attacked, said the court, was great enough to allow the school to ban the clothing.[38] The court neglected to mention whether bars could ban women from wearing short skirts, since it might encourage rape.

At California's Gavilan View Middle School in Santa Rita, a teacher told a student not to draw a picture of the flag with the words "God Bless America." "You can't draw that—that's offensive," said the teacher. Another student, fortunately, provided a more palatable picture for the teacher: a red, white, and blue drawing of President Obama. She loved it.[39] Undoubtedly, the latter student will grow up to be a higher-up in the Democratic Party establishment, mocking the former for being a "bitter clinger."

In Albany, Oregon, management of the Oaks Apartments told Jim Clausen that he had to take a flag off his motorcycle. Said management, "Someone might get offended." Other residents were told they couldn't fly any flags on apartment premises. Several residents fought back by carrying around American flags and wearing flag pins;[40] eventually, the management backed down. The property manager did admit, however, "What we were trying to do was to keep the peace. Obviously, we were wrong. If the peace needs to be kept, it belongs to the police department." She *was* offended that one of the residents had gone to the media. "He's just a romping, stomping patriot," she said with some scorn. She refused to say who had originally complained about the flags.[41] Hint: it might have been the woman who describes pro-flag residents as "romping, stomping patriots."

In Oshkosh, Wisconsin, an Iraq War veteran was told to remove an American flag from the window of his apartment. If he didn't, he was told, he'd be evicted. The management company explained, "This policy was developed to insure that we are fair to everyone as we have many residents from diverse backgrounds. By having a blanket policy of neutrality we have found that we are less likely to offend anyone and the aesthetic qualities of our apartment communities are maintained."[42] Wouldn't want any multicultural apartment residents getting huffy over a man who risked his life to protect their rights flying the flag that represents those rights. That's just bigoted.

In the Coney Island section of Brooklyn, New York, Greta Hawkins, principal of the Edna Cohen School, stopped kindergartners from singing Lee Greenwood's "Proud to Be an American" at their graduation. During a rehearsal, she showed up and stopped the CD player. "We don't want to offend other cultures," she said. One of the teachers said, puzzled, "I've never come across anyone who felt it insulted their culture." But that teacher obviously didn't get it—diversity trumps Americanism. That's why the students were allowed to sing both Justin Bieber's "Baby" and "The World Is a Rainbow," with lyrics that state: "The world is a rainbow / That's filled with many colors: / Yellow, black, and white, and brown." Not coincidentally, this was the same principal who told teachers upon arriving at the school, "I'm black. Your previous principal was white and Jewish. More of us are coming."[43]

These are somewhat minor incidents of bullying, of course. But they're not all that rare. Fifty years ago, you'd be hard-pressed to find *one* such incident. The anti-flag phenomenon is indicative of something far deeper and broader: the general sense that the American flag itself is a representation of something nefarious. Flags are dangerous. Wearing branded designer labels while rocking out to Green Day in a flea-infested tent in downtown Los Angeles next to a homeless man with meningitis—now *that's* patriotic.

That's not a joke. Tea Party patriots are derided on a regular basis for donning Revolutionary War garb; the media gleefully realized that "teabagging" was a slur for a fringe sexual act often linked with gay men, and began calling Tea Partiers "teabaggers." Rachel Maddow, who knows nothing about the practice, used it as a substitute for "Tea Partier"; Bill Maher did the same. (Not coincidentally, Maher also said to the applause of his audience of trained primates, "Would it be better if the country just got over this notion of American exceptionalism? Oh, I think it would.")[44] Even President Obama has reportedly used the term *teabagger*. The *Oxford English Dictionary* actually labeled the term its second most popular word of the year.

The NAACP characterized the Tea Partiers' dress this way: "The Revolutionary War–era costumes, the yellow 'Don't tread on me' Gadsden flags from the same era, the earnest recitals of the pledge of allegiance, the over-stated veneration of the Constitution, and the defense of 'American exceptionalism' in a world turned towards transnational economies and global institutions: all are signs of the over-arching nationalism that helps define the Tea Party movement."[45] Cue the spooky music—those Tea Party Jasons are all donning their star-spangled hockey masks. They carry the flag. They like the Constitution. Now they're coming for your children.

ANGRY "PATRIOTIC" MALES

The left has bullied Americans into believing that mere belief in the superiority of their country constitutes dangerous intolerance of others. No wonder the Department of Homeland Security (DHS) released a report shortly after Obama took office decrying "Rightwing Extremism" and suggesting that "Current Economic and Political Climate [Are] Fueling Resurgence in Radicalization and Recruitment." Its own admission that they have "no specific information that domestic rightwing terrorists are currently planning acts of violence" didn't stop DHS from releasing the report, which said that the election of a black president and the shoddy economy were going to cause an upswing in Timothy McVeigh types. "Rightwing extremists are harnessing this historical election as a recruitment tool," said the minions of the historic election winner. "Many rightwing extremists are antagonistic on a range of issues, including immigration and citizenship, the expansion of social programs to minorities, and restrictions on firearms ownership and use. Rightwing extremists are increasingly galvanized by these concerns and leverage them as drivers for recruitment." What's more, said DHS, those psycho right-wingers might recruit soldiers, forming an army of insane conservatives with paramilitary skill sets.[46]

Those jingoistic morons tend to grab their guns and go postal when they can't afford their cigs and lottery tickets, after all. Meanwhile, Occupiers who poop on themselves, hit cops with frying pans, rape and kill people, cause tens of millions of dollars in property damage, and wear shirts featuring noted murderous maniac Che Guevara are deemed American patriots by the left.

Every time an insane person decides to shoot a politician or bomb a building, the left immediately pegs him or her in the press as a right-winger. When a psychopath named Jared Lee Loughner shot Representative Gabrielle Giffords (D-AZ) through the head at a "Congress on Your Corner" event in Tucson, Arizona, in January 2011—along with seventeen others, including a Republican-appointed federal judge, resulting in six deaths—the media labeled him a conservative who had been influenced by Sarah Palin. In particular, the media cited an obviously figurative map on Palin's website that showed targeted political districts by placing a crosshairs on those districts. There was zero evidence that Loughner had ever visited Palin's website. Zero.

As it turns out, Loughner had a serious history of dangerous behavior and was mentally unstable; the Giffords event had no police presence. Actually, like most of the murderers in the United States, Loughner was a left-winger. He was a pothead. He said that he liked both *The Communist Manifesto* and *Mein Kampf*. He cut a video of himself burning an American flag. But that didn't stop leftist politicians and media folks from speculating as to Loughner's motives. "You look at unbalanced people, how they respond to the vitriol that comes out of certain mouths about tearing down the government," said Pima County sheriff Clarence Dupnik. "The anger, the hatred, the bigotry that goes on in this country is getting to be outrageous. . . . We have become the mecca for prejudice and bigotry.[47] He doubled down on the statement on Megyn Kelly's show on Fox News: "There are a whole lot of people in this country who are very angry about the politics of people like Gabrielle." Kelly then forced him to admit that he had no evidence whatsoever that Loughner was even listening to radio or watching television or was inspired by politics.[48]

In a shocking coincidence, it turns out that Dupnik was a vocal opponent of the Tea Party; he said that it was racist, evidence that "bigotry is alive and well in America," "the worst in America."[49] He called Arizona's SB 1070, the state's anti–illegal immigration law, "unwise," "stupid," and racist. But according to Dupnik, dastardly right-wing rhetoric caused the shooting, and certainly not his department's failure to investigate Loughner.[50]

None of that stopped the left from bringing out rhetorical firearms to assassinate conservative reputations. "When you heard the terrible news from Arizona, were you completely surprised?" wrote Nobel Prize–winning bearded moron Paul Krugman of the *New York Times*. "Or were you, at some level, expecting something like this atrocity to happen? Put me in the latter category. I've had a sick feeling in the pit of my stomach ever since the final stages of the 2008 campaign." In fact, Krugman cited the bogus DHS report as background to support his evidence-less argument.[51] Jon Stewart, the comedian-no-wait-I'm-a-reporter-no-wait-I'm-a-comedian comic/left-wing hack/journalist, agreed with Krugman, suggesting that in this case, "actions match the disturbing nature of words."[52]

Keith Olbermann, the prettier Rachel Maddow, put down his

vat of hydrochloric acid long enough to sanctimoniously lecture conservative Americans, and Sarah Palin in particular, that "this age in which this country would accept 'targeting' of political opponents and putting bullseyes over their faces and of the dangerous blurring between political rallies and gun shows, ended."[53] Olbermann said that Palin, Representative Allen West (R-FL), Nevada U.S. Senate candidate Sharron Angle, and the Tea Party had to be "repudiated" by the Republican Party. "If all of these are not responsible for what happened in Tucson, they must now be responsible for doing everything they can to make sure Tucson doesn't happen again," the dumbest Cornell graduate in history intoned.[54] The new advocate of civility had, over the course of his MSNBC show, called conservatives "terrorists" and "fascists," suggested that Rush Limbaugh had "blood on [his] hands," accused the Tea Party of wanting to return America to the era of Jim Crow and destroy the country outright, called Michelle Malkin a "big mashed-up bag of meat with lipstick on it," slurred Chris Wallace of Fox News as a "monkey posing as a newscaster," and compared Kenneth Starr to Nazi thug Heinrich Himmler, "including the glasses."[55]

The point of all of this was obvious: shut up, conservatives. *Civility* is the left's code word for silence. Historically speaking, America's politics today is *far* more civil than at any other time during our history. During the founding era, people tarred and feathered each other—literally, they poured hot tar over people and then doused them in feathers—over politics. The left never seems to care about left-wing civility—they said nothing about Olbermann causing violence when stalkers began threatening Sarah Palin, or about the Democratic Leadership Council posting a map with shooting targets on particular districts—but they're quick to blame right-wing rhetoric when a left-wing nut job kills a Republican judge and shoots a blue-dog Democrat. That wasn't rare. Virtually every major American shooting of an elected official during the twentieth century was committed by a left-winger. Leon Czolgosz, who murdered President William McKinley in 1901, was a left-wing anarchist. Giuseppe Zangara, who tried to shoot FDR and succeeded in murdering Chicago mayor Anton Cermak, confessed, "I have the gun in my hand. I kill kings and presidents first, and next all capitalists." Sirhan Sirhan was a Palestinian terrorist who hated Robert F. Kennedy's pro-Israel record. Lynette "Squeaky" Fromme, who tried to kill President Gerald Ford, was a former member of the insane radical left Manson family. It's far more common for leftists to routinely pick up weapons and try to kill those with whom they disagree than it is for those on the other side of the ideological spectrum.

The most infamous assassin of all, Lee Harvey Oswald, defected to Soviet Russia and tried to emigrate to communist Cuba before killing JFK. As with Loughner, leftists attempted to label Oswald a right-winger, or at least thrust collective responsibility on conservatives across America. When Lady Bird Johnson asked Jackie Kennedy if she wanted to change out of her blood-spattered clothes on Air Force One after JFK's assassination, Jackie said, "No. I want them to see what they have done." What did she mean? As James Piereson details in *Camelot and the Cultural Revolution*, she meant the same thing Jon Stewart did: conservatives didn't shut up, so JFK had been shot. Sure, Oswald was a commie. Jackie later lamented, "He didn't even have the satisfaction of being killed for civil rights. It had to be some silly little Communist." But that didn't matter. The left quickly turned Oswald into a hero of the right.

New York Times columnist James Reston wrote a piece after the assassination that might have been plagiarized by Krugman some fifty years later. The title: "Why America Weeps: Kennedy Victim of Violent Streak He Sought to Curb in Nation." Said Reston, "America wept tonight, not alone for its dead young president, but for itself. The grief was general, for somehow the worst in the nation had prevailed over the best. . . . From the beginning to the end of his administration, he was trying to tamp down the violence of the extremists from the right."

Supreme Court Chief Justice Earl Warren seconded the motion, stating in his eulogy on the Capitol steps, "It is not too much to hope that the martyrdom of our beloved president might even soften the hearts of those who would themselves recoil from assassination, but who do not shrink from spreading the venom which kindles thoughts of it in others." Was he talking about communists? Of course not. He was talking about Kennedy's political opponents.

Lyndon Johnson himself played this card: "It is this work that I most want us to do—to banish rancor from our words and malice from our hearts—to close down the poison springs of hatred and intolerance and fanaticism." He'd have no such words for SDS or the violent leftists who would plague the nation for the next decade. After all, they were leftists. And LBJ's agenda was leftist. So instead of telling the truth about Oswald, LBJ twisted it, standing on JFK's coffin to ram through his legislative agenda.

In fact, in the wake of the JFK assassination, LBJ was most concerned that Americans would turn against the communists for the killing. As Reston reported, "One of the things President Johnson is said to be concerned about is that the pro-Communist background of Lee Harvey Oswald . . . may lead in some places to another Communist hunt that will divide the country and complicate the new President's relations with Moscow."[56]

Hand it to the left: from Oswald to Loughner, they're unbelievably consistent.

Even after a leftist had shot the president of the United States, the right had to be blamed. Because, after all, we wouldn't want those flag-waving idiots pushing for a stronger pro-American foreign policy, would we?

"ISLAMOPHOBES"

Fast-forward almost four decades from the JFK assassination.

On September 11, 2001, three thousand Americans were murdered in flame and ash.

The left responded with fury and fear—not about the Muslim terrorists who had forced Americans to leap to their deaths from the World Trade Center or crash a plane in a field in Pennsylvania, but about those dastardly conservatives, who would no doubt start burning mosques.

The left quickly proclaimed that Islam meant peace, and that Americans had to be policed for signs of Islamophobia. If we weren't, they implied, we were sure to go around burning crescents into lawns and stringing Iranian shopkeepers up on lampposts. This philosophy was so deeply rooted that it became a hallmark of the Bush administration, which routinely implied that Americans were on the verge of rioting in the streets, throwing lard on Muslim kids.

It was a subtle bully tactic. And it worked. It taught Americans that any action against any Muslims in any country—no matter how guilty they were—would only enmesh America in a cycle of violence. President Bush, infected with the spinelessness of a perversely Arabist State Department, said in the days after September 11, "We must be mindful that, as we seek to win the war, we treat Arab-Americans with the respect they deserve. There are thousands of Arab-Americans who live in New York City who love their flag. We should not hold one who is a Muslim responsible for an act of terror."[57] This was a warning that would go unheeded by actual racists—after all, why would they care about what Bush said?—but it would infect the American mentality with the notion that any anti-Muslim action had to be secretly linked with xenophobia.

That sentiment broke out into the open immediately after September 11, when members of the far left began complaining about American action in Afghanistan. International Act Now to Stop War and End Racism (ANSWER) began marching against action in Afghanistan immediately. Not coincidentally, ANSWER's steering committee was composed of groups like the Free Palestine Alliance, the Muslim Students Association, and the Party for Socialism and Liberation. Actually, ANSWER was closely associated with the Stalinist Workers World Party. They were anti-Semitic and anti-American. But their accusations—that America wanted war with brown people to gain oil—began to seep into the public consciousness.

A more subtle form of the argument came from the less openly ridiculous left. They suggested that September 11 was itself a symptom of evil American foreign policy in the Middle East. Howard Zinn's popular *A People's History of the United States* informed the American people that "terrorism was rooted in deep grievances against the United States. . . . However, these issues could not be addressed without fundamental changes in American foreign policy." Those changes, however, could not be undertaken, thanks to the interference from "the military-industrial complex that dominated both parties."[58] Ron Paul, a leftist on foreign policy, echoed this perspective. Osama bin Laden, said Paul, was driven by anger at the Gulf War in 1991, which had been fought to "protect our oil. . . . Muslims see this as an invasion and domination by a foreign enemy, which inspires radicalism."[59] In this perspective, Americans were "little Eichmanns" (Professor Ward Churchill's words), and America's "chickens were coming home to roost" (the perspective of Obama spiritual mentor Jeremiah Wright).

By the time the Bush administration began pushing for military action against Saddam Hussein, this underground view became full-blown leftist bullying. There were many legitimate reasons to attack the war in Iraq. Supposed racism was not one of them. Neither was supposed profit-making for Halliburton and the oil industry. But that didn't stop the left, which now accused the Bush administration—the same Bush administration that had been parroting the liberal line that Americans were secret anti-Muslim, anti-Arab racists—of racism and imperialism.

The "America fights racist wars" perspective is now common parlance on the left. Tom Hanks, producer of *Saving Private Ryan* as well as HBO's *Band of Brothers* and *The Pacific*, said that the wars in Iraq and Afghanistan were just like the American war against the Japanese: "Back in World War II, we viewed the Japanese as 'yellow, slant-eyed dogs' that believed in different gods. They were out to kill us because our way of living was different. We, in turn, wanted to annihilate them because they were different. Does that sound familiar to what's going on today?"[60] Tom must have forgotten about that whole Pearl Harbor thing.

This sort of bullying by the left teaches Americans to back down in the face of *real* threats. Americans have been taught by the left that they're like Bruce Banner—if something, *anything* bad happens, we've been told, we immediately go berserk, transforming into a ten-foot-tall green monster that likes to bash minorities against walls. And if we *do* push for military action, all we're doing is participating in a racist cycle of violence.

This has become a regular media narrative. On the second anniversary of September 11, the BBC ran a piece titled "US Muslims fight 9/11 backlash."[61] On the eighth anniversary of September 11, the Associated Press ran a long piece decrying the treatment of Muslims in America. "There is the dread of leaving the house that morning. People might stare, or worse, yell insults." The AP reported, disapproval dripping from its pen, "A poll released this week by the Pew Forum on Religion & Public Life found that 38 percent of Americans believe Islam is more likely than other faiths to encourage violence." That might have something to do with the fact that Islam is more likely than other faiths to encourage violence. But the point of the AP story was obvious: Americans are racists. The 9/11 attacks just showed it.[62]

And because Americans are racists, they must be stopped from interfering in world affairs.

On the tenth anniversary of September 11, the *New York Times* ran an editorial by Ahmed Rashid proclaiming just that. "After 9/11," he said, "Hate Begat Hate." Because of America's knee-jerk intolerance of Islam, said Rashid, "the wave of anti-Americanism is rising in both Afghanistan and Pakistan, even among many who once admired the United States, and the short reason for that is plain. . . . The more belligerent detractors of America will tell you that Americans are imperialists who hate Islam, and that Americans' so-called civilizing instincts have nothing to do with democracy or human rights. A more politically attuned attitude is that the detractor doesn't hate Americans, just the policies that American leaders pursue." How can we solve this problem? Says Rashid, "The questions about who hates whom will become only more difficult until the warfare ends and national healing begins."[63]

In other words, leave those terrorists alone, dammit.

This has an impact. The "cycle of violence" rhetoric, which implies that our response to Muslim violence springs from xenophobia and corruption, cows Americans into inaction when we're attacked. That, of course, is the goal of the left, which doesn't want America fighting back.

BULLYING THE TROOPS

The left bullies Americans into fearing their own patriotism. But since the 1970s, they haven't attempted to bully Americans into fearing or disowning the military.

That's not to say their anti-military bias doesn't come creeping out at inopportune moments. When Hillary Clinton was first lady, she may not have been able to control her husband's pants, but she tried to control the wearing of military uniforms in the White House. And every so often, you get an honest leftist appraisal of the military from geniuses like Senator Dick Durbin (D-IL), who compared military treatment of terrorist detainees to "Nazis, Soviets in their gulags or some mad regime—Pol Pot or others—that had no concern for human beings."[64] But overall, the left has been on its best behavior about our troops since the halcyon Kerry Winter Soldier days.

That's because the left has found a far better use for the military: as tools in their anti-patriotic bullying agenda.

The left has a tremendous advantage when it comes to the military: the military works for the government, and military men and women are bound by law from speaking out *as* military folks. Required to remain largely silent, expected to stay apolitical, men and women of the military are instead utilized as cannon fodder for the liberal agenda.

The left says that only those who have served in the military can be pro-war. This is the scurrilous so-called chickenhawk argument—you can't have been a "chicken" (a person who didn't serve in the military) and be a "hawk" on foreign policy. As Michael Moore put it, a chickenhawk is "[a] person enthusiastic about war, provided someone else fights it; particularly when that enthusiasm is undimmed by personal experience with war; most emphatically when that lack of experience came in spite of ample opportunity in that person's youth." The "chickenhawk" argument was picked up by government actors like Senator Frank Lautenberg (D-NJ), who, campaigning for John Kerry, labeled Vice President Dick Cheney a "chickenhawk."[65] Leftists routinely called President Bush a chickenhawk, even though he served in the Air National Guard, because his daughters didn't join the military. (Bill Clinton, who actually dodged the draft, was not a chickenhawk, presumably because he is pro-abortion and raised taxes.)

These days, it's 2012 Republican presidential candidate Mitt Romney who gets tarred with the "chickenhawk" argument—not President Obama, who has actually ordered troops into action. "Frankly, I'm getting tired of hearing pandering politicians cast about for votes by offering up the lives of other people's kids in the name of national security," writes Paul Whitefield of the *Los Angeles Times*. "Take Romney's sons: Did he offer *them* up as cannon fodder?"[66]

These folks suggest that you can't be a hawk unless you or your kids are in the military. Then they try to make sure that actual military folks can't vote (see absentee ballots, Florida).

The assumption behind the chickenhawk argument is simple: the horrors of war are so great that all soldiers and ex-soldiers are secretly pacifists. The only problem with this argument is that it's dead wrong. Every poll ever taken has shown that men and women of the military are significantly more conservative than the general civilian population. As a civilian, I'd be happy to establish a blanket policy that only military and ex-military men and women get to vote on foreign policy. But the left wouldn't like the result.

The left knows this, which leads to their second bully tactic against the military: they're victims. According to the left, even though the men and women of the military are all volunteers, they're also idiots, suckered into the armed services by promises of glory and grants. Nobody with an education ever goes into the military. Only if you ignore education, as John Kerry put it, do you "get stuck in Iraq."[67] That's why the left ardently opposes the presence of the Reserve Officers Training Corps on high school and college campuses—you never know when those uniformed devils will pounce on an unsuspecting goober and convince him to sign his life away.

The corollary of this argument is that most of these poor goobers are black, Hispanic, and undereducated—or some combination of all the above. In December 2002, gravel-voiced Representative Charles Rangel (D-NY) proposed reinstating the draft, since a "disproportionate number of the poor and members of minority groups make up the enlisted ranks of the military, while most privileged Americans are underrepresented or absent." Bob Herbert of the *New York Times* followed suit, stating that "very few" of the soldiers on the ground in Iraq "are coming from the privileged economic classes." His point: if rich kids had to fight, there would be no wars.

None of this is true. Soldiers are more educated than the general population—98 percent of those who enlist already have high school diplomas (as opposed to 75 percent of the general population); since 9/11, enlistment has been disproportionate among middle- and upper-class men and women; racially, the military is almost directly proportional to the country (77 percent of Americans are white, and so are 76 percent of its military volunteers). As Tim Kane and James Jay Carafano of the Heritage Foundation write, the left wants to "manufacture the oxymoronic case that volunteers are coerced."[68]

The left goes even further than the slur that volunteers are coerced. They aren't just coerced—they're nuts. The crazy-vet theme goes all the way back to the Vietnam War, when Hollywood decided that veterans had been victimized by the military-industrial complex. Hollywood "sympathetically" turned them into drooling psychopaths, epitomized by Sylvester Stallone in *Rambo*, Christopher Walken in *The Deer Hunter*, Robert De Niro in *Taxi Driver*, and Bruce Dern in *Coming Home*.

It's why the left insisted that Major Nidal Hasan, the Islamist terrorist who stands accused of murdering thirteen people and wounding twenty-nine others at Fort Hood, Texas, in 2009, was a victim of post-traumatic stress disorder. Sadly, that narrative fell apart when it turned out that Hasan had never deployed to a battle zone. So the left came up with a new idea—he was the victim of "secondary trauma." The *New York Times* contended that "repeated stories of battle and loss can leave the most professional therapist numb or angry. . . . That was the world that Maj. Nidal Malik Hasan, an Army psychiatrist, inhabited until Thursday."[69] Forget all that shouting about "Allahu akhbar!" The real problem is that Hasan had to listen to people talk about their deployments.

Hasan, then, was a victim. A victim of the military-industrial complex. A victim of war. Sure, he'd never seen war. But he'd heard all about it. And that was just as good as the real thing.

Not only that—the military, pushed by the Obama administration, promptly declared that Hasan was a victim of both war *and* xenophobia. In fact, if we had learned anything from a radical

Muslim shooting American soldiers, it was that we had to protect radical Muslims in the army. "Our diversity," said General George Casey, top officer of the U.S. Army, "not only in our Army, but in our country, is a strength. And as horrific as this tragedy was, if our diversity becomes a casualty, I think that's worse."[70]

Probably not. Diversity doesn't bleed out and leave behind widows and orphans.

What's the point of the "soldiers are victims" slur? It means that good-hearted Americans, if they truly love the troops, will keep them out of harm's way. In the leftist view, there are only three types of soldiers: antiwar soldiers, who have learned the brutality of battle and embraced pacifism (Tom Cruise in *Born on the Fourth of July*); pro-war soldiers, who are barbarians looking to "get some" (Matt Dillon in *Platoon*); and ignorant soldiers, who are just too dumb to get anything (everybody in *Apocalypse Now* except Martin Sheen and Marlon Brando). The soldiers who want to do their job and go home? They don't exist. They didn't choose freely to be there. It's *our* job to ensure that they are never asked to fire their weapons. And if we *do* ask them to go into battle, we have somehow befouled our own patriotism.

Hence the left's paternalistic view of soldiers as inanimate objects to be waved in the faces of nonliberals. President Obama does this routinely. He sees the soldiers as "photo ops" and that means he can use them for his own ends.

And he uses them and throws them away like Kleenex.

On Memorial Day, during that Vietnam War speech in which he ripped the left's prior treatment of Vietnam vets, he subtly ripped President Bush and implied that many Americans are too cavalier about the deaths of soldiers—an absolutely scurrilous suggestion. And he used his favorite line: "[L]et us never use patriotism as a political sword. Patriots can support a war; patriots can oppose a war. And whatever our view, let us always stand united in support of our troops, who we placed in harm's way."[71]

Nice words. But Obama's support for the troops was a cynical campaign ploy, as he made clear just a month earlier when he flew to Afghanistan to claim credit for the Osama bin Laden kill. Sure, he praised the troops—he's an exploiter, not an idiot. And exploit he did. With the troops coming home, the only way to make their sacrifice worthwhile, said Obama, was to embrace his domestic agenda. "We must redouble our efforts to build a nation worthy of their sacrifice," he said. "As we emerge from a decade of conflict abroad and economic crisis at home, it is time to renew America."[72] In case you missed it, Obama spelled out the message more clearly in his weekly YouTube address: "[A]fter more than a decade of war, it is time to focus on nation building here at home. As a new greatest generation returns from overseas, we must ask ourselves, what kind of country will they come back to? Will it be a country where a shrinking number of Americans do really well while a growing number barely get by? Or will it be a country where everyone gets a fair shot, everyone does their fair share, and everyone plays by the same set of rules—a country with opportunity worthy of the troops who protect us?" Obama explicitly called for more spending on "clean energy," on "education and medical research," and on "newer, faster transportation and communications networks."[73]

So, we should never exploit patriotism to pursue a political goal—like, say, defeating communism or Nazism or radical Islam. But we should exploit patriotism to pursue high-speed rail.

Imagine if George W. Bush had said something similar: "Well, folks, we need to build a nation worthy of our troops by enshrining my new tax rates and minimizing burdensome environmental overregulation." Do you think the left *might* have suggested that such a tactic was a disgrace to the troops?

Using the troops as political cannon fodder is bullying. And that's what Obama and his ilk do daily.

What's more, they don't care about the military *unless* they're using it for political cannon fodder. The left routinely seeks to cut military funding. When Democrats negotiated a deficit reduction plan with Republicans, their default position was military cuts before domestic cuts. Liberals constantly leap on incidents like Abu Ghraib or marines urinating on terrorist corpses in Afghanistan as evidence that our troops are out of control. They *live* for moments when they can channel their hippy parents' outrage over My Lai. They long desperately for the moral clarity of *Casualties of War* and sob in confusion over the ambiguities in *We Were Soldiers*. When Scott Thomas Beauchamp wrote long diaries about his time in Iraq for the *New Republic*, suggesting that Americans were engaging in war crimes, the magazine couldn't wait to print it—without any evidence.

The left truly bullies the military when it gets the chance by reining them in.

They are always on the lookout for signs of overweening nationalism among the troops. When American soldiers took Baghdad, tore down a massive statue of Saddam Hussein, and draped an American flag over its face, liberals—and the supposed conservative castrati—were aghast. It didn't matter that the flag itself had been carried all the way over from the Pentagon, where it had been hanging on September 11. "That should have been the Iraqi flag," said a miffed announcer on Al Arabiya.[74] "The flag incidents reinforced Arab fears that occupation is the hidden motive behind the U.S. invasion of Iraq," tut-tutted the *Chicago Tribune*. The Army quickly ordered that nobody display the U.S. flag on cars, buildings, statues, or virtually anything else. The order: "[D]isplaying the American flag counters the perception that we are liberators and allows enemy and other bad actors to use the images of our flags prominently displayed to reinforce their message that the U.S. is here to oppress the Iraqis."[75] Wouldn't want to offend the natives for whom American soldiers had just bled and died, would we?

But the truly serious bullying of the military comes in the form of civilian-issued rules of engagement. The rules of engagement are simply not built for actual combat situations. They are written by those who are afraid that American soldiers will turn baby-killers the moment they're let off the leash. Cultural sensitivity takes precedence over preserving the lives of our soldiers. Army Staff Sergeant David Bellavia writes about his tour in Iraq in 2004—and his stories leave you with your jaw on the floor. In one village, the sheikhs suggested that for cultural reasons Americans could not enter the area in vehicles or tanks. "Our platoons basically said, 'Yes,'" said Bellavia. "We were sent to fight al-Qaeda and in that situation we were forced to fight on al-Qaeda's terms."[76] The first Battle of Fallujah was stopped just short of its goal—defanging Muqtada al-Sadr, then the leader of the Shiite insurgency—because American brass didn't want Americans entering a mosque.

In 2010, General Stanley A. McChrystal laid down the so-called Karzai 12 rules of engagement in Afghanistan. "It's a framework to ensure cultural sensitivity in planning and executive operations," explained Captain Casey Thoreen. Meanwhile, Americans were dying.[77]

Is some of this a strategic decision designed to win hearts and minds? Certainly. But some of it is sheer absurdist leftism that has infiltrated the hearts and minds of the military leadership. According to the *Military Times*, "A certain group of Marines in Afghanistan were asked by their leaders to avoid farting audibly around their Afghan partners because they are offended by flatulence."[78] Seriously. Farting.

CONCLUSION

"If fascism ever comes to America," leftists misattribute Sinclair Lewis as stating, "it will be wrapped in a flag and carrying a cross." Actually, when fascism tried to come to America, it was the left that wrapped itself in a flag to promote it. Today's conservatives wrap themselves in the flag to fight dictatorial regimes across the globe and overreaching government at home. Those who uphold the flag typically uphold American values.

A recent Harvard study showed that July Fourth celebrations tend to make children more Republican. "The political right has been more successful in appropriating American patriotism and its symbols during the 20th century," wrote the researchers. "Survey evidence also confirms that Republicans consider themselves more patriotic than Democrats. According to this interpretation, there is a political congruence between the patriotism promoted on Fourth of July and the values associated with the Republican party." One sunny July Fourth celebration prior to reaching age eighteen, says the study, will increase the likelihood of voting Republican by 2 percent, and 4 percent over the course of their young adulthood.[79]

No wonder. Ask the average leftist in an honest moment whether they'd be more comfortable wearing an American flag T-shirt in multicultural company or an Obama T-shirt, and they'll tell you the truth: the red, white, and blue *O* takes precedence over the flag our fathers fought for. The problem is that the left has translated that discomfort to a broad swath of Americans, who now feel a vague sense of unease—the feeling that they're being somewhat rude—if they stand up for American exceptionalism. They've been bullied. And deep down, they know it.

In 1968, in response to the actions of groups like SDS and the Weathermen, Congress passed the Flag Protection Act. Then, in 1988, a communist burned a flag at the Republican National Convention. When he was arrested, he sued; the Supreme Court of the United States, by a vote of 5–4, overturned two centuries of American law and announced that the First Amendment was designed to protect flag-burning. "It is poignant but fundamental that the flag protects those who hold it in contempt," wrote Justice Anthony Kennedy.[80]

The flag may protect those who hold it in contempt. But those who hold it in contempt have bullied Americans into believing that only Americans' silence to anti-patriotism makes them patriots. They have bullied Americans into accepting the false and pernicious notion that dissent is the highest form of patriotism, and that nationalistic pride is jingoistic nonsense. The only cure for traditional patriotism, the left insists, is a *new* kind of patriotism—one that rejects America as an exceptional nation, and instead embraces her as one nation among equals.

That is the left's anti-patriotic message. It cuts the heart from American assertiveness, gladdening dictators and dooming millions across the globe to darkness. And at home, it dooms us to gradual abandonment of the very values that make us great. After all, if we can be bullied into silence, who will be left to fight for founding principles?

3.

RACE BULLIES

On March 23, 2012, President Obama announced that Americans had to do some "soul searching." The reason? A seventeen-year-old young man named Trayvon Martin had been shot and killed in Sanford, Florida.

Now, what separated young Trayvon from all of his teenage peers shot across the country? What made him special, worthy of presidential comment? Was he an honor student? Was he a potential president of a Fortune 500 company? Was he on the fast track to curing cancer?

Probably not. Shortly before his death, Trayvon had been suspended from school for ten days for carrying around a Baggie with pot residue. He'd been suspended two other times, once for missing school, and a second time for tagging "WTF" on a hallway locker; a security guard searched his backpack and found women's rings, earrings, and a screwdriver. Authorities described the screwdriver as a "burglary tool."[1] He wore a grille in his mouth. He was tattooed. He dressed like a punk.

His Twitter feed was filled with misogynistic, drug-loving garbage. Reading the tweets makes you weep for America and her education system. His Twitter handle? @NO_LIMIT_NIGGA. There are precisely zero members of the Mensa Society with similar Twitter handles. He particularly enjoyed retweeting sexist comments from his friends:

"RT@x_highlyfavored:f— a bitch. any bitch. who you want? take yo pick, but you have gone have to take yo time."

"RT @Mitchell_Garcia: I'll slap a girl if she said suck my toes wtf, she must be giving some great dome for some s— like that u u u."

"RT @fukunurhoexxx: #youthetype of b— that give up your p—y for free and think its cool #p—yaintfree #fb."

"RT @x_highlyfavored: '@Slim_Nigga: I wanna experience a white girl just one time.'"

And he used some hieroglyphics of his own:

"BEND IT OVA HOE!!→_|¯|o"[2]

Which, loosely translated, means "I hate women." Or "I hate English." Martin's parents should have slapped a bumper sticker on their car: "If my child can't read, write, or tweet coherently, blame a teacher . . . and his parents."

Trayvon's classy friends tweeted him about whether he punched a bus driver: "<<<<yu ain't tell me yu swung on a bus driver," tweeted @RIP_TRAY9. They tweeted over and over about smoking marijuana. One @MrMonopolSKEE tweeted a picture of a rolled marijuana cigarette in tribute to Trayvon. One of his Facebook friends messaged him prior to his death, "damn were u at a nigga needa plant."

So this was the young man Obama chose to eulogize.

Now, none of this is to say that Martin should have been shot and killed. But it was quite odd for Obama to single out Martin's death, as opposed to other victims with less-checkered histories.

According to Obama, we were all supposed to search our collective souls about Trayvon Martin's death. We weren't supposed to consider the actual facts surrounding his shooting. We weren't supposed to consider his prior behavior, his penchant for drug use, his previous disciplinary actions.

We were supposed to consider one fact, and one fact only: Trayvon Martin was black. Or, as Obama put it, "If I had a son, he'd look like Trayvon."[3]

Apparently, all black people look alike to Obama. In reality, Trayvon would look nothing like Obama's potential son. But the important thing was that Trayvon shared a skin color with the president.

Unlike the famed Henry Louis Gates Jr. incident, in which President Obama slandered the Cambridge, Massachusetts, police for arresting a black Harvard professor, this remark wasn't off-the-cuff. It was well planned and well executed. White House Press Secretary Jay Carney said that Obama had known about the Martin story for days, and "clearly had some thoughts about it and—as a parent, and expressed those to [the media] today." Earlier in the week, the White House had ignored the question; now, said Carney, Obama was "certainly prepared to answer a question if he were to get one." Said Obama, "When I think about this boy, I think about my own kids."[4]

Of course, that wasn't all it took for Trayvon Martin to become a household name. He also had to be shot to death by a supposed white person.

The word *supposed* is used advisedly here, because Trayvon Martin's shooter was a fellow named George Zimmerman. The media quickly labeled Zimmerman "white." In actuality, Zimmerman was of Hispanic origin, but that didn't matter to either the media or to the Democratic Party and liberal organizational establishment. They wanted a racist shooting in preparation for the 2012 election so that they could claim that America was still a racist country. The implication would be clear: the only way Americans could prove that they *weren't* racist was by reelecting President Obama. Hence President Obama's bizarre self-insertion into the story. It was no coincidence. Dozens of black teens are gunned down each year in major cities across the United States. None of them has a face or a name that anyone knows. But Trayvon did, because he was a bullying tool for Obama and his minions.

The left never cared about Trayvon Martin or his family. They didn't give a damn. They didn't care about him when his parents split. They didn't care about him when he misbehaved in school. They didn't care about him when he started doing drugs, and possibly dealing drugs. They didn't care about him when he got tattoos, dressed like a thug, and tweeted misogynistically. They cared about one thing and one thing only: achieving their political ends by exploiting a dead black teen. The minute Trayvon's story hit the press, the left began drooling. That's what they do when they see an opportunity to bully Americans using race as a club. Their goal: silence Americans who disagree with the liberal agenda by labeling them part of the unalterably racist white majority. The bullies were people of all races united by a common cause: using race to bully their political opponents into submission.

It's important to note that there's a pattern to racial controversies in America. Usually it begins with a flash-point event—some event occurs that may or may not have anything to do with race. The media, in coordination with leftist groups, then launches a smear campaign to turn the event into the Biggest Event Ever, evidence that racism is rife in America. With that groundwork in place, they then proclaim that events like the Biggest Event Ever will continue to take place unless vaguely defined, albeit nonexistent systemic racism is removed from the equation—which, of course, can happen only if liberal policies are enacted, and if conservatives shut the hell up.

The Trayvon Martin case played out the leftist strategy perfectly.

ANATOMY OF A RACIAL BULLYING: THE FLASH POINT

The real story of the Trayvon killing began three weeks earlier. George Zimmerman, a Hispanic American, lived in a gated community in Sanford, Florida, called the Retreat at Twin Lakes. He was a twenty-eight-year-old insurance fraud investigator with a religious Catholic background. According to Reuters, "He was raised in a racially integrated household and himself has black roots through an Afro-Peruvian great-grandfather—the father of the maternal grandmother who helped raise him." During his young adulthood, he and a black friend partnered in starting a business. Now, Zimmerman was no angel. He had two prior arrests, one for assaulting a police officer, and one for domestic abuse. The charge for domestic abuse was dropped; the charge for assaulting a police officer was reduced to resisting arrest without violence. So there was evidence that Zimmerman had serious temper issues. There was *zero* evidence he was a budding KKK member.

After Zimmerman moved to the Retreat, which was 20 percent black, the neighborhood fell victim to a series of crimes perpetrated by young men who looked like Barack Obama's fictional son. Vandalism and robberies became commonplace, and drug activity became a serious problem. From November 2010 to February 2012, there were at least eight burglaries in the neighborhood. Dozens more reports of attempted burglaries made the neighborhood gossip rounds. In July 2011, a young black man stole Zimmerman's bicycle from his home. In August 2011, Shellie Zimmerman, George's wife, saw a young black man fleeing a nearby home during a robbery. "We were calling the police at least once a week," said a neighborhood resident. By September 2011, the neighborhood had asked Zimmerman to lead their neighborhood watch program. In February 2012, the Retreat's monthly newsletter stated, "The Sanford PD has announced an increased patrol within our neighborhood . . . during peak crime hours. If you've been a victim of a crime in the community, after calling police, please contact our captain, George Zimmerman."

On February 2, 2012, Zimmerman called 911 after he saw a young black man possibly scouting out a robbery location—an empty home. "I don't know what he's doing," said Zimmerman. "I don't want to approach him, personally." Zimmerman didn't. The cops sent a car; by the time it got there, the suspect was gone.

Four days later, two young black men burglarized another home in the Retreat. The police caught one of the suspects, eighteen-year-old Emmanuel Burgess, and found stolen property on him.[5]

About three weeks later, on February 26, 2012, Zimmerman was driving to the grocery store when he spotted a young black man walking around the neighborhood. He immediately called the nonemergency number at the Sanford Police Department. "Hey," said Zimmerman, "we've had some break-ins in my neighborhood, and there's a real suspicious guy, uh, it's Retreat View Circle, um, the best address I can give you is 111 Retreat View Circle. This guy looks like he's up to no good, or he's on drugs or something. It's raining and he's just walking around, looking about." The dispatcher asked if the suspect was "white, black, or Hispanic?" Zimmerman answered, "He looks black." The dispatcher asked what the suspect was wearing. "A dark hoodie, like a gray hoodie, and either jeans or sweatpants and white tennis shoes. He's here now, he was just staring," said Zimmerman.

The suspect, said Zimmerman, was "looking at all the houses. . . . Now he's just staring at me. . . . Yeah, now he's coming towards me. . . . He's got his hand in his waistband. And he's a black male. . . . He's got buttons on his shirt, late teens. . . . Something's wrong with him. Yup, he's coming to check me out, he's got something in his hands, I don't know what his deal is. . . . See if you can get an officer over here. . . . These a—h—, they always get away." Zimmerman then told the dispatcher that the suspect was running.

Zimmerman apparently got out of his car. Still on his phone, he told the dispatcher he was following the suspect. "Okay, we don't need you to do that," said the dispatcher. At some point during the call, Zimmerman lost track of the suspect. The conversation continued, with Zimmerman saying he would meet law enforcement. Then he hung up.[6] The time was approximately 7:13 p.m.

What happened next remains controversial.

Martin's defenders maintained that Zimmerman provoked a physical confrontation with Martin, then shot him in cold blood.

Zimmerman claimed that Martin confronted him and demanded to know why Zimmerman was following him; Martin, said Zimmerman, then punched him in the face.

Whatever happened, Zimmerman clearly fell backward onto the ground.

At this point, witness testimony takes over. Trayvon jumped on top of him and began beating him savagely, pounding his head into the ground. Zimmerman, according to witnesses, was screaming for help. According to one witness, Trayvon was pummeling Zimmerman "MMA-style"—mixed martial arts, a brutal form of combat with no holds barred.[7]

Zimmerman then reached into his waistband, pulled out his handgun, and shot Trayvon in the chest, killing him.

Zimmerman's story was corroborated by all available evidence, including the physical evidence: Martin's body was undamaged except for the gunshot wound and injuries to his knuckles, indicating that he had been hitting someone, while Zimmerman's head had massive lacerations, he had two black eyes, and his nose had been broken.[8]

The Sanford Police Department arrested Zimmerman and brought him to the police station for questioning. He asserted self-defense, and the police found no evidence to disprove it. While the police filed a "capias request," which suggests that criminal charges be filed, investigators decided that such a request was inappropriate in this case.[9]

ANATOMY OF A RACIAL BULLYING: THE SMEAR CAMPAIGN

And that's where the case lay for one day. Two days. A week. A full eleven days. While local media covered the story, that's what it remained—a local story, one of dozens of shootings around the country every week.

Then, on March 8, 2012, the mainstream media finally decided to weigh in.

The Associated Press wrote a nationally syndicated story highlighting specific facts that made the killing seem racial in nature. Trayvon's family's attorneys, the AP reported, "said they believed Trayvon Martin was being profiled at the time of the encounter because he was a young black man. The neighborhood watch leader is white. The attorneys also questioned why a neighborhood watch leader would carry a gun. 'He was stereotyped for some reason,' attorney Ben Crump said of the victim. 'Why was Trayvon suspicious? There are hundreds of children in that community.'"[10]

It was an entirely one-sided hit piece on Zimmerman—and the fact that it labeled Zimmerman "white" sparked a firestorm. Now the story wasn't a Hispanic man killing a young black man who was ramming his skull against the sidewalk. It was a white guy straight from *Birth of a Nation* stalking a young black man and murdering him in cold blood.

This was a much sexier narrative than the truth. And so it became common belief. Only later, when it came out that Zimmerman was in fact Hispanic, did the media back down—and they did so only by coining a new term, "white Hispanic," since Zimmerman was of mixed parentage. By that standard, Barack Obama is "white black."

In any case, the media coverage was black-and-white.

Al Sharpton—an alleged news host for MSNBC, which would be like Fox News hiring David Duke to do a show in prime time—

quickly jetted down to Florida, eager to get his shaggy mane before a camera. It wasn't enough that this was the man who had disgraced himself repeatedly in the Tawana Brawley case, in which he falsely accused a white man of raping a black woman, and the Duke lacrosse case, in which he falsely accused several white men of raping a black woman—now he wanted to play the race card on George Zimmerman, with the help of the NBC News brass. His National Action Network immediately released a statement calling for a "full investigation"—and then simultaneously stated, "The fact that a young unarmed man could be killed by a neighborhood watch captain while his family was blatantly misled by local police as to the background of the shooter is disturbing. Further, the fact that we are told that racial language was used when the young man reported his suspicions to police . . . is a compelling reason for NAN and I to become involved."[11] So Sharpton had two problems: he didn't care about the facts, and he didn't care about grammar.

The next night, Sharpton interviewed Martin's family attorney. The attorney called Zimmerman "white." Sharpton didn't contradict him. But then again, you couldn't expect Sharpton to "resist he much."

The media quickly supplemented the narrative by presenting George Zimmerman as a racist monster, and Trayvon Martin as a darling little angel. Charles Blow of the *New York Times* wrote a race-baiting masterpiece centered on a simple fact: "Trayvon is black. Zimmerman is not." He continued, "As the father of two black teenage boys, this case hits close to home. This is the fear that seizes me whenever my boys are out in the world: that a man with a gun and an itchy finger will find them 'suspicious.' That passions may run hot and blood run cold. That it might all end with a hole in their chest and hole in my heart. That the law might prove insufficient to salve my loss. That is the burden of black boys in America and the people that love them: running the risk of being descended upon in the dark and caught in the cross-hairs of someone who crosses the line." And then, ominously: "that is the burden of black boys, and this case can either ease or exacerbate it."[12] In other words, if Zimmerman wasn't arrested, tried, and convicted, it meant that America was deeply racist. Even if he *was* arrested, tried, and convicted, "black boys" would still carry their burden. But if he *wasn't*, it just showed that America was still racist.

Zimmerman's 2005 arrest mug shot (for battery) was flashed across televisions throughout the nation, unshaven, heavy, and menacing. Meanwhile, the pictures of Trayvon Martin used by the media and supplied by the family showed a kid who *did* look like Obama's hypothetical son: twelve years old, clean-cut, bright smile. To look at the pictures, you'd assume that Zimmerman was a linebacker attacking a waif; in reality, Zimmerman was five foot eight and 185 pounds, while Trayvon was five foot eleven and clocked in at 158 pounds. Newer photos showed Trayvon sporting tattoos and a grille, and looking significantly more menacing than he had at age twelve. When this was pointed out, of course, the left-wing media called *that* racism, suggesting that it was fine to bias the pictures against Zimmerman, but to do so against Trayvon was George Wallace lite.[13]

The New Black Panther Party showed up outside the Sanford, Florida, police headquarters three days later demanding an arrest.[14] Three days after that, a massive crowd, including leaders from the NAACP, the Urban League, and the Sanford City Commission, massed at Allen Chapel AME Church to call for Zimmerman's arrest. Local city officials called on the police chief to resign. Rev. Jamal Bryant, a Baltimore preacher, came to put the Zimmerman case into a broader racial context: "We call for an immediate arrest. We want him behind bars," said Bryant. "Because you have arrested a lot of black men without probable cause." He then led the crowd in chants of "If there is no justice, there is no peace." He railed, "This is a wake-up call for the state of Florida, and for any racist who has a gun and thinks it's a license to kill our children."[15]

This was disgusting. Bryant and company spoke from complete ignorance. Was Zimmerman a racist? There was no evidence to that effect. Did he hunt down Trayvon in cold blood, looking to kill him? Certainly not. But that didn't matter to them. They wanted a race case, and they were going to fit this square peg into that round hole no matter what. The Zimmerman lynching had begun.

And it *was* a lynching.

On March 23, President Obama stepped into the case—not coincidentally, just three days before Obama's signature health-care legislation came up for hearing before the Supreme Court. Obama wanted Americans' attention on what was happening in the Florida courtrooms, not the halls of Washington, D.C. It was brilliant misdirection. And it succeeded.

Now Obama had opened the floodgates. The next day, the New Black Panthers led a protest in Sanford. There, leader Mikhail Muhammad—someone who certainly needs a day job—put a bounty on George Zimmerman's head: ten thousand dollars. Someone asked him whether he meant to cause violence to Zimmerman. "An eye for an eye, a tooth for a tooth," said Muhammad. The Panthers also suggested that ten thousand black men should go on the hunt for the fugitive Neighborhood Watch volunteer Zimmerman. "If the government won't do the job, we'll do it!" he yelled. The city begged for quiet. The Panthers wouldn't let up. Instead, when the police arrived to keep the peace, Muhammad shouted, "If you'd had shown this much concern, Trayvon may still be alive today!" Even black residents were getting freaked out by this point. "I'm as much for black power as anybody," said one puzzled resident. "But this is going to alienate the white friends we need to get things done." The Panthers were less concerned about alienating whites than about milking blacks for cash—they wanted to raise $1 million for their anti-Zimmerman campaign.[16]

Where there's money to be made, Rev. Jesse Jackson is never far behind—and he, too, told the fictional story of poor little Trayvon, stalked and killed by George "Hitler Youth" Zimmerman. Preaching before 1,600 people in Eatonville, Florida, the Rhyming Race-baiter launched into full campaign mode. He compared Trayvon's death to the murders of Emmett Till in 1955, civil rights leader Medgar Evers in 1963, and Martin Luther King Jr. in 1968. Because as we all know, pounding a man's head into the ground and then being shot is the same as leading a struggle for equal rights for millions of black Americans.

But at least Jackson was honest. He didn't care about Trayvon in the slightest. He cared about using Trayvon as a tool to push his brand of liberalism. Trayvon, said Jackson, was "killed because he was black." Trayvon, said Jackson, was a "martyr." And that meant it was time for some leftist solutions to America's problems. It was time for war. "How do we go from a moment to a movement that creates fundamental change?" he asked. "If it's a moment, we go home. If it's a movement, we go to war." What kind of war? Political war. "I would hope that movement would turn into Trayvon Martin voter-registration rallies," said Jackson.[17] Now, put aside the passion for a moment. Martin was seventeen years old. He had never voted. And Jackson was using him as a martyr for *voter registration*?

And in his efforts to advance his cause, Jackson appears to have misstated the facts of the case. In reports from the church that were later pulled by the media, Jackson reportedly said, "Zimmerman told police he had killed him. Shot him in the back of the head in self-defense." Jackson's surrogates across the country echoed the malicious and false charge.[18]

His allies in the media, meanwhile, were spinning away furiously on behalf of Obama and his team of race-baiting liar allies. On March 26, NBC News played a tape on the *Today* show from the Zimmerman 911 call. It had been selectively edited to make Zimmerman seem racist. "This guy looks like he's up to no good. He looks black," said the tape. As you'll remember from the more complete transcript above, Zimmerman said that Trayvon looked like he was "up to no good, or he's on drugs or something. It's raining and he's just walking around, looking about." The 911 operator then *prompted* Zimmerman on Trayvon's race, to which Zimmerman said that he looked black.[19]

But the media wasn't done lying yet. CNN isolated audio that made it sound as if Zimmerman used a racial slur, mumbling about "f—ing c—ns." Mediaite repeated the falsehood. Soon it was zooming around the news sphere—Zimmerman was a racist! He'd used a fifty-year-old slur that nobody knows anymore![20] CNN even called their favorite legal nonexpert, Jeffrey Toobin, to explain that the finding was "extremely significant" and could lead to hate crimes prosecution for Zimmerman.

Oops. As it turned out, Zimmerman had said that it was "f—ing cold," since it was raining that night. Now Toobin retracted his former enthusiasm for the "c—n" charge: "[T]his certainly sounds like cold. . . . Again, everybody wants this case to be wrapped up tomorrow. This just shows why it's important to say, let's get all the best evidence we can."[21]

That was a laugh. A few days later, the media doubled down on its opposition to Zimmerman. Now he wasn't just a racist—he was lying about his own wounds. And he wasn't the only liar—the police lied, too, to cover up the murder. On March 28, ABC News released a poorly pixelated videotape of George Zimmerman in the police station after the killing. The report by Matt Gutman pulled no punches: "A police surveillance video taken the night that Trayvon Martin was shot dead shows no blood or bruises on George Zimmerman. . . . The initial police report noted that Zimmerman was bleeding from the back of the head and nose. . . ."[22] NBC News agreed. The video, they said, "shows no blood or bruises on George Zimmerman."[23]

Oops. Within a week, ABC News released enhanced video showing massive gashes on Zimmerman's dome.

It was obvious that the so-called objective news media was in the tank on the story. And they were going to ruin a man's life to achieve their political ends.

But that was the media. Surely government officials would be more responsible.

Or they could wear hoodies and complain about Zimmerman's supposed racism on the House floor.

They chose the latter. On March 20, just before President Obama took to the Rose Garden to announce the skin color of Trayvon Martin, colorfully behatted Representative Frederica Wilson (D-FL) got up on the House floor and went berserk. "Mr. Speaker, I am tired of burying young black boys. I am tired of watching them suffer at the hands of those who fear them and despise them. I am tired of comforting mothers, fathers, grandparents, sisters and brothers after such unnecessary, heinous crimes of violence." She wasn't tired, however, of a permanent black underclass brought about by a purposefully implemented regime of government dependency—after all, that's what she does for a living. Well, when she's not blaming whites for all the problems of blacks, that is: "Trayvon was running for his life. He was screaming for help, fighting for his life, and then he was murdered, shot dead. . . . No more racial profiling. I am tired of fighting when the evidence is so clear, so transparent."[24]

The evidence was clear and transparent: Frederica's hatband was too tight. But she was too busy bullying George Zimmerman—and white America—to worry about either poisoning the jury pool in the Trayvon case or pursuing the facts.

She wasn't the only one. Representative Maxine Waters (D-CA), who routinely defends violent action by black Americans, called the situation a "hate crime." Representative Emanuel Cleaver (D-MO) joined Waters in her outrage. He claimed, "The issue is the low esteem in which black life is held, particularly black males." He neglected to mention that the people who apparently hold black life in least regard are other black males, who murder blacks at rates that far outpace white-on-black murder.[25]

Meanwhile, congressional Democrats invited Trayvon's mother, Sybrina Fulton, to a hearing where she announced, "Trayvon was our son, but Trayvon was your son." Actually, his behavior was such that you could argue he was nobody's son—his parents were divorced, and he was on his way to his father's girlfriend's house when he had his fatal encounter with Zimmerman. Yet now, both of Trayvon's parents were touring the country preaching about their son. And they were toeing the liberal line, suggesting that people live "the legacy of Trayvon and [make] sure that he did not indeed die in vain."

Democrats took up the battle cry. "If you review the case, every aspect of it has been handled very poorly," said Representative Corrine Brown (D-FL), whose district includes Sanford. "I don't know whether it's incompetence, or whether it's a cover-up, or all of the above. But we have got to make sure that what has happened in Sanford, with the police department and how they have handled this situation, never happens again in the United States." Representative Sheila Jackson Lee (D-TX) said she wanted Zimmerman arrested, too.[26]

But the mother of all rants was reserved for Representative Bobby Rush (D-IL). Rush bought into the press angle that it was Martin's hoodie that led to his death—a meme repeated by celebrities from LeBron James to Chris Brown to Jamie Foxx to P. Diddy, who all donned hoodies to proclaim their support for Trayvon. Of course, one of those folks urging kids like Trayvon to go to school, stay away from drugs, and not steal things might have been more useful to Trayvon. Maybe it wouldn't have stopped him from being killed—maybe Zimmerman really went off that night. But it would have served him better during his life. Then again, such advice wouldn't have been nearly as emotionally cathartic as whining about hoodies.

Bobby Rush wanted that same catharsis. So he headed for the floor of the House, wearing a hoodie sweatshirt. There, according to the *Washington Post*, Rush delivered a "rousing speech." "I applaud the young people, all across the land who are making a statement about hoodies, about the real hoodlums in his nation, specifically those who tread on our law wearing official or quasi-official cloaks," Rush ranted. "Racial profiling has got to stop. Just because someone wears a hoodie does not make them a hoodlum." Rush was then tossed from the floor for breach of sartorial protocol.[27]

There was only one problem: hoodies do make you more suspicious. Or at least they should. Within days of Rush's House speech, hoodie-wearing gunmen shot thirteen people and killed two in Rush's district in Chicago.[28] As it turns out, wearing a hoodie to commit a crime is a great way to cover your face and prevent identification.

The Los Angeles Police Department actually admits as much. The LAPD North Hollywood Division is fine if you wear a hoodie—but they don't want you to do so inside places of commerce. In October 2011, they told store owners in the area to be on the lookout for people wearing hoodies, and asked customers to take off their hats and pull down their hoodies to prevent suspicion. "The LAPD isn't anti-hoodie," said LAPD Lieutenant Alan Hamilton. "If you walk into the LAPD academy, one of the first things you will see selling are LAPD hoodies. We are not asking you to take off your hoodie. Just take down the hood when you enter a business. It is not raining in the bank." As the *Los Angeles Times* reported, "The anti-crime tool dates at least to King Carlos III of Spain, who banned the wearing of broad-brimmed hats in the 1700s to deter robberies and other crimes."[29] Of course, the article doesn't mention that King Carlos III did it because he hated black folks.

But the fight for hoodies was a transitional moment for the Trayvon story. Until the hoodie fight, everyone had focused on Zimmerman himself, as well as the local police force—were they racist? Should Zimmerman have been arrested? With the transition to the hoodie conversation, the left was beginning to direct America's attention to policy.

And that was the final step in the Race Card Mazurka.

ANATOMY OF A RACIAL BULLYING: THE PAYOFF

While Martin's supporters—or supposed supporters—marched throughout America, protested on the floors of legislatures, and generally kicked up a fuss about the shooting of one young black man by one young Hispanic man, they didn't give a damn about Trayvon's case. If they had, they would have stopped poisoning the jury pool, making it that much more difficult to convict Zimmerman in a trial by giving his lawyers the ability to appeal any verdict.

No, they were interested in something much more valuable than Zimmerman's scalp: they were interested in political point-scoring. And if it took violence to make those political points, so be it.

Even as the left decried racial profiling and violent action from Zimmerman, they had nothing to say about the violence they were themselves breeding. When Zimmerman was actually arrested and then released on bail, Twitter went wild with thugs calling for riots across America. And the left said nothing at all.

That's because the violence they were breeding was *good* violence.

The leftist philosophy of violence is simple: It's good when it's being used for leftist causes. It's bad when it's being used for any other purpose. When Twitter nuts call for the murder of George Zimmerman,[30] or when Al Sharpton threatens the entire town of Sanford,[31] or when Spike Lee tweets the address of Zimmerman's parents' house (and gets the address wrong, threatening the lives of the actual residents),[32] that's not really a huge deal because . . . well . . . shut up, you racist! But when anyone speaks out in favor of policies that the left doesn't like, they are quickly lumped in with the racists. They're just like George Zimmerman, gunning down black folks at will, if they don't approve the straightforward leftist agenda.

This has long been the leftist pattern. Take, for example, the Rodney King riots in Los Angeles in 1992. As with Trayvon Martin, the liberal media turned an ugly incident into the pretext for a broader push for liberal policies. They started with a flash point—the beating of King—and then proceeded to ignore many of the relevant facts, including the facts that there were two other black men in King's car, neither of whom was beaten; King was speeding at 115 mph through a residential area in an attempt to avoid police so that he wouldn't be taken back to jail for violating his parole; he resisted arrest; he was Tasered, then got back up and began attacking police again, which made them believe he was on PCP. None of that justified the extent of the beating he received. But it certainly gave the beating some much-needed context. Rodney King was no victim. He was a career scumbag and criminal who beat up women, drove drunk, and robbed stores with tire irons. And, as the beating death of homeless white man Kelly Thomas in Fullerton, California, in 2011 shows, police occasionally (and wrongly) excessively beat those who resist arrest because they're *resisting arrest*, not because they're black.

But the media thought this was Bull Connor, the Birmingham commissioner of public safety who turned fire hoses on civil rights protesters, all over again. And so they played the tape over and over and over again. They cited endemic police racism as the background for the King beating. When three of the officers were acquitted and the jury split on the fourth, blacks in South Central Los Angeles immediately rioted.

Now, you'd think that when a group of folks randomly loot, beat, murder, and destroy entire neighborhoods, that would be seen as a bad thing—especially when the neighborhood they're destroying is majority black, and many of the businesses they're destroying are Korean. Fifty-three dead, 2,400 injured, 3,000 businesses ruined, and $1 billion in damage—normally, that's seen as a problem.

But not according to the left. Because the left wanted to achieve certain goals—in particular, the hamstringing of the Los Angeles Police Department, as well as the defeat of President George

H. W. Bush—these thugs became freedom fighters. Representative Maxine Waters actually encouraged the rioting, suggesting that Bush had to sic the Justice Department on the officers. Waters called the rampage "a spontaneous reaction to inequality and injustice." She called it "righteous anger, and it's difficult for me to say to the people, 'Don't be angry.' When people are angry and enraged, they do do senseless things, they do act even sometimes out of character, and that is why it is the responsibility of America to try and avoid putting people in these kinds of situations."

It was now America's fault that the scum of the earth were stealing TVs from the local Kmart.

But she wasn't done. Waters actually threatened the rest of the country with similar violence if the Bush administration didn't sic the Justice Department on the police officers. "Many other cities could go the way that Los Angeles went last night unless the president is willing to step in and take some strong action," she said. What was her ultimate goal? "We have a moral responsibility to share the resources of this country," she said. The Marxist–Race Bully Horsemen of the Apocalypse were riding again. Waters still calls the riots the "Los Angeles Rebellion." And when the National Guard came to South Central to stop the rioting, she called it an "occupation." "Riot," she blithely explained, "is the voice of the unheard."[33] In Los Angeles, of course, riots were the voice of the morons who wanted new tape decks. But same difference.

Just as with the Los Angeles riots, the left used the Trayvon case to push anticapitalism. The same day that Barack Obama claimed quasi-parentage of Trayvon, smelly, anarchist Occupy idiots joined the "Million Hoodie March"—and then proceeded to sprint through the streets of New York, overturning barricades, assaulting and taunting police officers, climbing public monuments. The videos flooded YouTube. And the mainstream media said nothing. The *New York Times* reported on the rally but said nothing about the violence; the *Los Angeles Times* talked about the glory of social networking, which had allowed the rioters to organize.

But the Occupy movement knew exactly what it was doing: they were bullying the American public with the race club, pushing for their own agenda at the same time. They didn't give a hoot about Trayvon. They just thought Trayvon would be a good excuse to bash capitalism. As Natasha Lennard, a former freelance *New York Times* reporter and Occupy Wall Street organizer, said, "It might at first seem confusing that a solidarity march over justice for a murdered Florida teen would involve mass support from Occupy Wall Street. But those who still see Occupy as limited to contesting corporate greed and the influence of money in politics have fallen behind the movement. Occupy actions take aim at all oppressive, hierarchical systems—capitalism and racism (and their interplay) among them. Indeed, a popular printed-out sign held by many on Wednesday's march read, 'You can't have capitalism without racism.'" And you can't have riots without falsely invoking racism, these days.[34]

Occupy isn't about racism. It's about anticapitalism. But the bullies saw their opportunity, and they conflated the two. Of course, as we'll see, there's a long history of Marxism infiltrating the race card movement and radicalizing it; by now, the two movements are so comfortable working together, they don't even know where they shift from black and white to red.

Capitalism wasn't the left's preferred Trayvon target—after all, they may be nasty bigots, but they're not idiots. They knew that they weren't going to overthrow the American economic system because a black teenager got shot after pounding a Hispanic man's noggin into the ground.

But the left could, at least, take out some smaller, more cohesive targets.

One of the first targets they settled on was the American Legislative Exchange Council. ALEC is an organization dedicated to advancing "the fundamental principles of free-market enterprise, limited government, and federalism at the state level." They're highly successful, and they pose a huge threat to Democrats at the state and local level, since they lobby effectively for their positions.

That's why ALEC became a target. Thanks in part to ALEC, at least eighteen states enacted or were poised to enact measures opposing Obamacare, including six states proposing constitutional amendments. Thanks in part to ALEC, states have opposed raising taxes and greater encroachment of federal legislation.[35]

They had to be destroyed. So the left went to work bullying them by wielding the corpse of Trayvon Martin.

ALEC happened to back state legislation like Florida's "stand your ground" law, which provided, essentially, that if you are in a place where you have a right to be, and you're attacked physically, you don't have a duty to retreat—you can stand your ground and "meet force with force, including deadly force" if necessary to save your own life. This isn't self-defense, which is a defense to a charge—it provides immunity from criminal prosecution and civil action.[36] Florida isn't the only state with such laws; over twenty other states have them.

As soon as the media focused its ire on George Zimmerman, it began claiming that Zimmerman had not been arrested due to the stand-your-ground law. Jonathan Capehart of the *Washington Post* called the law "insane" and suggested that it was a "license to kill" invoked by police to protect Zimmerman.[37] So did Eugene Robinson of the *Post*. Robinson went further—not only was the law wrong, it was . . . wait for it . . . racist! "Imagine that Martin, not Zimmerman, had been carrying a legal handgun—and that it was Zimmerman who ended up dead. The law should have compelled police to release Martin, a young African American in a hoodie, without charges. Somehow, I doubt that would have happened."[38]

There was no actual evidence that Zimmerman had been released thanks to "stand your ground." In fact, there were *zero* contemporaneous media reports claiming that Zimmerman had cited the stand-your-ground law to justify his actions. He instead said what all nonlawyers would say: self-defense. As for the police, while later reports claimed that they cited "stand your ground" to release Zimmerman, contemporaneous reports said he was released because they had no evidence to contradict his self-defense claims.

Yet the stand-your-ground meme was picked up by the *New York Times*, *Los Angeles Times*, and virtually everyone else in the mainstream media.

This was deliberate. Zimmerman wasn't arrested initially because police often don't arrest in clear cases of self-defense, which is what Zimmerman claimed. Only after an arrest does stand-your-ground come into play—a lawyer can ask for a hearing on the stand-your-ground issue, which can result in a case being dismissed. But Zimmerman's first lawyer suggested that stand-your-ground wasn't even applicable to the case—"this is self-defense, and that's been around forever," he said.[39]

But if Zimmerman had claimed self-defense, the media and Obama's organizational allies would have no weapon to wield against ALEC.

So the left homed in on ALEC for pushing for stand-your-ground laws—even though such laws were completely irrelevant to this case. On March 29, the NAACP, the National Urban League, the AFL-CIO, Service Employees International Union (SEIU), Van Jones's ColorOfChange, People for the American Way, and several members of Congress, among others, all came together in front of ALEC's headquarters to demand that ALEC stop supporting "Kill at Will"—that is, stand-your-ground laws.[40] All of these groups are heavily linked to the Obama administration in terms of donations; many of them have a revolving-door staff relationship with the Obama White House.

They simultaneously targeted ALEC for its support of voter identification measures, which would require voters to show ID before casting a ballot. That policy is opposed by liberals on the grounds that it's "racist." What makes ID racist? Nothing, really—

you have to show ID to buy a beer, unless you can get the creepy guy on the curb to buy a six-pack for you. But what makes voter ID racist is that it stops voter fraud—and we can't have that, since Democrats are all too eager to find folks they can bus to the polls, with or without ID.

Since February 2012, the Obama administration had, through its liberal organizational allies, pressed against voter ID laws. In early March 2012, NAACP president Ben Jealous appeared at the UN Human Rights Council in Geneva to proclaim that America was racist for enacting such laws. "The power of the UN on state governments historically is to shame them and to put pressure on the US government to bring them into line with global standards, best practices for democracy."[41]

With the newfound publicity surrounding ALEC, however, the Obama administration and its allies knew that the campaign against voter ID could be piggybacked onto Trayvon Martin and the associated anti-ALEC cause.

"We are organizing. We are not agonizing," railed Representative James Clyburn (D-SC). "We have staffed up." ColorOfChange tweeted "@CocaCola is helping undermine voting rights. Tell them to stop."[42] "The clear and simple message was that you can't come for black folks' money by day and try to take away our vote by night," blathered Rashad Robinson, ColorOfChange director.[43] ColorOfChange, it is worth noting, has been a powerful tool for the left, standing behind boycott attempts on Fox News' Eric Bolling and Lou Dobbs, among others. Overall, ColorOfChange supposedly got 85,000 people to sign an anti-ALEC petition directed at Coke.[44]

Coke quickly pulled out of ALEC. "The Coca-Cola Company has elected to discontinue its membership with the American Legislative Exchange Council (ALEC)," Coke spokespeople told the *Washington Examiner*. "We have a long-standing policy of only taking positions on issues that impact our Company and industry."[45]

By April 18, 2012, ALEC corporate sponsors, including Mc-

Donald's, Coca-Cola, and Kraft Foods, had pulled their involvement from the group. And so, that day, ALEC's legislative board voted without dissent to shut down its noneconomic focuses. "We hate to see any members leave," said spokeswoman Kaitlyn Buss. "[W]e hope to work with these companies that have had problems again in the future."[46] In May, Wal-Mart followed suit.

Suddenly, one of President Obama's greatest political adversaries had been castrated.

This is how the left bullies. They use a racial incident to stir up fervor about the generally racist United States of America (remember, as we've learned so far, America is a racist and imperialist hellhole), portray conservative legislation as emblematic of that racism, and then fight to shut down any groups promoting that conservative legislation.

That same logic applies to the greatest of all causes: the cherished and powerful Obama administration.

YOU DON'T LIKE OBAMA BECAUSE YOU'RE RACIST

Remember how President Obama said that Trayvon looked like his fictional son?

That wasn't an accident.

During the 2012 election cycle, President Obama was unable to settle on any workable theme. Hope and change were done. Obama had clearly underperformed, broken his campaign promises, utterly failed to reunite the country after the divisive Bush years. In fact, he had been the most divisive president since the pre–Civil War era.

But he had a reason for that: it wasn't him, it was you.

See, you were a racist if you didn't like what Obama was doing. In April 2008, in the secrecy of a fund-raiser in liberal heaven San Francisco, President Obama explained what he really thought of Americans: they're a bunch of bigots. Small-town Americans—the same Americans who didn't really like candidate Obama—were, not coincidentally, "bitter, they cling to guns or religion or antipathy toward people who aren't like them or anti-immigrant sentiment or anti-trade sentiment as a way to explain their frustrations."[47]

It was a theme he'd return to over and over again. If Americans didn't like him, it was because his middle name was Hussein or because he didn't look like all the other fellas on the dollar bills. For Obama, the only reason somebody would dislike his policies had to be the level of melanin in his skin. Or at least, that's how the bully strategy went. Because the contrapositive was obvious: if you don't want to be seen as a racist, back Obama.

It was no wonder, then, that Obama's followers and backers got the message.

In 2009, when the Tea Party formed spontaneously from the vehement backlash against Obama's high-spending bailout policies, the Obama administration panicked. They insisted that the Tea Party had started not because of opposition to anti-constitutional values, but because Tea Party was short for Tea and Lynching Party. Obama was black; the Tea Party wanted to throw him into Boston Harbor.

The media jumped on this meme quickly. National Public Radio's then-CEO and president Vivian Schiller called the Tea Party "racist."[48] MSNBC was so eager to paint the Tea Party as racist that they simply made things up. Contessa Brewer showed video of Tea Partiers legally carrying guns, then said somberly, "There are questions about whether this has racial overtones . . . white people showing up with guns." Only one problem, Contessa: the footage of the "white person" with a gun was actually a black guy. They'd chopped off his head on the footage. Dylan Ratigan of MSNBC then piped up, "they get the variable of a black president on top of all these other things and that's the move—the cherry on top, if you will, to the accumulated frustration for folks." Only on MSNBC would figuratively cutting off a black man's head be considered antiracist, but carrying a gun at a Tea Party while *being black* be considered racist.[49]

Obama's Hollywood friends turned out to explain to the benighted American public that all those folks protesting with flags had picked up Old Glory because they ran out of replicas of the Confederate Stars and Bars. Morgan Freeman, once again playing God by reading people's minds, said that the Tea Party was "going to do whatever [they] can to get this black man outta here. . . . It is a racist thing."[50]

Sean Penn, taking a break from hanging with South and Central American dictators, called the Tea Party the "Get the N-word out of the White House Party," and said that the Tea Party wanted to "lynch" President Obama.[51] Alan Cumming, the voice of Gutsy from *The Smurfs* movie, said the Tea Party was both homophobic and racist—a twofer! Janeane Garafalo told Keith Olbermann that the Tea Party love for Herman Cain hid "racist elements of the Republican Party."[52]

For good measure, Obama himself said the Tea Party was racist. According to Kenneth T. Walsh's book *Family of Freedom*, "Obama, in his most candid moments, acknowledged that race was still a problem. In May 2010, he told guests at a private White House dinner that race was probably a key component in the rising opposition to his presidency from conservatives, especially right-wing activists in the anti-incumbent 'Tea Party' movement that was then surging across the country."[53] There was more evidence that Tea Partiers hated Obama for his inability to dunk than for his race. But to Obama, who thinks that all must love him naturally, the only rationale for his dipping popularity had to be his father's racial heritage.

All this was lies. It was nasty, baseless, and ridiculous—there was far more evidence of anti-Semitism in the Occupy movement than there was evidence of racism within the Tea Party. But that didn't stop the media from trying. In fact, they and their friends tried so hard to label the Tea Party racist that they stooped to planting faux racists, including faux Nazis, at Tea Parties, just to gin up racial controversy. The Tea Parties threw the infiltrators out.[54]

But facts didn't matter to the media. The greatest anti–Tea Party hoax of all came on the day that Nancy Pelosi and her radical minions staged a signing of the Obamacare bill. Tea Partiers showed up en masse on Capitol Hill. They were polite, courteous, and predictably, loud.

It was that noise level that allowed Democrats a chance to pounce on made-up Tea Party racism. First, Representative André Carson (D-IN) said that there were incipient KKK members in the crowd chanting "the N-word, the N-word, 15 times." Carson walked alongside civil rights leader Representative John Lewis (D-GA). "It was like going into the time machine with John Lewis," said Carson. "He said it reminded him of another time."

Opposition to Obamacare was now racism. And it was the worst kind of racism. Bull Connor was lurking somewhere in that crowd with a fire hose and a tricorner hat.

There was only one problem: it didn't happen.

Andrew Breitbart took the lead in proving it. He offered $10,000 for any tape of the n-word being shouted on Capitol Hill—the money would go to the United Negro College Fund. "It's time for the allegedly pristine character of Rep. John Lewis to put up or shut up. Therefore, I am offering $10,000 of my own money to provide hard evidence that the N- word was hurled at him not 15 times, as his colleague reported, but just once. Surely one of those two cameras wielded by members of his entourage will prove his point," wrote Andrew. "Rep. Lewis, if you can't do that, I'll give him a backup plan: a lie detector test."[55]

Predictably, Lewis could provide no tape, and wouldn't take a lie detector. But the myth lives on: to this day, leftists cite the phantom n-word incident as proof that the Tea Party was ready to reopen the Triangle Trade.

Despite the media's complete assault on the Tea Party—despite their racial bullying—the Tea Party drove the Republican Party to a historic landslide in the 2010 congressional elections.

And Obama got more desperate. Which meant it was time to up the racial ante.

That's where Trayvon Martin came in.

By the time the Trayvon Martin story broke in 2012, Obama's approval ratings had fallen dramatically. He was in serious trouble. He needed a boost. And what better way to boost his sagging campaign than by labeling all Americans racists? Even better—label them George Zimmerman–style racists who secretly want to kill black folks.

It was a foolproof strategy. So naturally, the Obama folks found the biggest racial fool they could to prime the pump: MSNBC contributor and 9/11 truther Touré, their resident racial analyst, who grew up in an upper-middle-class white enclave. "Historically, after a surge in black power there is a retort, a reassertion of white power," wrote Touré. "Now in the wake of the rise of Obama, we see the power structure responding by continuing to implement voter ID laws tailored to functionally disenfranchise poor blacks. We see an increase in violent crimes that target blacks but not specific blacks, any black person will do. . . . The anxiety about Obama's success has led to many reactions, most of them not physical but still emotionally violent." (This sort of nastiness isn't unusual for Touré; later in the campaign, he actually suggested that Mitt Romney had engaged in "niggerization" of Obama by accusing Obama of running an "angry" campaign.)

Touré's masterful bit of propaganda tied together all the loose ends: Trayvon Martin happened because Obama was elected; voter ID laws sprang from the same racism that brought about Trayvon Martin. In the end, it was the White Man's Fault for not loving Obama.[56] Jesse Jackson seconded the motion: "[Obama's] victory has triggered tremendous backlash. Blacks are under attack."[57] Heather Horn of the *Atlantic* even wrote a piece saying that Europeans thought white Americans hated President Obama and killed Trayvon Martin for the same reason. "Most significantly, articles tend to connect Trayvon Martin, American history, and Barack Obama," she wrote. Articles like . . . for example . . . Heather Horn's.[58]

Michael Eric Dyson, who talks as though he should be reading commercial liners for the side effects of Cialis, was the worst. In an interview with Touré—and it should be noted here that it is a wonder the earth didn't implode with stupidity at this pairing—he said, "Now it is the case that whatever hoods we wear, sagging pants, those become part of the folklore of American racism because it now signifies to white America that this is a hood, this is a thug, and the suspicion that is cast not only on Trayvon Martin. Look at the President of the United States of America. Here is a guy who do it the right way. He went to Harvard, he's the President. Look at the—the ready—the—the steady stream of racism and bigotry . . . the—the—the stereotypes that prevail, right, I'm afraid of him, he's a—he's a moron, he's an orangutan, he's an animal. Look at all of that."[59] Technically, Dyson is the moron. Everyone agrees that Obama is brilliant, even if he's a rotten president.

One question remained unanswered: if racist white Americans wanted to kill black teens like Trayvon and hated President Obama, why did Senator Obama become President Obama? Perhaps it was all a dark, clever scheme to suck victims like Trayvon into complacency so white folks could release their white Hispanic hounds.

The Trayvon angle, needless to say, didn't work.

But that didn't mean that Obama and his friends would stop invoking racism every time somebody looked cross-eyed at the president.

On June 15, 2012, President Obama announced that his executive branch would stop enforcing federal immigration law with regard to people aged sixteen to thirty who had resided in the country for at least five years, among other qualifications. In essence, he granted them amnesty.

That afternoon, the First Immigrant President (after all, according to the press, he's also been the First Gay President, the First Female President, the First Jewish President, and, of course, the First Slow-Jamming President) held a press conference in the Rose Garden. He blabbed on and on about why he was the First Cool President for ignoring Congress, unilaterally undermining enacted immigration law in violation of constitutional limits on separation of powers. Then a journalist from the *Daily Caller* had the temerity to shout a question to him. Obama responded as though he'd taken a bullet à la Teddy Roosevelt. "Excuse me, sir. It's not time for questions, sir. Not while I'm speaking." When the Great One finally deigned to answer the reporter's question, and the reporter asked a follow-up, he tut-tutted, "I didn't ask for an argument, I'm answering your question."

The *New York Times* breathlessly reported—as though they had just found a tape of Mitt Romney having sex with a horse—that the "interruption stunned White House correspondents and television viewers . . . [the reporter] violated decorum at the White House and generated online shouts of disapproval from other reporters, analysts and historians."[60]

Somehow, the mainstream press didn't seem to object nearly as much when President Clinton violated decorum on the Oval Office rug. Or when Sam Donaldson abused President Reagan on a regular basis.

But it wasn't enough to feign outrage over an interruption. The press had to go whole hog and paint Obama's entire opposition as racist—just because one guy didn't have the manners to wait until Obama finished his sentence.

That night, Touré explained that only Obama's blackness could explain the interruption. "This disrespect of this human being cannot be disconnected from the fact that he's black," said Touré. "There is a basic, lesser humanity generally ascribed to black people, even one this alpha, this much in power, this much in control."[61]

Now, Touré admittedly has the IQ of a kumquat. But other, smarter people tried to make the same point: opposing Obama made you a racist. The late Sam Donaldson, the White House correspondent who had heckled Ronald Reagan, denied that he had ever interrupted a president; he said that the reporter reflected not only "the growing incivility of the times," but "let's face it: Many on the political right believe this president ought not to be there—they oppose him not for his policies and political view but for who he is, an African American!"[62] Donaldson failed to explain whether Dan Rather had presented forged documents about President Bush to the American people because Bush, of course, was black.

Politico, the house organ for the Democratic Party, agreed; Joe Williams said, "It's very, very difficult to place race outside of this context. Mostly because a lot of the interruptions, a lot of the disrespect has been unprecedented. We haven't seen anything like this before."[63]

It was one thing to suggest that Bush had lied America into a war for oil. It was another to speak while Obama was speaking. Why, the latter was just degrees from enslaving blacks again! Or, as Joe Biden would later put it about Republicans, "they gonna put y'all back in chains!"

President Obama *was* elected, at least in part, because he was black. It was a positive for him. Many Americans believed that America needed to elect its first black president to move beyond issues of race once and for all. Instead, they got a champion race bully masquerading as a racial unifier.

THE HISTORY OF RACIAL BULLYING

During the Trayvon Martin case, a reporter asked Representative Emanuel Cleaver (D-MO) whether he was exploiting Martin's death to push a political agenda. "Any time somebody is forcefully stepped up and speaking out against injustice, there are those who say they are using it for their own purposes," said Cleaver. "We have always had to face people making those accusations since the civil rights movement began; that's not going to stop."

He's right, and he's wrong.

He's right that civil rights workers often faced accusations that they had a political agenda rather than a justice-oriented agenda. He's wrong if he thinks that such accusations are as untrue now as they were originally. Yesterday's race-baiters were brutal white bullies. Today's are left-wingers invoking fictional white racism to achieve their goals.

At the beginning, the race bullies were race victims. Blacks were, of course, a victimized class. They did face brutal and evil systemic discrimination, from lynchings to race laws to the voting booth to restaurants to government agencies. But the victims fought back, and the victims won. Martin Luther King Jr.'s admonition to create a society in which people were judged by the content of their character rather than the color of their skin was the opposite of bullying—it was full-fledged tolerance.

The problem began to arise as soon as African-Americans won their initial victories. Liberals insisted that it wasn't enough to push for a color-blind society. Instead, they claimed—not without some justification—that the systemic racism of the American system had to be undone only by instituting reverse racism in favor of blacks. If blacks had been coerced under the Jim Crow system, now whites would be coerced to push society back to a stable center. If society had been bent too far in the direction of racism, now it would be bent just as far in the opposite direction.

The left saw measures like affirmative action and school integration in this way. They were explicit about it. In *Green v. County School Board of New Kent County* (1968), the Supreme Court okayed a mandatory busing system that would take children from one end of town to the other to achieve certain racial quotas in schools. The purpose, they said, was to establish a color-free system—but that couldn't be created by being color-free in the treatment of children. Instead, said the court, *Brown v. Board of Education* (1955), which mandated desegregation, didn't mean that schools could just open their doors to anyone. It was "a call for the dismantling of well-entrenched dual systems tempered by an awareness that complex and multifaceted problems would arise which would require time and flexibility for a successful resolution." If whites didn't choose to go to black schools, they could be forced to do so . . . temporarily.[64]

Nobody expected affirmative action—an inherently coercive, bullying system—to last beyond a few years, in which blacks would achieve equality and the racism of the old system would be wiped away. That's exactly what the Supreme Court said in *Regents of the University of California v. Bakke* (1978). In that case, a white male with high scores was refused admission to the University of California, Davis, thanks to racial quotas. Though the Supreme Court said that hard-and-fast racial quotas were no good, they did say that affirmative action—giving people special treatment based on race—was justified, again as a temporary measure.[65]

These were not effective policies. Forced busing had the unintended consequences of destroying many public schools, as well as many well-integrated communities. The problem was obvious: black schools had been historically mistreated, and the students weren't properly educated. That was the fault of a deeply racist system. But forced busing was not the solution. Creating an influx of undereducated students into previously white schools ended up lowering standards across the board—including for many black students, who fell behind quickly and never caught up. Meanwhile, many white parents weren't happy sending their kids across town on buses to historically black schools, many of which were located in lower-income areas. Instead, they fled to the suburbs and enrolled their kids in local schools or private schools.

Affirmative action was similarly counterproductive. Instead of providing a leg up for equally qualified students who had seen difficult circumstances growing up, race-based affirmative action created stigmas on blacks who did make it into top colleges—stigmas that last until today. The fail rate for affirmative action admittees at top schools is far higher than the fail rate for non–affirmative action admittees at the same schools.

Although these policies turned out rotten, they were justifiable on a moral level. Unfortunately, they became the basis for racial bullying by the left, which saw affirmative action, forced busing, and the growth of the welfare state, among other causes, as the only solutions to racism. Anybody who opposed these policies became, by definition, racist.

This is where victims began to turn into perpetrators. Where civil rights leaders had once called for equal rights, now they called for special rights.

Again, it is worth remembering that at the beginning, these special rights were seen as temporary remedies for the ills of Jim Crow. But they soon became permanent features of the political landscape. Crime and poverty were blamed on white people; calls for harsher policing and less welfare cash were labeled racist. Suddenly it was racist to call for equal treatment under the law.

But this presented a bit of an issue. For equal treatment under the law to truly be racist, America had to be portrayed as a place of endless racism—not a country transitioning from racism to acceptance, but rather an incurable mass of bigoted whites who had to be curbed by the power of government. All black ills had to be presented as results of white racism. The system was unfixable. And white people had to get used to it and bend over backward to make amends. But no matter what sort of amends they made, they'd never be done paying the piper.

This was a pretty nasty point of view. It suggested the collective guilt of nonblacks in America. Forever. Do not pass Go; do not collect $200. It was racist. And it was bullying.

That point of view was articulated in nasty ways, too. Even as Martin Luther King Jr. dreamed of a postracial day, Malcolm X was preaching hatred of the "white devil" keeping him down—even though he says in his autobiography that he had a chance at becoming a lawyer, and could undoubtedly have made his way in America without becoming a career criminal, and then a racial rabble-rouser. Instead, he chose to denigrate America and create paranoia-driven false histories of white man's racism invariably leading to black man's downfall. "Every white man in America, when he looks into a black man's eyes, should fall to his knees and say 'I'm sorry, I'm sorry—my kind has committed history's greatest crime against your kind; will you give me the chance to atone?' But do you brothers and sisters expect any white man to do that? *No*, you *know* better! And why won't he do it? Because he *can't* do it. The white man has *created* a devil, to bring chaos upon this earth. . . ."[66]

But, of course, that's *precisely* what liberals did: they spent the decades since the civil rights movement trying desperately to buy the love of radicals like Malcolm X. But the radical race bullies wanted no part of them, because even the *existence* of such white folks disproved the very case they were making. That's why Malcolm X rejected a young white woman who asked what she could do to help him. Malcolm X was, in short, a racial bully.

Even Malcolm X recognized that, which is why later in life he rejected his earlier racist teachings. And then he was shot by members of the Nation of Islam, many of whom had bought into his earlier agenda.

Malcolm X's radical teachings lived on; his less bombastic statements about peace and racial harmony did not. After all, the nastier teachings were attractive to many blacks, who had an easier time addressing ills of the black community as the fault of whites rather than looking to fix them from the inside out. Even President Obama admitted his sympathies for Malcolm X's teachings in *Dreams from My Father*.

The Black Panther Party formed in the aftermath of the murder of Malcolm X. They espoused precisely his old program, with an added twist: they bred Marxism into the mix. After all, America was capitalist, and everything associated with America was racist; communism, by contrast, was *not* American, class- rather than race-conscious. Huey Newton and Bobby Seale formed the group in 1966; their program was a blatant combination of Lenin and Malcolm X. Racism inherently dominated all aspects of social life; therefore, anything bad that happened to black folks resulted from racism. So they called for the release of all blacks from prison; all blacks had to be exempted from military service; they wanted to rewrite history in a way that would "expose the true nature of this decadent American society." As Stokely Carmichael, their honorary prime minister, said, "This country is a nation of thieves. It stole everything it has, beginning with black people."

They didn't bully nonblack Americans just with their rhetoric. They bullied nonblack Americans with all-out violence, working in coordination with their leftist friends in the Weather Underground. In 1968, Newton murdered a police officer. Thanks to the sympathies of liberal whites, he walked free within two years. Seale allegedly issued kill orders against suspected informants to the police. Angela Davis, a prominent member of the party and a communist, helped criminal black high schooler Jonathan Jackson and two of his allies kidnap and murder a judge, a juror, and a prosecutor. Overall, the Panthers injured dozens of police officers.

The bullying worked. They drew precisely the same pathetic white liberal admirers Malcolm X had. Tom Wolfe documented in his hilarious 1970 essay "Radical Chic: That Party at Lenny's" how New York literati like Leonard Bernstein invited Panthers to his house to show off to his liberal friends: "That huge Panther there, the one Felicia [Bernstein] is smiling her tango smile at, is Robert Bay, who just forty-one hours ago was arrested in an altercation with the police, supposedly over a .38-caliber revolver. . . . The very idea of them, these real revolutionaries, who actually put their lives on the line, runs through Lenny's duplex like a rogue hormone." It's their violence, their nastiness, their downright refusal to recognize the good in America that turned on liberals like Bernstein, as Wolfe describes: "*These are no civil-rights* Negroes *wearing gray suits three sizes too big*—no more interminable Urban League banquets in hotel ballrooms where they try to alternate the blacks and whites around the table as if they were stringing Arapaho beads—*these are* real men! Shoot-outs, revolutions, pictures in *Life* magazine of policemen grabbing Black Panthers like they were Vietcong—somehow it all runs together in the head with the whole thing of how *beautiful* they are. *Sharp as a blade*." The attendees ignore Black Panther references to violence and racism and drug dealing. They were just happy to bask in the forgiving glow of the Panther sycophancy.[67]

Eventually, the Black Panthers disbanded, crippled by their consistent fighting with the law. But their legacy had already pervaded the black community—and the liberal white community, who became their enablers. The media now chalked up every black riot to white racism; every serious societal problem in the black community was seen as the inevitable result of a white legal system. White liberals made common cause with black radicals: both became race bullies, targeting conservative principles.

This newfound consonance between traditional white liberals and black radicalism needed to be upgraded, however. The Black Panthers may have been sexy, but they were vulgar. So was Malcolm X. They were crude, blunt instruments in the arena of political discourse. White liberals needed a better partner, a more palatable partner, than folks who walked around talking about CIA conspiracies to distribute drugs in the inner cities.

And so the race bullies went upscale. Sure, there were still old-school race-baiters like Jeremiah Wright, who railed from the pulpit about the "US of KKKA"—and President Obama was only too happy to sit in his pews for decades on end. There were racial hucksters like Al Sharpton, the man who in 1991 incited riots against Orthodox Jews in the Crown Heights section of Brooklyn by shouting about "diamond merchants" at the funeral of a black kid, and who accused a white prosecutor of raping a black girl without any evidence whatsoever—and a man who is still welcome in Obama's White House.

There were charlatans like Jesse Jackson, shaking down businesses for cash while threatening to call them racist—and Jackson, too, gets to visit the White House. And there were outright scumbuckets like Louis Farrakhan, whose virulent anti-Semitism and racism are well-known—and who thinks Obama is a messianic figure.

But Obama is embarrassed of all these people. That's because, at heart, Obama is stuck somewhere between the white liberals and the black radicals. He needed a unifying philosophy of race that would justify his politics while allowing him to sympathize with the race bullies.

And he found one at Harvard Law School.

Professor Derrick Bell was the father of a school of thought called critical race theory (CRT). CRT was a subset of a Marxist philosophy called critical theory, which taught that all law, and particularly the Constitution, had been pervaded by the capitalist system. In order to get rid of inequality, critical legal theory said, the legal system would have to be deconstructed—criticized—and torn to the ground. Endless criticism; hence, critical theory. Once scholars had razed the current legal system, the theory said, a new Marxist superstructure could be built.

Critical race theory also posited that the Constitution—indeed, the entire legal system—was a creation of racists, and that all laws resulting from it were inherently racist, no matter what they said. Laws against robbery: racist. Laws against drug use: racist. Laws of neutral applicability—laws that on their face had nothing to do with race—were racist.

In order to make that case, the critical race theorists had to engage in a fair bit of historical revisionism. They had to argue that the founders were racists, that the system they designed was inherently and incurably racist, and that even the Civil War and civil rights movement could not wipe away that stain. And that's precisely what Professor Derrick Bell argued.[68]

In Derrick Bell's view, even *Brown v. Board of Education* becomes a way for the white man to keep the black man down.[69] Bell actually spun *Brown v. Board* as a way for the United States' white majority to fight the Soviet effort to portray America as racist.

If the system is inherently racist, and there's no way to change it, then liberalism is always the answer. Affirmative action becomes a permanent feature of the political landscape, not a temporary attempt to solve a deep wrong. School busing becomes a permanent corrective mechanism.

Meanwhile, facially neutral statutes become racist. All statistics suggesting that blacks commit a disproportionate share of crimes, for example, are racist in and of themselves, since they reflect the underlying racism of the society. When Mumia Abu-Jamal murders a white police officer, it's not because he's a violent piece of human feces—it's because he's the product of a racist system. That's why Derrick Bell signed a petition on behalf of Mumia.

It is no coincidence that Barack Obama saw Derrick Bell as a philosophical mentor during his halcyon Harvard Law School days, rallying for him and hugging him, explaining to classmates that they ought to "[o]pen up your hearts and your minds to the words of Professor Derrick Bell." Even the lower-class race-baiters embraced this race theory. Jeremiah Wright loved it so much that he invited Bell to speak at his church—the same church where Barack Obama would sit in the pews for twenty years.

There is no worse form of bullying than racial bullying. Because America has been cursed with the blight of racism for centuries—and because it is such a deep and at one time pervasive evil—the word *racist* ought to be reserved for actual racists. But now the term *racist* is applied to every conservative cause—hell, every non-racially-discriminatory-in-favor-of-minorities cause.

ENFORCING THE LAW = RACISM

Because white America is so irredeemably racist, the Obama administration has deemed it hunky-dory to allow black thugs to stake out polling places to intimidate potential voters. When two members of the New Black Panthers hung out outside a polling place in Philadelphia on Election Day 2008 brandishing nightsticks and wearing military gear, the Eric Holder Justice Department quashed an investigation. "There is no doubt that some people were hostile to this case," said Justice Department lawyer J. Christian Adams, who quit the department over their selective prosecution.[70]

According to Adams, some of his fellow Justice Department officials suggested that "the law should not be used against black wrongdoers because of the long history of slavery and segregation. Less charitable individuals called it 'payback time.'" The left called Adams a liar.

Then the New Black Panthers opened up on the issue. Malik Shabazz, who is notable for two reasons—having two *z*'s in his name, and heading up the New Black Panthers—spoke to a Panther event in July 2010. There, he joked, "You know we don't carry batons . . . PSYCHE! I'm just playin'." He then followed up that sliver of comedic genius with this stunning justification for the nonprosecution of the Panthers: "Justice Department leadership changed into the hands of a black man by the name of Eric Holder."[71] Shabazz reiterated that two years later, explaining, "[The Democrats know] that it's not fair to persecute [the New Black Panthers] group and we're not going to back down even though it's hurting us politically, even though it's being used every day against us politically. That's what you call 'mercy.' Really, it's fairness, which is what we deserve anyway. . . . And so we have mercy, really, right now. We will receive no mercy under these new enemies that are now taking over really right now [Republicans] and controlling the action." He lamented the fact that Obama and Holder might not be able to hold out in favor of the Panthers. He also said that Obama and Holder owed the Panthers "some favors."[72]

The idea that enforcing the law is racist has become a pervasive pattern in liberal America. The most obvious example is the left's bullying take on illegal immigration, in which they label anyone who wants to police the southern border a bigot. Now, obviously there's nothing racist about opposing illegal immigration. For the love of God, it's *illegal* immigration. You can have a ton of sympathy for the poor unfortunates who risk their lives to cross the American border—I fully understand and sympathize with people who simply want to escape the current drug cartel regime cesspool in favor of the beacon of hope that is America. But that doesn't mean that the United States can afford to continue to usher across its borders people who don't pay into the system yet do reap the benefits of our generous social services.

That sympathetic but pro-legal perspective makes you a racist, according to the left. Many Democrats, *Time* reported in 2006, say that "a hint of racism or nativism" really underlies the immigration debate. "I have no doubt that some of those involved in the debate have their position based on fear and perhaps racism because of what's happening demographically in the country," said Senator Ken Salazar (D-CO). Of course, *Time* agreed. It wasn't a "political ploy"—instead, "there certainly is a case to be made that racial fears are informing some of the debate on immigration policy."[73]

The issue truly came to a head in 2010, when Governor Jan Brewer (R-AZ) signed into law Arizona's senate Bill 1070, the Support Our Law Enforcement and Safe Neighborhoods Act. The bill merely allowed local law enforcement to act in accordance with federal immigration law, allowing officers to ask for identification during traffic stops if there was reasonable suspicion that the person was an illegal immigrant. The law explicitly barred racial profiling.

There could not have been a more race-neutral law than this. We have to show ID every time we buy a beer, every time we get on an airplane. When we're stopped for a traffic ticket, we have to show ID. There is nothing racist about having to show identification, especially when such checks can help enforce the border.

Arizona had good reason to pass the law. There were nearly half a million illegal immigrants in the state in April 2010, when the bill became law. Violence along the Arizona border had become a massive issue for the state; much of it was driven by Mexican drug cartels, which also funneled agents across the border.

Yet Brewer was quickly raked over the coals and labeled a racist. Cardinal Roger Mahony of Los Angeles suggested that Arizonans were "reverting to German Nazi and Russian Communist techniques." Protesters flooded Arizona, threatening Brewer personally and comparing her to Hitler; local congresspeople suggested that white supremacist groups were behind the law. Meanwhile, outside the state, the media pressured Major League Baseball to move the All-Star Game out of state; the Los Angeles City Council voted to divest from Arizona; the Phoenix Suns donned *Los Suns* jerseys in an attempt to make a statement. Al Sharpton, always in search of a camera without a face before it, dragged his bloated carcass down to Arizona to sneer, "The Civil War is over. Let's not start it again with states' rights."[74] Because, of course, asking people for ID was exactly the same as shackling them in the hold of a cargo ship and moving them to plantations in Alabama. As usual, Sharpton also called for civil disobedience.

President Obama himself led the charge against the law. He said, "You can try to make it really tough on people who look like they, quote, unquote look like illegal immigrants. . . . Now suddenly if you don't have your papers and you took your kid out to get ice cream, you're going to be harassed, that's something that could potentially happen."[75] Obama hosted Mexican president Felipe Calderon, who had done nothing to stem the tide of illegal immigrants crossing the American border; at that meeting, he told Calderon, "[T]he Arizona law has the potential of being applied in a discriminatory fashion." Minorities, he said, could be "harassed and arrested."[76] On the day Brewer signed the law, Obama held a press conference at which he said that the law would "undermine basic notions of fairness that we cherish as Americans."[77]

Attorney General Eric Holder announced that the Obama administration would be bringing a federal lawsuit against the state of Arizona . . . for *enforcing federal law*. So the Justice Department *wouldn't* prosecute Black Panthers intimidating voters but *would* prosecute a state for obeying the law. Said Holder, SB 1070 "has the possibility of leading to racial profiling." He then admitted he hadn't actually read the law.[78]

But he didn't have to read the law. Liberals never do. The law is made in the United States. That means it's racist. And that means it should be disobeyed, whenever and however possible.

Brewer tried to meet with Obama for months over SB 1070. He routinely ducked her. When they finally *did* meet, he was "patronizing," according to Brewer's book, *Scorpions for Breakfast*.

The next time they met, in January 2012, *Scorpions for Breakfast* had already come out. Somebody in Obama's inner circle had read it. So Obama confronted Brewer about it on the tarmac of the airport in Arizona. There, he promptly lectured her; she responded by pointing her finger at him. She later said she felt "a little bit threatened."

And, sure enough, the liberal bullies called her a racist for daring to point her finger. The NAACP told *Politico* that Brewer was playing on racist stereotypes. "What were you afraid he would do, steal your purse?" sneered Hilary O. Shelton of the NAACP. Al Sharpton used his show to promote the notion that Brewer was disrespecting Obama because he was black.[79] Perhaps Brewer was a little bit afraid that the president of the United States might come after her personally, or her state. After all, he'd already done it over and over again.

CONCLUSION

In May 2012, a few weeks after George Zimmerman was arrested, the George Soros–funded Center for Social Inclusion held a special session for House Democrats. The purpose? According to the organization's founder and president, Maya Wiley, the session would teach Democrats how to decode "racially coded . . . conservative messages" and inform them how to "raise racial disparities" in public policy contexts. In other words, Wiley taught Democrats how to play the race card. A staffer for Representative Barbara Lee (D-CA) told the *Washington Examiner* that Wiley would walk Democrats "through their strategy and how they message and talk about stuff."

What exactly were those "racially coded" conservative messages? According to Wiley, it was racist when Newt Gingrich called Barack Obama the "food stamp president," even if Gingrich "did not intend racism." Rick Santorum's statement that the Obama administration wanted to hand out "more food stamps, give them more Medicaid" was racist, too. House Majority Leader Eric Cantor (R-VA) stating that he was against raising "taxes on those that are paying in, taking from them, so that you just hand out and give them to someone else"—that was racist, too. Said Wiley, "It's the emotional connection, not rational connection that we need."[80]

That's how political bullies operate. They manipulate emotion by claiming victimhood, then bludgeon political opponents into submission. Thus a Hispanic man who had his head bashed against pavement by a black man ends up a symbol of white racism—and that racism justifies the entire plethora of leftist causes. Thus organizations that support conservative, race-neutral laws end up on the wrong end of boycotts, for no apparent reason at all.

Everything becomes racist.

In 2009, James O'Keefe worked with Andrew Breitbart to release video of O'Keefe and his partner Hannah Giles infiltrating branches of the Association of Community Organizations for Reform Now (ACORN), showing that ACORN employees were willing to help pimps and prostitutes engage in tax evasion and child sex trafficking. In those videos, O'Keefe posed as a pimp and Giles as one of his prostitutes; they asked ACORN employees how they could avoid tax consequences for shipping in illegal underage prostitutes. The ACORN employees were only too happy to offer their assistance. Shortly after this blockbuster story, ACORN was defunded by the federal government and then fragmented.

Now, child prostitution should be a nonracial issue. But it wasn't for the left. That's because ACORN was a tool of the race-bully community, constantly working to threaten businesses and government agencies in order to obtain special benefits, generally for minorities. So when O'Keefe took down ACORN, he poked the hornet's nest. Sure enough, within weeks, the liberal media was suggesting that O'Keefe was a racist. Mediaite suggested that the pimp costume O'Keefe donned in the videos had "racial subtext."[81] Salon.com, which had attempted to downplay the ACORN story, now ran a big piece by slimy smear artist Max Blumenthal suggesting without a shred of evidence that O'Keefe was somehow a white supremacist.[82] The *Economist* called O'Keefe's tape a "minstrel show."[83]

The left was so desperate to protect ACORN from the group's own willingness to engage in *child sex crimes* that it pulled the race card.

Neither O'Keefe nor Andrew ever backed down on the story. The left tried to cudgel them into silence. And they refused to be bullied.

That's a tough stand to take. Typically, white Americans—with good reason—are so afraid of being called racist that they will do just about anything to avoid it. They'll embrace liberal positions. They'll soften their language. They'll avoid difficult issues that could even tangentially touch on race. They'll go completely silent.

That is how the race bullies win.

Ironically, the greatest victims of the race bullies are minorities who don't buy into the anti-American theory that the United States is so racist that it requires constant liberalism. No group is more bullied than black conservatives, who must face down charges of racial disloyalty every day—just ask Ward Connerly, Larry Elder,

Herman Cain, Condoleezza Rice, or Clarence Thomas. Many minorities are cowed into silence. Meanwhile, the racial thugs like Jesse Jackson and Al Sharpton—and yes, Barack Obama—are glorified.

The race bullies win by relying on racial guilt. But collective racial guilt can only separate Americans. We are individuals, not homogeneous members of racial subsets. Only when we learn to cherish the words of Martin Luther King, judging people as individuals, will we truly have the guts to stand up to the race bullies. After all, to paraphrase a man who once stood for unification rather than division, we're not black America or white America. We're the United States of America. We're brothers and sisters.

If we don't begin to recognize that simple truth—and recognize the inherent goodness of America, and our ability to look beyond skin color and ethnic heritage—the race bullies will continue to tear America down for their own political gain, brick by brick.

4.

★

CLASS BULLIES

In 2008, the American economy essentially melted down. Thanks to decades of government interventionism in the free market, the American financial system hit a crisis point.

Fortunately, government was only too happy to step in and spend taxpayer money to fix up the perverse system it had created in the first place. On March 16, 2008, JPMorgan Chase bought up Bear Stearns at $2 per share in a government-brokered deal that required $30 billion in federal investment. Just fourteen months earlier, the stock had been trading at $171 per share. On July 30, 2008, President Bush signed the Housing and Economic Recovery Act of 2008, effectively guaranteeing $300 billion in federal funding for subprime borrowers; on September 7, 2008, the government nationalized Fannie Mae and Freddie Mac, which owned half the mortgage debt in America. Taxpayers absorbed Fannie Mae's loss of $25.2 billion in the last quarter of 2008 alone, and ponied up another $15.2 billion to pay off additional debt. On

September 14, 2008, the federal government rammed through a deal for Bank of America to acquire Merrill Lynch. On September 15, 2008, Lehman Brothers went bankrupt. On September 17, the Federal Reserve "lent" $85 billion to American International Group (AIG) to bail them out. At the same time, Citigroup took $45 billion of government cash; by January 2009, the U.S. government owned 36 percent of Citigroup. Finally, on September 18, 2008, Bush Treasury secretary Henry Paulson and Federal Reserve chairman Ben Bernanke met to propose a $700 billion bailout plan that would buy up "toxic" assets—the Troubled Assets Relief Program. Instead of buying up the assets, however, the $787 billion TARP ended up being a series of bailouts to the banks.[1]

From October 1 to October 10, the stock market dropped nearly 2,400 points, losing more than 20 percent of its value. The real estate market utterly collapsed, with housing prices dropping nearly a third. Overall, between 2007 and 2010, Americans saw 40 percent of their net wealth disappear.[2]

Normally, you'd think this would be a bad thing.

For liberals, it was a dream come true.

Class bullies—socialists—love crisis. When everyone is fat and happy, there is no great furor for redistribution of income, for a leveling of the economic playing field. Marx was wrong when he said that capitalism carries the seeds of its own destruction thanks to inequalities between rich and poor—the fact is that capitalism *helps* both rich and poor, even if the rich get richer faster than the poor get richer. When everybody's getting richer, nobody really cares about income inequality.

But recessions—those are another story. When economic times get tough, the knives come out. When the rich get poorer and the poor get poorer, things get ugly. When the rich get *richer* and the poor get poorer—then things *really* get ugly. Suddenly earners find themselves under scrutiny. Violence against the wealthy and the not-so-wealthy becomes something tolerable. The class bullies begin engaging in threats and brutalities. After all, they can't just let a good crisis go to waste.

The Obama administration certainly wasn't going to let a good crisis go to waste.

On April 3, 2009, President Obama met with the CEOs of thirteen of America's biggest banks. Obama seated them at a table with no food, and one glass of water per person. No refills. Then he told them he'd have to cut all the top salaries at the banks.

For some of these companies, that was fair. For others, it wasn't. Certain firms had been forced to take TARP money. And many of the firms weren't being allowed to *pay back* the TARP money. The government wanted to own a piece of the banks. And the banks would have to deal with it. Around the time of the meeting, Stuart Varney of Fox News reported that the Obama team had turned down repayments from a bank that had been forced to take cash, "since unlike smaller banks that gave their TARP money back, [the bank at issue] is far more prominent. The bank has also been threatened with 'adverse consequences' if its chairman persists."[3] The Obama administration even began administering "stress tests" to the banks—tests that determined whether the banks were "stable." If they weren't, they'd be forced to take more TARP money, raise capital, or allow the government to convert its preferred, nonvoting shares into common stock, which would give the government greater ownership of the company.[4]

Back to the meeting. Obama apparently looked around the room at the various CEOs of the banks. As they told him that they needed to be able to compete for top management talent, his temper flared. "Be careful how you make those statements, gentlemen. The public isn't buying that," he said.

This was sheer bullying. As one person who attended the meeting later said, "The signal from Obama's body language and demeanor was, 'I'm the president, and you're not.'"

Then Obama got to the punch line. "My administration," he spat, "is the only thing between you and the pitchforks."[5]

Of course, Obama had been ginning up those pitchforks for months. In his Inaugural Address, Obama blamed "greed and irresponsibility" for the economic collapse, rather than governmental interventionism. He called for "hard choices"—choices that would, of course, be hard for the earners, and relatively easy for everyone else.

And now, like Gaston in *Beauty and the Beast* urging the ignorant townspeople to march on the castle and bring back the Beast's head, Obama was going to put those pitchforks to use. Rather than acknowledging that the banking firms had made crucial mistakes, pushed and aided by the federal government, Obama blamed it all on the rich folks. The financial crisis became a divisive rather than a unifying moment. It was all the fault of those wealthy New Yorkers and their big wallets.

And they had to be taken down a peg. "We all need to take responsibility," said Obama in a February 2009 speech. "And this includes executives at major financial firms who turned to the American people, hat in hand, when they were in trouble, even as they paid themselves their customary lavish bonuses. . . . That's shameful. And that's exactly the kind of disregard for the costs and consequences of their actions that brought about this crisis: a culture of narrow self-interest and short-term gain at the expense of everything else."[6]

Since his inauguration, the threat of the pitchforks has never been too far away. From the Occupy Wall Street movement, coordinated and organized with the help of Obama's allies and with Obama's explicit approval, to the union movement, which pours hundreds of millions of dollars into Obama's campaign machine, President Obama has never—not for a single moment—let up on his class bullying. When he says that he wants people to pay their "fair share," he never means that he wants *all* Americans to pay a fair share. He just means that those who earn should continue to pay for those who don't. And if you disagree, he'll target you. Personally.

Just ask Joe the Plumber. Now, Samuel Joseph Wurzelbacher wasn't rich. As it turned out, he earned $40,000 per year. But he made one big mistake that put him on the Obama radar: he asked Obama a question about class warfare. On October 12, 2008, just a few days before John McCain was scheduled to debate Barack Obama for the last time in the election cycle, Obama stumbled on Wurzelbacher while wandering around his Ohio neighborhood. "I'm getting ready to buy a company that makes about $250,000 . . . $270–280,000 a year," said Wurzelbacher. "Your new tax plan's gonna tax me more, isn't it?"

This was like waving a red flag before a bull. Obama just couldn't help himself. "I'm going to cut taxes a little bit more for the folks who are most in need, and for the 5 percent of the folks who are doing very well, even though they've been working hard. . . . I just want to make sure that they're paying a little bit more in order to pay for those other tax cuts. Now, I respect your disagreement, but I just want you to be clear. It's not that I want to punish your success. I just want to make sure that everybody who is behind you, that they've got a chance at success, too."

Except, of course, that Obama *did* want to punish success—or at least, spread it around—as he made clear moments later: "I think when you spread the wealth around, it's good for everybody."[7]

Now, this was a stupid line—an insanely stupid line, as it turned out. It was a line so stupid that even the insipid McCain campaign wasn't dumb enough to squander it. But that was the extent of the exchange with Wurzelbacher. You'd imagine that Wurzelbacher would have faded off the stage.

But he didn't.

Within hours, the media was digging on this nefarious Wurzelbacher character. They dug up information about his income, his family, his profession. Meanwhile, state employees at the Ohio Department of Job and Family Services were illegally using state computers to make inquiries about Wurzelbacher. Helen Jones-Kelley, the director of the department, later insisted that the checks had been done not as dirt-digging on Wurzelbacher, but rather because he said he wanted to buy a business. This did not pass the smell test, particularly since Jones-Kelley had also donated $2,500 to the Obama campaign.[8] She later resigned her position, and two of her coworkers were fired.

Was this connected to the Obama administration? It's hard to imagine it wasn't. Since the Joe the Plumber incident, the Obama camp has gone out of its way to wage class warfare by bulling wealthy individuals, suggesting that any political involvement by them is evil and retrograde. It's one thing to sleep in a park and fling feces at passersby, say the class bullies—that's just political discourse. It's another to ask the president a question about taxes or spend money on political advertising. That's living on the back of the poor, and must be stopped at all costs.

This class bullying is aided and abetted by the mainstream media, which constantly calls for greater wealth redistribution, portraying the rich as greedy fat cats rather than job creators. And, shockingly enough, it's also backed by many corporate bigwigs themselves, who may disdain nasty class bully rhetoric but are all too happy to buy their way into the favor of the class bullies (see Buffett, Warren). There's a reason that Wall Street gave heavily to Obama in 2008. They caved to the class bullies. They figured that if they couldn't beat 'em, they should join 'em.

THE ORIGINS OF AMERICAN CLASS BULLYING

Teddy Roosevelt is widely respected and admired by Americans on both sides of the political aisle.

He shouldn't be.

Teddy Roosevelt was the first American president to truly embrace class bullying. He didn't understand economics particularly well. What he *did* understand was terrible European progressive philosophy. He believed that anyone who earned a lot of money had entered the realm of evil. "The really big fortune, the swollen fortune, by the mere fact of its size, acquires qualities which differentiate it in kind as well as in degree from what is possessed by men of relatively small means," he said in 1910 while labeling himself a "New Nationalist." It didn't matter if you made your fortune creating bandages for impoverished children. If you made a lot of money, you were a *bad guy*, and you deserved to have your money taken away from you.

The government, said Teddy, would allow rich folks to make money only if they didn't make money in doing so.[9]

Because Teddy didn't like guys who made a lot of money, he felt it necessary to break up their businesses. Antitrust legislation soon became the order of the day. Teddy wanted a "square deal" for the little guy—but he wanted a raw deal for those who actually hired the little guy.

And he didn't care if he had to enable the world's worst people to make his attacks on capitalists happen. During Teddy's presidency, socialist Upton Sinclair took it upon himself to expose the meatpacking industry in *The Jungle*. "I wished to frighten the country by a picture of what its industrial masters were doing to their victims," he wrote. The book itself claimed that the meatpacking industry was "the incarnation of blind and insensate greed . . . the Great Butcher . . . the spirit of capitalism made flesh." His book sold 150,000 copies and made him rich (but he was a class bully, so he was allowed to be rich).

Now, Teddy knew this was bunk. He actually wrote that he had "utter contempt" for Sinclair, that Sinclair was "hysterical, unbalanced, and untruthful," and that "three-fourths of the things he said were absolute falsehoods."[10] But why would the truth stop a class bully?

It wouldn't. Teddy rammed through the Pure Food and Drug Act, dramatically regulating the meatpacking industry, as well as the pharmaceutical industry. This despite the fact that there were already hundreds of meat inspectors policing plants across the country. The result was a dramatic decrease in medical patents, laying the groundwork for today's slow and ineffective Food and Drug Administration.[11]

That's how Teddy ran his administration. Prosperous individuals could be bullied and branded; the lower classes needed protection from them. No matter that many men of property hadn't been born to the purple, as Teddy had—Teddy grew up in a four-story home in Manhattan where his parents hired tutors for him, then went to Harvard—the rich were the victimizers. As for the Constitution, that guardian of individual liberty and freedom of wealth creation, Teddy didn't want to hear about it. "To hell with the Constitution when the people want coal!" he said.

Teddy's class bullying had one unintended consequence—it brought some corporate quislings out of the woodwork. One of them was Thomas Edison, perhaps the most successful inventor and entrepreneur in American history. Recognizing that the class bullies were in ascendance, he decided that he could be either the bully or the bullied—and he wasn't going to be the guy shoved into the locker. Instead, he decided that he would run all industry. "What is wanted is some person familiar with the selling and buying, the technical as well as the financial end of all industries, to devise some generic scheme that business can work on," Edison said with himself in mind. Edison wanted to run the economy for the benefit of all. As his model, he used the ultimate class bully, protofascist Kaiser Wilhelm of Germany.

But Teddy was just the beginning of class bullying in America. Woodrow Wilson, who was elected president in 1912, was fond of posing false choices between wealth and happiness—as though only by making America poor could anyone truly experience the joy of life. "Property as compared with humanity, as compared with the vital red blood in the American people, must take second place, not first place," said the pointy-headed Princeton professor.

Why property had to be compared with humanity, or with blood, or with rainbow unicorns, Woodrow didn't explain. He just placed money in opposition to humanity, and that was that.

Of course, it didn't help that Woodrow was basically a socialist. "Men as communities are supreme over men as individuals," he said. No greater recipe for bullying has ever been created.

To that end, he emboldened labor unions.

Wilson saw unions as the chief tool for stripping the wealthy of their power. He was truly the first president to run a Department of Labor, and his department was explicitly dedicated "in the interest of the wage earners." He was such an ideologue that in the middle of World War I, when war production was paramount, he insisted on strengthening rights of collective bargaining. Not surprisingly, after World War I, with the influx of young men coming home, the very unions Wilson created went ballistic, striking against their employers.[12]

And so the American people fell out of love, for a time, with the class bullies. Republicans dominated politics for the next decade after Wilson left the White House. And because of that, the economy boomed. The rich got richer, and so did everybody else.

Then the Great Depression hit.

The Great Depression—not unlike today's Great Recession—was the greatest single event in history for the Democratic Party. The Democrats, who had been largely tied down to the South and the legacy of Jim Crow, finally found what they had been looking for: a class war.

They moved quickly to exploit it.

In spring and summer of 1932, with the economy deeply depressed thanks to the stock market crash of 1929 and the interventionism of President Herbert Hoover, an enormous mass of World War I veterans began crowding the streets of Washington, D.C. They had been promised war bonuses years before that were not due for delivery until 1945. Now they were showing up to collect early. The press quickly dubbed the event the Bonus March.

The earliest protesters were Pennsylvanian veterans led by Father James Renshaw Cox, a labor organizer; he wanted to soak the rich by introducing a 70 percent inheritance tax and a huge government hiring program. Over time, their numbers grew. They set up tents and small hovels in the Anacostia Flats; by this time, such encampments had been dubbed "Hoovervilles."

And there they stayed. They marched every day. One observer called them "an immense hobo jungle." Their leader was one Walter W. Waters, an unemployed soldier from World War I.[13]

Waters was anticommunist; he had been helped to leadership by the local police chief.[14] But soon enough, the Communist Party saw their opportunity. John T. Pace, a member of the Communist Party, testified in 1951 about what happened next: "Well, we were using Almen [a Bonus March leader and rival to Waters] to get control of the rank and file. It was the plan of the party to use Almen as a front for gaining control of the entire bonus expeditionary forces . . . . It is my candid opinion that had this thing gone on for another week, the Communists would have gained the leadership of the bonus expeditionary forces . . ."[15] Pace's orders from Moscow, he said simply, were "to provoke riots." The riots, it was hoped, would provoke revolution.[16]

The Democratic Party, too, was eager to jump into the Bonus Army fray. Bullying the wealthy—and bullying Hoover with extralegal force—certainly didn't bother one particular governor, Franklin Delano Roosevelt. This, Roosevelt knew, was an army of "Forgotten Men." And FDR would manipulate those Forgotten Men into doing whatever he wanted them to do.[17] It was something he had been contemplating for a long time—in April 1932, he had called on Americans to form the "infantry of our economic army . . . the unorganized but the indispensable units of economic power."[18] He planned a radio address for shortly after his inauguration that would call for Americans to become his foot soldiers. Literally: "I reserve to myself the right to command you in any phase of the situation which now confronts us," he would tell his subjects.[19]

Governor Roosevelt played the benevolent father to the Bonus Marchers, sending Nels Anderson of the New York Temporary Emergency Relief Administration to visit the encampment. He then told the Bonus Army that they'd get jobs and free transportation to New York if they dispersed. When the army turned him down, Anderson publicly declared that Hoover ought to leave them be.[20]

The battle lines were drawn. And with the communist infiltration now at crisis levels, according to communist sources including Pace, President Hoover had no choice but to act. That became especially clear when, on July 28, 1932, two Washington, D.C., policemen were forced to shoot two veterans who rushed them. Hoover saw it the same way. So did General Douglas MacArthur, who headed the troops sent to put down the Bonus March. He forced the shutdown of the Bonus March, at the cost of fifty-five injured and 135 arrested—in other words, a typical day in a major city. One of the members of the Bonus March burned down the Hooverville. MacArthur said that night that he had saved the nation from "incipient revolution" by "insurrectionists."[21] He had probably saved the city from a bunch of ragtag veterans being misled by communists. But the Democrats couldn't wait to jump in and condemn Hoover as though he'd herded veterans into the Anacostia River itself.

"Well, Felix," FDR apparently said to future Supreme Court justice Felix Frankfurter upon hearing of the events, "this will elect me."

As Hoover later wrote, "The Democratic leaders did not organize the Bonus March nor conduct the ensuing riots. But the Democratic organization seized upon the incident with great avidity. Many Democratic speakers in the campaign of 1932 implied that I had murdered veterans on the streets of Washington."[22]

And, of course, FDR won the election in a landslide. He was promptly feted by liberal Hollywood in *Gabriel Over the White House*, a movie featuring a president who, instead of rushing the camps, simply hired everybody at the camps. FDR essentially did just that the next year when the Bonus Marchers returned.

Now empowered by his successful seizure of a mass class bully movement, FDR grabbed control of the entire financial infrastructure in pursuit of his antibusiness agenda. This was necessary, he said, because "the train of American business" had "to be loaded more evenly." He compared financial firms to "kidnappers and bank robbers," luring "the unsuspecting and the unwary to financial destruction."[23]

One of FDR's biggest targets was Henry Ford—yes, founder of the all-American car company. Ford didn't buy into FDR's view of business. So FDR went after him as though his name were Joe Wurzelbacher. "The Republican campaign management and people like Henry Ford," he charged, "are guilty of spreading the gospel of fear." Once in office, FDR quickly moved to regulate the automobile industry and help the unions. His National Recovery Administration (NRA) forced American businesses to sign codes of behavior organizing all companies operating within particular industries. Products produced by NRA signatory companies were branded with the Blue Eagle.

Public hearings would allow the administration to decide fair work hours, pay, and price of products. FDR announced, "The challenge of this law is whether we can sink selfish interest and present a solid front against a common peril." Hugh Samuel "Iron Pants" Johnson, an army general who led the effort, was named *Time*'s 1933 Man of the Year. Johnson was fond of passing out a tract on corporatism titled "The Corporate State," written by one of Mussolini's favorite advisors.

Ford fought back. "I do not think this country is ready to be treated like Russia for a while," Ford wrote. But the FDR administration didn't stop bullying him. General Johnson announced,

"I think maybe the American people will crack down on Mr. Ford when the Blue Eagle is on other cars and he does not have one." Johnson and FDR actually initiated a government boycott of Ford. In many cases, that meant the taxpayers paid more for cars produced by other manufacturers. FDR basically drove Ford into the ground. According to *Life* magazine, its market share was over 60 percent after World War I, but was just 20 percent by the beginning of World War II. Its more pliant competitors benefited, with General Motors picking up 50 percent of market share and Chrysler rising to 20 percent.

But FDR wasn't done yet.

In 1935, FDR followed in Wilson's footsteps and rammed through Congress the National Labor Relations Act. It prohibited companies from doing anything to fight against the formation of labor unions, including firing prospective union members, or most importantly, declining to bargain with a union once it had been formed. The union bullies were now in the industrial henhouse.

The results were dramatic. With government backing their play, the United Auto Workers, led by communist fellow-traveler Walter Reuther, began implementing sit-down strikes. Government actors, including the governor of Michigan, Frank Murray, stepped in to act as negotiators. Within a few years, the entire automobile workforce was unionized—a welcome change for politicians, who could now use those unions to raise funds and pound pavement on their own behalf. Ford was the last company to break, but in 1941, it did.

Of course, FDR wasn't alone in his quest to bully the earners and the investors. He was actually the *least* offensive of the class bullies. Father Charles Coughlin, an early supporter of FDR, led the charge—and, not unlike his modern liberal descendants, tempered his class warfare with the delightful hint of anti-Semitism. "We have lived to see the day that modern Shylocks have grown fat and wealthy, praised and deified, because they have perpetuated the ancient crime of usury under the modern racket of statesmanship," he railed in 1930 to millions via radio. Human rights, said Coughlin, should outweigh property rights. And "international bankers"—code for those big-nosed Hebraic folk—were to blame for the Depression.[24] Coughlin was one of FDR's most strident early backers. "If Congress fails to back up the President in his monetary program, I predict a revolution in this country which will make the French Revolution look silly!" he predicted before Congress.[25]

Huey Long, the wildly popular and corrupt governor and senator from Louisiana, preached something similar from his pulpit. A stem-winding speaker, Long thought that fortunes should be capped. His program was simple: Soak the rich. Bully them. Destroy them. "[T]he rich people of this country—and by rich people I mean the super-rich—will not allow us to solve the problems, or rather the one little problem that is afflicting this country, because in order to cure all of our woes it is necessary to scale down the big fortunes, that we may scatter the wealth to be shared by all of the people."[26] Because, as we know, when you scatter the wealth around, everybody's better off.

No wonder the economy stagnated during the FDR years. Anybody with money was probably scared to go outside with a fat wallet, lest a politician or union thug grab it and pummel them senseless.

But FDR's class warfare truly opened the door to American class bullying. Every Democratic president since has cited FDR as a transformative figure; the unions are still living off the class warfare regime FDR created; the activation of the dissatisfied poor against capitalism started with FDR.

And Obama has certainly studied his FDR.

UNION BULLYING

If Obama learned one thing from FDR, it was that every socialist needs his foot soldiers.

And what better place to get them than the unions?

FDR created the massive union infrastructure that would pave the way for nearly a century of Democratic political dominance; Obama inherited that infrastructure. During the 2008 election cycle, unions spent in excess of $200 million to help get Obama elected.[27] They did that because Obama wasn't just a friend of the unions—he was a former union lackey. In 2007, Obama admitted as much to the Service Employees International Union (SEIU). He told them, "I've got a history with this union. When I was a young organizer, I had just moved to Chicago. I started with working with SEIU Local 880, home health care workers, to make sure that they were registered to vote."[28] To be more honest, Obama had done more than simply help register people to vote. He'd worked with the SEIU's race-baiting love baby, ACORN. And the SEIU helped him right back in 2008, sending out one hundred thousand volunteers to work the pavement for him and dropping $60 million to back his play.[29]

It wasn't just the SEIU. He told the AFL-CIO, "I know the AFL-CIO is tired of playing defense. We're ready to play some offense."[30] They dropped some $50 million. The National Education Association backed him to the tune of $50 million, too.

Obama made sure that his own personal Bonus Marchers got their bonuses. His stimulus package was heavily geared toward the unions. One Department of Labor grant handed $7.4 million to the SEIU for "green jobs" training programs. As Van Jones, Obama's "green jobs czar" admitted, there were no such things as "green jobs."[31] More than $115 billion of the stimulus package went to education—which meant, in essence, that it went to teachers' unions.

Obama stacked the National Labor Relations Board, which oversees business relations with unions, with union cronies. That meant that cases of union intimidation went unprosecuted. In one particular case, pro-union employees physically threatened anti-union employees in advance of a union election. The NLRB ruled that was no problem at all.[32] Obama also pursued the notorious card-check legislation, which would allow union thugs to intimidate employees into voting to unionize.[33]

Obama's biggest union giveaway of all, though, was Obamacare. It's incredible that the media never got curious about union support for Obamacare. After all, unions have the best health-care plans on the planet—those Cadillac health-care plans in which union members essentially get to walk into the Mayo Clinic, slap down twenty dollars, and get diagnosed for a serious case of the cooties. So why would they support government intervention in health care?

The answer is obvious: today's unions are for the most part government sector unions, staffed by government employees who bargain collectively with politicians. The more government employees, the more union members. Observers expect more than 20 million additional government workers to join the union rolls under Obamacare.[34] The vast majority of the cash that these unions receive comes through forced dues—the ultimate form of bullying, in which union members don't get a say in how much they wish to send to their unions or how the dollars are spent.

In any case, the unions didn't really have to worry about losing those Cadillac plans anyway. As it turns out, Obama handed out waivers to the unions like Pacman Jones making it rain at a strip club. Meanwhile, everyday Americans watched their ability to choose their own health care get washed down the union toilet.

While Obama stacked legislation with union giveaways at the expense of the American people, that's not truly bullying—it's legislation approved by a majority of Congress, which at least in theory represents the people of the United States. Where things truly get ugly is in the thug tactics used by the Obama administration to target individuals who get in the way of the union agenda.

Take, for example, the auto bailouts.

President Obama got a nice big chunk of cash from the United Auto Workers during his 2008 run. When Chrysler found itself in financial ruins, Obama did the only logical thing: he decided to turn over the company to the UAW to pay them back for all their support. In order to make that happen, he shafted longtime investors in the company, including pensioners; secured creditors received just 29 cents on the dollar, while unsecured creditors—namely, the UAW—got 55 percent of the company. It was the same deal at GM, where the UAW owned $20 billion of GM's debt but somehow ended up owning 17.5 percent of the company and $9 billion in cash. Meanwhile, bondholders got shortchanged dramatically.[35]

This deal was pure bullying. Obama wanted a payoff for his cronies, so he rammed it down the throat of the bondholders. While the unions insisted all the bondholders were rich fat cats—which, by the way, wouldn't make this tactic any less thuggish—the truth was different. The bondholders included people like the family of Vicki Denton, a woman killed in a Dodge crash, who was owed some $2.2 million by Chrysler. Now the family got nothing.[36]

Unions have nothing to fear in pursuing their thuggery—politicians like Obama are always willing to bail them out. No wonder they strike against the public interest. Historically, some police and firefighters unions have actually committed arson during strikes in order to pressure the cities with which they bargain.[37] Literally thousands of violent incidents by union members have been reported over the past few decades. The concept of kneecapping didn't come from nowhere.

The unions are so used to bullying their opponents at this point that they simply don't know what to do when people fight back. In Wisconsin, Governor Scott Walker moved to curb collective bargaining for unions, since they'd bankrupted the state. The unions responded by occupying the state capitol, camping inside the building,[38] screaming and chanting in absolutely frightening fashion. Jesse Jackson, drawn to the bevy of orgasmic reporters like a moth to the flame, showed up to threaten violence: "So they're going to escalate the protests—you will either have collective bargaining through a vehicle called collective bargaining or you're going to have it through the streets. People here will fight back because they think their cause is moral and they have nowhere else to go."[39]

Normally, Jackson's threats are empty when they don't rhyme. This time, they didn't rhyme . . . but the threats weren't empty. One union member was arrested after threatening to shoot Walker. Ironically enough, he worked at a prison, so at least his workday didn't change all that much.[40] Dan Kapanke, a Wisconsin state senator who stood with Walker, got an email from a delightful probable union member, suggesting a playdate: "I will have your decapitated head on a pike in the Madison town square. This is your last warning."[41] Other emails were just as delightful: "Please put your things in order because you will be killed and your families will also be killed."[42] At least the assassination threat was polite. So polite, in fact, that the author of that missive ended up being treated leniently, because, as case management said, "she never intended to truly threaten or disturb anyone."[43] When *I* don't want to threaten or disturb anyone, I have a weird habit of *not threatening or disturbing anyone*. When union thugs want to avoid threats and disturbances, they send emails threatening to murder people. But they use the word "please," to tip off caseworkers that they're not serious about it.

Unbelievably enough, even people who had nothing to do with the Walker fight received such nonthreats from the unions. One of Wisconsin's biggest chain stores received a nonthreat from the unions if its management decided to stay neutral.[44] Which union sent the nonthreat? The police union. But according to liberals, being threatened by the police counts as something bad only if you're a black man driving 115 through a residential neighborhood. If you own a shop and don't actively oppose Scott Walker, you deserve whatever you get.

Teachers unions began protesting outside the capitol, busing in their students to help them. The teachers obtained fake signed notes from doctors so that they could ditch school.[45]

President Obama didn't think any of this was good. He thought it was downright fantastic. He called in Wisconsin reporters for an exclusive interview, in which he sided with the unions.[46]

Obama's Democratic Party friends in the Wisconsin state senate decided to help out, too, in the bullying. They fled to the state of Illinois in an attempt to forestall a quorum in the legislature. They stayed there for weeks.

This wasn't democracy or republicanism. This was fascistic bullying on a scale rarely seen in America.

In the end, the unions lost. Walker passed his bill, and when the unions recalled him, he won reelection in a landslide. But that wasn't about to stop the unions. They merely decided that they needed an army of their own. A bigger, better, stronger army. Of vagrants, homeless people, unemployed college students, ex-hippies, and the celebrities who love them.

They needed a better class of thugs.

The first indicator that the union bullying machine was about to become a permanent feature of the political landscape occurred in May 2010. On a Sunday, Nina Easton of *Fortune* reported, five hundred "screaming, placard-waving strangers" showed up on the front lawn of Easton's next-door neighbor, Greg Baer, deputy general counsel of Bank of America. "Waving signs denouncing bank 'greed,'" wrote Easton, "hordes of invaders poured out of 14 school buses, up Baer's steps, and onto his front porch. As bullhorns rattled with stories of debtor calls and foreclosed homes, Baer's teenage son Jack—alone in the house—locked himself in the bathroom. 'When are they going to leave?' Jack pleaded when I called to check on him." Baer called the police. Nothing happened. "Intimidation was the whole point of this exercise, and it worked—even on the police," Easton wrote. "A trio of officers who belatedly answered our calls confessed a fear that arrests might 'incite' these trespassers."[47]

All this was a great start for the unions—frightening children, staking out the front lawns of executives. The only thing missing was an enormous replica guillotine. But in order to really threaten the status quo, the unions needed a front group. If they did it themselves, there would be consequences. If they could get a dissolute group of rabble together to bother, threaten, and assault everyday Americans, they could achieve their goals.

They needed Occupy.

OCCUPY THE WHITE HOUSE

President Obama wasn't elected on a platform of class warfare. In the last weeks of the campaign, in fact, Obama lost ground to John McCain based on charges that he was too liberal economically. The Joe the Plumber incident clearly hurt him.

President Obama needed a groundswell in order to make FDR-like transformative change.

What he got, unfortunately for him, was the Tea Party. As President Obama forged forward with his program of crony bailouts and wild, uncontrolled spending, Rick Santelli of CNBC took to the airwaves. "Government is promoting bad behavior," he shouted to the traders standing behind him at the Chicago Mercantile Exchange. "Do we really want to subsidize the losers' mortgages? This is America! How many of you people want to pay for your neighbor's mortgage? President Obama, are you listening? How about we all stop paying our mortgages! It's a moral hazard." He then called on Americans to begin a second Tea Party.

All across America, citizens concerned about government spending and the destruction of constitutional principles answered the call. Thousands turned out at rallies to protest President Obama's massive expansion of the state.

This was not what Obama had in mind.

Obama responded by turning to his media cronies to demonize the Tea Party as enemies of the people. When the Tea Party tried to push Republicans to implement spending cuts before automatically raising the debt ceiling, the media went clinically insane. "Never negotiate with terrorists," wrote Joe Nocera in the *New York Times*. "It only encourages them. . . . Tea Party Republicans have waged jihad on the American people. Their intransigent demands for deep spending cuts, coupled with their almost gleeful willingness to destroy one of America's most invaluable assets, its full faith and credit, were incredibly irresponsible. But they didn't care. Their goal, they believed, was worth blowing up the country for, if that's what it took."[48] This was shades of Father Coughlin.

But Obama had many Father Coughlin stand-ins on whom he could rely. Steven Rattner, his former car czar, took to the MSNBC airwaves to explain that Tea Partiers were waging a "form of economic terrorism"; they had, he said, "strapped [themselves] with dynamite standing in the middle of Times Square at rush hour, and saying 'either you do it my way, or we're going to blow you up.'"[49] The Obama administration couldn't label real terrorists terrorists—the war on terrorism became an overseas contingency operation. But when it came to people who thought the government should spend less—then it was shoot to kill.

Joe Klein of *Time* pulled the same nonsense. "Osama bin Laden, if he were still alive, could not have come up with a more clever strategy for strangling our nation," Klein fumed.[50] William Yeomans of *Politico* echoed the same message: "It has become commonplace to call the tea party faction in the House 'hostage takers.' But they have now become full-blown terrorists. They have joined the villains of American history who have been sufficiently craven to inflict massive harm on innocent victims to achieve their political goals."[51] Yup—Hitler and that random guy in the flag T-shirt. They're one and the same.

Scapegoating and bullying the Tea Party has remained a mainstay of the Obama administration all the way to the present. In May 2012, Joe Biden announced that all the failures of the Obama economic plan should be dumped at the feet of those Gadsden-flag-carrying morons: "Imagine where we'd be if the Tea Party hadn't taken control of the House of Representatives," he said.

"They have one overwhelming goal: prevent President Obama from a second term, with no—apparently no care of the consequences to the economy."[52]

Obama failed in his effort to shut up the Tea Party. So he, along with his union cronies, decided that they needed a Tea Party of their own. Not a group of patriotic Americans who would gather peacefully, clean up their own trash, and sing American songs while wearing red, white, and blue.

Rather, they needed a large group of smelly, violent, stupid people who could take over large swaths of public land and create a media center. The media's job in all of this would be to cover the Obama shock troops as a grassroots phenomenon, an unorganized and unled movement of the people.

They would call this movement Occupy Wall Street.

Now, occupying Wall Street didn't make a whole hell of a lot of sense from any rational perspective. Wall Street is a series of private firms bent on making profit for their investors. No amount of public outcry could have any real effect on private businesses—it could just serve to intimidate them into silence. If the Occupiers had truly cared about bank bailouts and crony capitalism, they would have shown up in Washington, D.C., to occupy outside the White House and Congress.

But, of course, Occupy Wall Street wasn't about folks who cared about the bailouts. It was about anticapitalism.

Naturally, Obama's other shock troops—the unions—showed up in force for Occupy. "We're in it for the long haul," said George Aldro, a member of the UAW. "We are here to support this movement against Wall Street's greed," shouted Victor Rivera, a vice president for the 1199 SEIU. "We support the idea that the rich should pay their fair share." Unions donated cash, blankets, office space, and food to the protesters.[53] Former SEIU head Stephen Lerner got together with other extremists at New York University in March to discuss the real Occupy agenda: "The Abolition of Capitalism." He suggested that Occupiers take over foreclosed homes, take over shareholder meetings, and shut down places of work.[54]

They also helped "train" Occupiers—which really meant organizing them and giving them the ability to continue breaking the law. The SEIU actually advertised on its website for a "Lead Internal Organizer," who would earn $65,000 to "train and lead members in non-violent civil disobedience, such as occupying state buildings and banks, and peaceful resistance . . . plan and execute strategic direct action field plans including banner drops, bank takeovers, and capitol occupations with membership, other local unions, and coalition partners."[55]

So, who showed up to Occupy? When I visited Occupy Los Angeles, it was clearly a group of homeless people, extreme anarchists, and anticapitalists—many of whom were anti-Semitic—and some students with nothing better to do. These were not peaceful, decent citizens simply attempting to express their outrage over excessive government relationships with Wall Street. These were incompetent would-be violent revolutionaries.

It wasn't just my perception. They self-perceived that way. An April 2012 poll of the occupiers of New York's Zuccotti Park—the leading wing of the Occupy Wall Street crowd—showed that 53 percent opposed "American-style capitalism," 71 percent wanted "massive redistribution of wealth," and almost 80 percent wanted free health care, education, and retirement. Were they violent? You bet they were: 63 percent said they had engaged in civil disobedience, and 13 percent said they'd gotten violent before.[56]

The Occupiers followed through on their violent rhetoric, too. Just as the SEIU did with Greg Baer, Occupiers made routine practice of invading private property, or staking out private persons unaffiliated with the government. In Los Angeles, one hundred Occupy protesters who wanted an eviction reversed pitched their poop-tents outside the home of a Bank of America executive.[57] Complaining about the "willingness to hoard wealth at the expense of the 99 percent," New York Occupiers descended on the home of Rupert Murdoch (who was not bailed out by the federal government), chanting, "Hey Murdoch, pay your fair share."[58] They descended on JPMorgan Chase executive Jamie Dimon's home. And who was heading up this activity? All the usual community-organizing suspects: the Working Families Party, UnitedNY, New York Communities for Change. All of Obama's friends, in other words.[59]

It wasn't just occupation. Rape reports spread across the Occupy movement. As it turns out, when you have a bunch of lawbreaking vagrants with degrees in mental illness, you end up with crime. Overall, there have been at least three murders at Occupy camps, 500 thefts, almost 7,000 arrests, and millions of dollars in property damage. On May 1, 2012, the authorities foiled an Occupy Cleveland plot to blow up a bridge.[60] Videos of Occupy violence cover the Internet.

And Occupy was insanely dirty. In fact, they're a public health hazard. In Occupy Santa Cruz, drug use, public defecation, littering, and vandalism were commonplace. The Santa Cruz sheriff's office stumbled upon a two-hundred-pound pile of human poop near the Veterans Memorial Building.[61] In Occupy Atlanta, tuberculosis broke out. As it turns out, when you live like residents of Sudan, you end up with their health problems, too. The only difference is that the people of Sudan are victims of outside forces; the people of Occupy are victims of their own stupidity.

Nonetheless, the Occupy slogan, "We are the 99 percent," quickly gained ground in media coverage—and in political circles. Suddenly, it seemed, every major politician was separating Americans by income.

Including Obama. Just days after ripping Bank of America for instituting a $5 debit card fee—something that was not illegal—Obama went full-bore Occupy. "I think people are frustrated and the protesters are giving voice to a more broad-based suspicion about how our financial system works," said the president of the United States about this criminal enterprise.[62]

On October 14, 2011, Obama-friendly *Washington Post* reporter—but I repeat myself—Peter Wallsten ran a piece stating flatly, "President Obama and his team have decided to turn public anger at Wall Street into a central tenet of their re-election strategy." That decision sprang not only from Obama's FDR-esque populism but from his need to wield a club against Mitt Romney, who even then was presumed to be the presidential front-runner. "We intend to make it one of the central elements of the campaign next year," said Obama senior advisor David Plouffe.[63]

Sure enough, on October 16, 2011, one of Obama's press secretaries informed the media that Obama would represent "the interests of the 99 percent of Americans." Jay Carney, Obama's press secretary, repeated the same line to the press.[64]

The press itself decided to back Occupy to the hilt. They'd never seen anything this inspirational since their parents were engaging in mud-soaked threesomes with hirsute hippies back during the glorious 1960s. Some of the reporters were so inspired that they effectively joined Occupy themselves. Natasha Lennard of the *New York Times* joined a discussion at the radical bookstore Bluestockings on October 14. For background, Lennard had reported on the Occupy takeover of the Brooklyn Bridge; there, she'd been arrested, supposedly for being a member of the press. It's more likely she was arrested because she was one of the protesters.

At the Bluestockings event, she talked about how best to organize. "[B]eing an outright anti-authoritarian or an anarchist is not really something that people like to be live streamed around the world with a f—ing police pen around you," she explained.[65]

Lennard wasn't the only Occupier in a high place. NPR host Lisa Simeone began using her show, *World of Opera*, as a bully pulpit for Occupy. NPR had to can her.[66]

But the mainstream media support wasn't limited to actually protesting with Occupy. The media routinely compared the violent, thuggish, and downright nasty Occupy movement with the peaceful and well-behaved Tea Party. They ignored Occupy's ugly undercurrents of anti-Semitism—as Jennifer Rubin of the *Washington Post* observed, "In the millions of pixels devoted to the radical Occupy Wall Streeters, virtually nothing has been said about its anti-Semitic elements." But those elements were there, nonetheless—propaganda against Israel, talk about Zionist interests controlling Wall Street, ugly chatter about Jewish influence on fiscal policy.[67] The Occupy official Facebook page even posted a Naziesque Jew-hating cartoon depicting an ugly-looking rabbi with large nose and beard, wearing a Star of David hat, driving a car; the gearshift was topped by Barack Obama's head. The wheel was the logo of the United Nations. The message: the Jews control everything.[68] None of the big three networks were interested in covering any of this.[69]

The media didn't want to hear about Occupy's violent tendencies—they were too busy playing offense on behalf of the Obama-Occupy nexus. When the Cleveland Occupiers tried to bomb a bridge, the *New York Times*, CBS News, and *USA Today* ignored it completely. Other outlets like CNN and the Associated Press tried to downplay any Occupy associations.[70] When the Oakland police department accidentally wounded an Iraq War veteran at Occupy, the media responded with fury but largely ignored the fact that the Oakland Occupiers had been abusing cops.

Hollywood showed up to support these thugs, too. Kanye West hilariously showed up to the Occupy rally in Zuccotti Park to hang with the downtrodden; hip-hop mogul Russell Simmons joined him. Said Simmons: "It was amazing to see how people loved seeing Kanye West at Occupy Wall Street. His music and his art has always been about the voice and the power of the people. Kanye just wanted to come down and experience the growing movement that has opened the eyes of many around this country and around the world of the struggles of poor people." Kanye did not, however, want to experience what it was like to be a poor person—he wore a gold chain and a $300 shirt.[71]

Michael Moore took a break from the pork rinds to visit Occupy, too. He'd already denied that he was a member of the "1 percent"; he'd visited Occupy Oakland, which had been replete with violence, and told them, "We've killed despair across the country and we've killed apathy." After Oakland police cleared Occupy Oakland, the occupiers returned, and Moore celebrated: "Millions have seen this and are inspired by you because you came back the next night."[72] He headed to New York to do the same thing a couple of months later. The Occupiers were more than happy to chat with the big fella, although he wouldn't answer questions about his $50 million fortune, which puts him squarely in the 1 percent.[73]

The Hollywood who's who supported Occupy, too—from well within their gated communities off Sunset Boulevard, of course. "It seems great!" exclaimed George Clooney. Susan Sarandon and Mark Ruffalo hung out at Zuccotti Park—presumably before heading back to expensive hotels in stretch limos.[74]

The most stirring anthem on behalf of Occupy was penned by none other than Hannah Montana, Miley Cyrus, who put together a YouTube video titled "Liberty Walk." "This," she wrote, "is Dedicated to the thousands of people who are standing up for what they believe in." The song's lyrics are rousing: "It's a liberty walk, say goodbye to the people who tied you up. It's a liberty walk, feeling your heart beat again, breathing new oxygen." The video itself mashes together clips from the Arab Spring, the Iranian protests, and, of course, Occupy. No word on whether Miley will be handing out her spare millions to the lice-ridden specimens in the park.[75]

While Occupy didn't actually accomplish much, other than breaking windows, threatening violence, rioting, raping, looting, and spreading disease, they did win *Time* magazine's Person of the Year. And they're always lurking in the background, waiting for the latest astroturfing from Obama and his allies on behalf of the liberal agenda.

SHUTTING UP THE RICH

President Obama has read the FDR playbook. A copy probably sits inside his nightstand like a Gideon Bible at a low-rent motel (although Obama would never be caught dead reading a Bible—that's for bitter clingers).

And just as FDR targeted private citizens like Henry Ford for destruction, simply because they wouldn't back his fascistic economic plans, Obama has his own enemies list. He checks it twice. Then he pops down the chimney and proceeds to beat the snot out of anyone who has deigned to cross him.

On April 20, 2012, President Obama's "Truth Team" campaign website listed eight donors to Mitt Romney. "Behind the curtain," the caption read, as though readers were about to stumble into a clandestine orgy at the Skull & Bones club.

What was behind that curtain? Evil rich guys who had the temerity not to donate to President Obama. "A closer look at . . . donors reveals a group of wealthy individuals with less-than reputable records," said the website. "Quite a few have been on the wrong side of the law, others have made profits at the expense of so many Americans."[76]

String 'em up!

So, who was on this list of nefarious ne'er-do-wells?

Frank VanderSloot, CEO of Melaleuca Inc., led it off. In August 2011, VanderSloot gave $1 million to Mitt Romney's Super PAC. The Obama website named VanderSloot as "litigious, combative and a bitter foe of the gay rights movement." Shortly after that, an Obama surrogate tried to obtain divorce records for VanderSloot—the dirt-digger was a former Democratic Senate staffer. VanderSloot has been attacked by partisan Obama media hacks like MSNBC's Rachel Maddow and Salon.com's Glenn Greenwald. "I knew it was like taping a target on my back," said VanderSloot.[77]

VanderSloot is relatively lucky—the Obama campaign has gone after him directly only once. The Koch brothers, David and Charles, run Koch Industries, a massive American job creator. Unfortunately for them, they're also opponents of the redistributionist Obama economic agenda. That put them squarely in Obama's crosshairs. And they weren't just profiled on the idiotic website.

In 2010, Austan Goolsbee, then Obama's chief economic advisor, lied in public about the Koch brothers' tax status and said the company didn't pay income tax. That prompted a Treasury Department review of Goolsbee.[78]

On February 24, 2012, Obama campaign manager Jim Messina issued a letter to his millions-strong email list, targeting the Koch brothers for their support of Mitt Romney's campaign. "In just about 24 hours," the email stated, "Mitt Romney is headed to a hotel ballroom to give a speech sponsored by Americans for Prosperity, a front group founded and funded by the Koch brothers.

"Those are the same Koch brothers whose business model is to make millions by jacking up prices at the pump, and who bankrolled Tea Party extremism, and committed $200 million to try to destroy President Obama before Election Day."[79]

This was entirely false. First, the Koch brothers owned zero gas stations, and oil and gas refining—Koch Industries' real business—lowers cost at the pump. Second, the Koch brothers never pledged $200 million to "destroying" Obama. Third, Americans for Prosperity has tens of thousands of members and donors. As the Koch Industries' spokesperson stated, "It is understandable that the President and his campaign may be 'tired of hearing' that many Americans would rather not see the president re-elected. However, the inference is that you would prefer that citizens who disagree with the President and his policies refrain from voicing their own viewpoint. Clearly, that's not the way a free society should operate."[80]

Clearly, the Obama campaign disagreed—just a few months later, they issued *another* false attack on the Koch brothers personally. In early May 2012, deputy campaign manager Stephanie Cutter picked up Messina's torch, cutting a video labeling the Koch brothers as "secretive oil billionaires bankrolling Republican campaigns" and stating that the Koch brothers supported Romney just to prevent Obama from removing "billions of dollars in unnecessary oil tax breaks." The video was vitriolic, angry, vengeful. "They will literally say anything," said Cutter, playing the victim. But it was clear that the Obama campaign would say anything.[81] Their media friends, who are busy demonizing the Koch brothers, and their astroturfed friends, who shout "Koch-suckers!" at rallies, are willing to lend a hand.

VanderSloot and the Koch brothers have been joined on the Obama hit list by many others. Obama has even gone so far as to joke about using the IRS to audit his opponents.[82]

But he doesn't need to audit his opponents. He can just sic his allies in the press on them. During the primaries, Sheldon Adelson, who gave $20 million to Newt Gingrich's floundering presidential campaign, somehow merited an entire editorial in the *New York Times;* they called him "the perfect illustration of the squalid state of political money, spending sums greater than any political donation in history to advance his personal, ideological and financial agenda, which is wildly at odds with the nation's needs." What makes Adelson such a nasty character? "Mr. Adelson's other overriding interest is his own wallet." As opposed to the millions of voters who pull the lever for Democrats so they can assure their welfare benefits. Somehow, the *New York Times* has never made this argument about George Soros or Warren Buffett or any of the liberal megadonors who populate Barack Obama's speed dial.[83]

The anti-Adelson bullying magnified once it became clear that Mitt Romney would be the nominee. The Obama campaign sent out repeated emails railing against Adelson; when Republican vice presidential nominee Paul Ryan visited Adelson during a campaign stop in Nevada, the Obama campaign unleashed a borderline anti-Semitic screed accusing Ryan of "making a pilgrimage" to "kiss the ring" of Adelson. The message was clear: the Catholic Ryan was traveling to Vegas to bow before his wealthy Jew master. Just a couple of days after the email, the *New York Times* ran *another* editorial against Adelson. The editorial said that Ryan "made a pilgrimage" to see Adelson. Same words. No attribution to the Obama campaign. The *Times* editorial team was so far up the Obama team's posterior, it was now difficult to tell where one ended and the other began.[84]

Actually, the Obama administration and its media and organizational allies have decided that any Republican who spends a lot of money on elections must be stopped. Hence their disgust for the *Citizens United* Supreme Court decision, which made the eminently correct observation that under the First Amendment, government cannot stop groups of people from spending money on elections—even if those groups of people are called corporations. Corporations are evil—except when they're 501(c)3s run by President Obama's allies. Then they're spectacular. Same thing with Super PACs. Those things are the root of all evil, unless they're run by David Brock.

So, here's the bottom line: Scumbags who smash windows, destroy businesses, riot, and call for the murder of the rich are fine with liberals. Rich people, however, pose a serious problem.

Got it. Robespierre had nothing on these jerks.

With friends in government like this, it's no wonder that so many major corporations have done what so many corporations did in FDR's and TR's day: cave. A century ago, Thomas Edison bought into the notion that working with the government was more useful than fighting against it. Today, exactly 101 years later, Jeffrey Immelt, who now heads Edison's General Electric, says that business should work in cooperation with government, and he actually attacks businesses that are opposed to government regulation. "The people who are part of the business sector, the people in this room, have got to stop complaining about government and get some action underway," Immelt told a group of businesspeople in July 2011. Not coincidentally, Immelt is chair of President Obama's Council on Jobs and Competitiveness. Also not coincidentally, Immelt's GE has received millions of dollars in subsidies and billions' worth of friendly regulations that drive consumers toward their products. As Immelt stated in 2008, "We at GE will continue to support and advocate swift passage of [friendly] legislation that is acceptable to the Senate, the House, and the Administration, and that can be promptly signed into law by the President." GE spends millions on lobbying for such legislation each year.

If the class bullies continue to dominate American politics, it won't be long before every corporation is a GE, dependent on government giveaways. And it won't be long after that when our entire economy is bankrupt, since a pick-and-choose economy is no match for a free market one.

CONCLUSION

Long before Mitt Romney formally won the Republican nomination for president of the United States, Barack Obama had set his sights on the likely nominee. And he knew—he *knew*—that Romney was vulnerable based solely and completely on class bullying. As one Democratic strategist told *Politico*, "Unless things change and Obama can run on accomplishments, he will have to kill Romney." How would Obama accomplish this brutal task, aside from using a chain saw and crowbar? Said David Axelrod, "[Romney] was very, very good at making a profit for himself and his partners but not nearly as good [at] saving jobs for communities. He is very much the profile of what we've seen in the last decade on Wall Street."

To that end, the Obama campaign began portraying Romney as a serial outsourcer, somebody "rooting" for economic destruction. "He is a corporate raider," explained Axelrod. As Paul Kengor of the *American Spectator* pointed out, "[Axelrod] is slicing up Mitt for an Occupy Wall Street feast. He sees Mitt as a hunk of red meat for the Occupy movement, as the poster-boy for Wall Street greed."[85]

This was too much even for some honest liberals like Cory Booker, mayor of Newark, New Jersey, who said on national television that it was "nauseating" to attack "private equity." The Obama campaign promptly forced Booker to back down from his statements, then tossed his inert political body into the sewage-ridden Newark Bay. Booker, said a source in the Obama administration, is "dead to us."[86]

And they were just getting started. In August 2012, Priorities USA Super PAC, an organization run by former White House deputy press secretary Bill Burton and associated with Media Matters head David Brock, ran an ad about one Joe Soptic. Soptic, the ad proclaimed, was a former employee of GST Steel, a company once owned by Bain Capital. Bain Capital shut it down. Soptic lost his job and his health insurance, said the ad; his wife then developed cancer and died. Essentially, the Super PAC argued, Romney killed Joe Soptic's wife.

There were a few problems with the story. First, Bain shut GST Steel down after Romney ended active management of the company. Second, Soptic was offered a buyout package by GST. Third, Soptic's wife was diagnosed with cancer in 2006, five years after GST Steel shut down. Fourth, Soptic's wife didn't lose her insurance—she already had her own insurance. Other than that, the ad was right on the money.

So the ad was chock full of lies. The Obama campaign knew it. They knew Soptic's story, and they obviously knew about the ad. Their campaign spokespeople, especially Stephanie Cutter, simply lied about it—she said the campaign had no idea about Soptic's story. But then it turned out that Cutter had hosted Soptic, telling precisely the same story, on an Obama campaign conference call months before. The Obama campaign website had a slide featuring Soptic, trying to link the death of his wife to Mitt Romney. The Obama campaign still refuses to denounce the ad—or, for that matter, the Richie Riches standing behind the Super PAC that produced it.

Let's leave aside the fact that the ad lied about the facts. Assume for a moment that everything the ad said had been true: Romney ran Bain, Bain shut down GST, Soptic lost his insurance, his wife died of cancer. That *still* wouldn't justify the ad from any rational pro-business perspective. Businesses are not responsible for ensuring the health and welfare of former workers. Businesses are created to produce product and profit—product that is passed on to consumers, profit that is passed along to workers and yes, bosses. Blaming businesses for firing people is asinine. If Obama blamed Apple for every death of every relative of every employee Steve Jobs ever fired, the American people would laugh him off the political stage.

But if Steve Jobs had been a major Republican donor, Obama probably would have done just that. Obama is a class bully. And he's an anti-business bully. That's why, in July, Obama explained to businesspeople that they hadn't really built their own businesses. "Look," he said, off-teleprompter, "if you've been successful, you didn't get there on your own. You didn't get there on your own. I'm always struck by people who think, well, it must be because I was just so smart. There are a lot of smart people out there. It must be because I worked harder than everybody else. Let me tell you something—there are a whole bunch of hardworking people out there."

So if it wasn't your smarts or hard work that built your business, what did?

"If you were successful, somebody along the line gave you some help. There was a great teacher somewhere in your life. Somebody helped to create this unbelievable American system that we have that allowed you to thrive. Somebody invested in roads and bridges. If you've got a business—you didn't build that. Somebody else made that happen."

Business owners couldn't take credit for their own achievements, their own businesses. Business owners owed their fortunes to government, not to absence of government. Government had built their businesses. And Obama could destroy them.

The left's thuggery on economics hides the fact that it has been wildly unsuccessful at rectifying economic inequalities. Obama, the greatest class warrior of modern times, has created more economic inequality than President George W. Bush by a landslide. According to Robert Reich, President Clinton's secretary of labor and a supporter of Obama, "The top 1 percent got 45 percent of Clinton-era economic growth, and 65 percent of the economic growth during the Bush era. According to an analysis of tax returns by Emmanuel Saez and Thomas Piketty, the top 1 percent pocketed 93 percent of the gains in 2010. 37 percent of the gains went to the top one-tenth of one percent. No one below the richest 10 percent saw any gain at all." That despite Obama's stimulus packages, his bailouts, his unemployment benefits, his vast spending, and his attacks on those who make money in America.[87]

Obama shouldn't feel too bad. His predecessors didn't do anything to rectify poverty, either, despite their Marxist thug tendencies. LBJ's War on Poverty defined the term "epic fail." About 13 percent of Americans live in poverty today; forty years ago, that rate was 19 percent. We've spent some $8–10 trillion on antipoverty programs during those decades. About a sixth of the federal budget every year goes to antipoverty programs. And yet our inner cities are a wreck, income inequality has widened—and if we adjust for massive economic growth over the past four decades, the statistics look even worse.[88]

What's more, we're alienating everyone who earns. In May 2012, just before Facebook went public, Eduardo Saverin, cofounder of the company, renounced his U.S. citizenship.[89] Leftists didn't respond by recognizing that perhaps emboldening poop-covered pitchfork-carrying morons to attack rich folks was a recipe for disaster. Instead, Senator Chuck Schumer (D-NY) said, "It's infuriating to see someone sell out the country that welcomed him and kept him safe, educated him and helped him become a billionaire. . . . We plan to put a stop to this tax avoidance scheme." And Senator Bob Casey (D-PA) echoed that message: "We simply cannot allow the ultra-wealthy to write their own rules. Mr. Saverin has benefited greatly from being a citizen of the United States but he has chosen to cast it aside and leave U.S. taxpayers with the bill. Renouncing citizenship to simply avoid paying your fair share is an insult to middle class Americans and we will not accept it."[90]

No. Bullying earners to the point where they leave the country is an insult to Americans. What's worse, it bankrupts them. But that's precisely what Obama and his cronies want to do.

That's why they keep focusing on the "breathtaking greed" of capitalists, as Obama did in a 2011 speech in Osawatomie, Kansas. That's why they say, as Obama did in Kansas, that the rich aren't paying their "fair share" even if they pay the overwhelming majority of taxes.[91]

And, by the way, it's no coincidence that Obama chose to lay his class bully platform out in Osawatomie. That's where Teddy Roosevelt called himself a "New Nationalist" and targeted "swollen fortunes."

It's been a century since then, and nothing has changed except the players. The bullies keep on bullying. Until they're stopped.

5.

★

SEX BULLIES

The left hates Sarah Palin.

They don't hate her because she's a Republican, though that doesn't help—the left isn't fond of George W. Bush, but they hate Palin more than Bush by a factor of five. They don't hate her because she's charismatic—Marco Rubio is charismatic, and the left doesn't hate him with the passionate fury of a thousand burning suns.

No, the left hates Sarah Palin because she's a charismatic Republican *woman*.

The first sign that the left couldn't stand Sarah Palin came when she presented her son Trig to the world. Trig was born with Down syndrome, and yet Palin had the gall not to abort him. If she'd been a leftist, this would have been seen as an act of supreme self-sacrifice; because Palin didn't abort Trig out of pro-life principle, however, the left decided that she was a villain.

And so they targeted her.

Andrew Sullivan of the *Atlantic* led the way, giving legs to the underground radical rumor that Trig was not Sarah's son, but rather her grandson. "The birth of Trig was critical to appealing to a pro-life base, and was used as a political argument and weapon in the 2008 campaign and since," wrote Sullivan. "It cannot surely be 'embarrassing' for the media to ask for evidentiary proof—any more than it was inappropriate for Obama to produce proof of his birth in Hawaii. It may be awkward, but it isn't illegitimate." The implication: if she'd just had an abortion, we'd all accept that the fetus was hers, and we could just move on.[1] Sullivan, as it turns out, is one of Barack Obama's favorite bloggers.[2] Obama even invited Sullivan to a state dinner.[3] But then again, it's not as if Obama has reason to be especially suspicious of those who doubt the birth stories of others.

Then there was the hatred of the Hollywood crowd, who couldn't stand that this shockingly good-looking Alaskan governor was . . . gasp! . . . a Republican. Louis C.K., the balding reprobate drunk comedian, tweeted from an airplane about Palin: "I want to rub my father's c—k all over Sarah Palin's fat t—t." And "@SarahPalinUSA kudos to your dirty hole, you fucking jackoff c—t-face jazzy wondergirl." When he was slightly less drunk, he referred to Palin's "f— retard-making c—t." This delightful individual got invited to the White House, too, where he spent five hours hanging out with Obama speechwriter Jonathan Favreau.[4] Betty White took a break from being old long enough to call Palin a "crazy bitch" on the *Craig Ferguson Show*.[5] Thankfully, because of the show's ratings, just two people saw it—White and Ferguson.

Formerly funny dwarf commentator Bill Maher, whose brainpan is apparently losing the battle for headspace with his proboscis, has called Palin both a "dumb t—t" and a "c—t." President Obama's Super PAC accepted $1 million from Maher, no questions asked.

The "journalistic" world weighed in, too. Keith Olbermann, between bouts of self-righteousness and bloviation, told the *Hol-*

lywood Reporter that Palin is "very stupid. She's one of the few people in politics that most political writers and broadcasters can sincerely, legitimately look down on."[6] Bill Keller, executive editor of the supposedly objective *New York Times*, echoed Olbermann: "If the 2012 election were held in the newsrooms of America and pitted Sarah Palin against Barack Obama, I doubt Palin would get 10 percent of the vote. However tempting the newsworthy havoc of a Palin presidency, I'm pretty sure most journalists would recoil in horror from the idea." Read closely. He isn't saying that Palin is unpopular. He's saying she's reviled.[7]

The conspiracy was worse than that. As soon as Palin was nominated, leftist journalists united on the previously discussed secret Internet listserv JournoList, where they coordinated attacks on Palin. Michael Cohen of the New America Foundation, a liberal think tank, wrote, "Honestly, this pick reeks of desperation. How can anyone logically argue that Sarah Pallin [*sic*], a one-term governor of Alaska, is qualified to be President of the United States? Train wreck, thy name is Sarah Palin." This precipitated a conversation with Jonathan Stein of *Mother Jones*, Jeffrey Toobin of the *New Yorker*, Daniel Levy of the liberal Century Foundation, Ryan Donmoyer at Bloomberg News, and *Politico* reporter Ben Adler, who later ended up at *Newsweek*. "Doesn't leaving said baby without its mother while she campaigns weaken [her] family values argument?" asked Adler, ignoring the fact that this argument cut against decades of feminist thought. "Or will everyone be too afraid to make that point?"[8]

HBO spent millions of dollars producing a Palin hit piece with falsified material, *Game Change*. The porn industry put together a movie starring a Palin look-alike.

On Hollywood 2008, Wonkette ran a picture of Trig being held by Sarah's daughter Bristol. "Little baby Trig must be so glad he wasn't aborted for this, his first Halloween," snarked Wonkette, "because his parents dressed him up like a political party symbol to be carried around at snarling political events. Aww. Isn't life just grand?"[9] Even relatives of Palin came under attack. David Letterman infamously suggested that Willow Palin, then fourteen, was "knocked up by Alex Rodriguez" during a game at Yankee Stadium.[10] Of course, Letterman had already gone after Willow's mom, suggesting that Sarah "bought make-up from Bloomingdale's to update her 'slutty flight attendant look.'"

Of course, it isn't just Palin whom the left attacks with the rage of . . . well . . . a woman scorned. Another is Michele Bachmann, labeled the "Mata Hari of Minnesota" by Chris Matthews of MSNBC, a "phony-ass broad" and a "skank" by leftist radio host Mike Malloy, the "Hate Monger of Minnesota" by left-wing sleazebag Max Blumenthal, and "America's craziest member of Congress" by Michelle Goldberg of the *Daily Beast*. Matt Taibbi—you may remember him from his evil attack on Andrew Breitbart the day of his death in *Rolling Stone*—put together an endless profile on Bachmann labeling her a "batshit crazy . . . political psychopath" with a "gigantic set of burnished titanium Terminator-testicles swinging under her skirt." See, she wasn't even a girl, cuz she was conservative. These are the types of people who thought girls had cooties on the playground.[11]

Michelle Malkin has come in for her share of hate, too. Malkin fell under Taibbi's perverse scrutiny in *Rolling Stone* after she rightly ripped the media for embracing the sexual slang term *teabagging* to describe Tea Partiers. Here's Taibbi's genius: "[T]his move of hers to spearhead the teabag movement really adds an element to her writing that wasn't there before. Now when I read her stuff, I imagine her narrating her text, book-on-tape style, with a big, hairy, set of balls in her mouth. It vastly improves her prose." Taibbi was obviously breathing heavily as he wrote these words. As for Olbermann, when he's not too busy playing with his cats in his lonely, lonely apartment, he's criticizing Malkin as a "big, mashed up bag of meat with lipstick on it."[12]

When unions in Wisconsin were busily targeting Republican lieutenant governor Rebecca Kleefisch, some of their friends brought out their most misogynistic slurs. John "Sly" Sylvester of WTDY radio suggested that she had performed "fellatio on all the talk-show hosts in Milwaukee." He added that she had "pulled a train" on them—pulling a train being a euphemism for engaging in group sex, apparently.[13]

And don't even get started on what they say about Ann Coulter.

So, what's the point of recounting all of this leftist hatred for conservative women?

This is the same left that decided that it was a War on Women to suggest that people pay for their own birth control. This is the same left that says that the Susan G. Komen for the Cure breast cancer group is sexist because they don't want to fund Planned Parenthood, that Republicans are misogynists because they don't think that Head Start is an effective federal program, and that anyone who opposes gay marriage for any reason is a homophobe.

The left consistently bullies those who disagree with them by claiming they're sexist and "heteronormative." Those patriarchal males, according to the left, must be stopped from imposing their Neanderthal worldview on Americans—and so must their wives. Traditional values Americans who believe in legitimate and valuable differences between the sexes must shut the hell up . . . or be bludgeoned into silence.

ORIGINS OF THE SEX BULLIES

Men are, admittedly, by nature, sexual pigs. Let's just put that out there at the start. Many men, if left unchecked by the civilizing influence of women and the institution of marriage, will sleep around, abandon children, and generally act like animals. How do we know that? Because that's what teenage boys do before they grow up.

But marriage works. The fact is that even polls of Americans today—after the sexual revolution—show that the vast majority of married people are faithful and do not get divorced. Actually, just 22 percent of people in monogamous relationships—not even marriages!—cheat. The rate goes down among married couples, where 22 percent of men admit to cheating, but just 15 percent of women say they have.[14] Between 3 and 4 percent of spouses have cheated on each other during any given year.[15] That's today. Fifty years ago, the numbers were, according to most accounts, far lower.

But not according to Alfred Kinsey. Kinsey was personally a libertine of libertines—he was a sexual masochist, an amateur pornographer (who made videos starring his wife and other men), and a sexual harasser. He justified pedophilia. And he authored the most famous study of sexual behavior in American history, *Sexual Behavior in the Human Male*, and its riveting sequel, *Sexual Behavior in the Human Female*. In that study, he found that an astonishing 85 percent of American men had engaged in premarital sex, nearly 70 percent had slept with prostitutes, and 30–45 percent of all husbands had cheated on their wives. As it turned out, according to Kinsey, more than a third of men had engaged in homosexual behavior. Unfortunately, his research was just as bent as his personal life—he had skewed statistics regularly, utilizing sex offenders ranging from pedophiles to prostitutes in his surveys.

But the damage was done. Kinsey preached that Americans were sexual hypocrites and needed to change their standards. Traditional American society, it seemed, was a sham. The damage can still be felt today—Americans have a dramatically exaggerated view about how many people cheat on their spouses, for example. Even though only about a fifth of married people cheat, Americans think an incredible 44 percent of men and 36 percent of women are cheating. That's the effect of the media's compliance in the sexual revolution, which tells us that even if no one we know is cheating, everyone we know is cheating.[16]

With the groundwork set—with the notion emblazoned on American minds that Americans were all lying, cheating perverts—the sexual revolution began.

Feminism recognized the basic truth that men are naturally pigs, but bought into the Kinseyan notion that institutions of civilization were utter failures. So instead of requiring men to act according to the dictates of traditional sexual morality—monogamy, care for and support of spouses, not being a jerk—feminism suggested that the solution was for women to act like jerks. After all, people behaving themselves was just impossible. Thus, the sexual revolution.

Feminism rejected basic biology by stating that women and men were essentially the same, except they had different sets of genitals. In *The Feminine Mystique*, that's exactly what Betty Friedan, a politically radical leftist, argued. Because women had been oppressed by the patriarchal hierarchy, they were guaranteed to live unhappy lives, empty of all meaning—essentially, they were destined to become like Kate Winslet's character in the film *Revolutionary Road*, cheating on their husbands, drinking heavily, and then dying.

Friedan hated marriage. The feminist movement has carefully avoided quoting Friedan's heated rhetoric in *The Feminine Mystique*. There's a reason for that: it's sick-making. She argued that women who wanted to be housewives were "in as much danger as the millions who walked to their own death in the concentration camps—and the millions more who refused to believe that the concentration camps existed." She said that suburban homes were "comfortable concentration camps," and that women were "not, of course, being readied for mass extermination, but they are suffering a slow death of mind and spirit."

Friedan went on to found the National Organization for Women (NOW) and the National Association for the Repeal of Abortion Laws (now NARAL Pro-Choice America). Friedan's entire agenda was the remaking of modern marriage, without traditional sex roles; abortion was a vital component of the new feminism, since pregnancy clearly separated women's capacities from men's on a biological level. As the NARAL original charter stated, "NARAL, recognizing the basic human right of a woman to limit her own reproduction, is dedicated to the elimination of all laws and practices that would compel any woman to bear a child against her will. To that end, it proposes to initiate and co-ordinate political, social, and legal action of individuals and groups concerned with providing safe operations by qualified physicians for all women seeking them regardless of economic status." Of course, this ignored the humanity of the child and the woman's role in choosing to get pregnant in the first place. But the bottom line was that all obstacles to true equality—including physical equality—had to be discarded.

None of this is to argue that women are not capable of doing a great many things as well or better than men, including earning. True feminism would recognize the differences between the sexes while upholding the right of women to work in jobs for which they are qualified. My wife currently attends UCLA Medical School; my mother runs business affairs for major Hollywood firms. Women in the workplace are a tremendous good. So are women at home. Feminism should be about choice.

Instead, thanks to people like Friedan, it became about bullying.

Anyone who opposed the feminist agenda was quickly labeled a sexist and bullied into submission. When Phyllis Schlafly, a conservative woman, debated Friedan over the proposed Equal Rights Amendment in 1973—an amendment that would have removed dependent wife benefits under Social Security and exemption from Selective Service registration, and paved the way for same-sex marriage—Friedan growled, "I'd like to burn you at the stake!"[17] Such bully tactics have become common for the left—when Larry Summers, the former Clinton and Obama administration official, and then president of Harvard, suggested in 2005 that perhaps there might be innate differences between men and women with regard to scientific capabilities, he was quickly ousted from his position. I was at Harvard at the time. Summers was beloved by the student body and backed in the community. The feminist faculty, however, would brook no quarter. They got rid of him.

Every mildly comprehensive scientific study ever done has shown significant brain differences between men and women—with women having some advantages, and men having some advantages.[18] The science simply isn't on the feminists' side. But that's why they bully. The feminist left has rammed their version of reality down Americans' throats: Everyone, regardless of sex, is the same. Sex is the same as race—an irrelevant categorizer that can be ignored at will. Sure, that's dumb. But so what? Wanna fight about it?

By leveling the sexes, the feminist left paved the way, as Schlafly thought they would, for the gay movement. If men and women are exactly the same except for a few appendages and holes, then why shouldn't a man marry a man and a woman marry a woman? What's the difference between a man and a woman raising a child and two men? Or three men? Or four women? Or three men, a woman, and a transvestite hooker who hitched a ride with Eddie Murphy?

Like feminists, gay rights activists had a point: nobody really should care (and now, nobody does) about what gays and lesbians do in their bedrooms. And gays and lesbians *were* bullied about what they did in their private lives.

But the gay agenda has moved well beyond tolerance of private behavior to acceptance of public behavior that would make anybody's skin crawl. Parading assless chaps down the center of Santa Monica Boulevard on the taxpayer dime is not a right. Neither is ramming homosexual education down the throats of American schoolchildren. Neither, in fact, is gay marriage—marriage is restricted in every state in the union in one way or another, and the state has a legitimate and compelling interest in one man and one woman getting married, producing and raising children.

Like the feminist movement, the gay rights movement is based on a false premise: that homosexual behavior is the same as race. This is logically nonsensical. If behavior is inborn, then racists are right—populations with higher rates of crime must be "born that way," the same way that the gay population is "born that way," in the infamously moronic words of sterile autotuned sex symbol Lady Gaga. If all behavior is preordained by biology, we should open up all our prisons now, since nobody's at fault for any of their behavior.

The fact is that behavior is not like race—it is not an innate characteristic that cannot be changed. That doesn't mean that we should crack down on all behavior, or even most behavior. It certainly doesn't mean we should start policing bedrooms. It *does* mean, however, that what people do in the public square—not in the bedroom—falls under the purview of community standards.

But not for the gay bullies, who suggest that it's okay for them to wear banana hammocks on Fire Island but wrong for Christian students to wear shirts with Bible verses. Like the feminist bullies, they're not going to use things like logic to argue their case—they're simply going to slander people as gay-haters, incipient Matthew Shepard murderers riding the rails, looking for the next gay to beat to death with a tire iron. Don't agree with their agenda? You'll find yourself out of work in Hollywood, or boycotted, or cursed out.

This is the new sexual politics of America: devoid of reason, devoid of science, devoid of logic. Chock full of thuggery.

ABORTION BULLIES

Jane Fonda is not the smartest woman in the world. Actually, her greatest contribution to society has been a set of surprisingly effective exercise videos. That somehow doesn't outweigh traveling to Vietnam and helping the Viet Cong torture American POWs—she rightly should have been jailed for that act of treason.

But if there's one thing Jane Fonda is an expert on, it's abortion. Or at least, that's how she holds herself out. She's tied in deeply with Planned Parenthood and routinely rallies to their cause. And, of course, she bullies those who disagree. Abortion opponents, she says, are the worst people on earth. "Every dictator—Stalin, Ceaucescu [*sic*], Hilter [*sic*]—has made anti-choice a central component of their agenda," she said.[19] As somebody who had actively supported a dictatorial regime—the North Vietnamese communists—Fonda should have known just how wrong she was. The communist Chinese, who backed the Viet Cong, were ardent proponents of abortion and remain so to this day. But the point for the left is always to invoke Godwin's law as quickly as humanly possible—cite Hitler at the first instance, then wait for conservatives to start weeping softly in the corner.

Fonda may not be the ultimate feminist, but Gloria Steinem is. Steinem cofounded *New York* and *Ms.* magazines. She is also a full-fledged intellectual lightweight who suggested after 9/11 that a U.S. military response would create a "cycle of escalating violence," and thinks that boys should be raised more like girls. She also says that you can't be a conservative feminist—you can't be a feminist if you want to stop abortion. Katie Couric, who was interviewing Steinem, specifically asked Steinem if Sarah Palin could be a feminist. Steinem, of course, said no.[20] Of course, some of that may be self-justification, given that Steinem had an abortion herself at age twenty-two. No wonder Pennsylvania Democratic state representative Babette Josephs says that pro-life women are "men with breasts."[21]

This is the same notion with regard to sex that race bullies promulgate with regard to race. Clarence Thomas is an Oreo; Larry Elder is an Uncle Tom; Condoleezza Rice is a token and a sellout. So, too, are women who don't think it's morally sound to murder unborn children. They're not even women. Only women who think that prospective children are polyps earn the title "women."

It's not enough for the pro-abortion feminist bullies to force their opinions on all women and question their status as females if they don't agree with the pro-abortion agenda. Feminists expect taxpayers to fund their abortions. That's why their great focus these days is on Planned Parenthood, the country's leading provider of abortion. The organization, which originated with eugenicist Margaret Sanger in 1938, now has an annual budget of more than $1 billion and performs hundreds of thousands of abortions every year; about half of its budget comes from federal, state, and local governments. In 2009, they performed in excess of 330,000 abortions. More than a quarter of all abortions performed in the United States are performed at Planned Parenthood clinics. Estimates state that nearly 100 percent of pregnant women who come to Planned Parenthood for supposed prenatal care show up to end the "prenatal" part of that care.[22] Estimates place Planned Parenthood's income on abortion at hundreds of millions of dollars.

Planned Parenthood doesn't just rake it in from taxpayer dollars, though. They take grants from other charitable organizations. Here's where the bullying *really* comes in. If one of those groups should choose to end those grants, they wind up in the public relations toilet. Planned Parenthood, which funds political campaigns for Democrats across the country, has friends in high places. And they have plenty of friends in the media, too. When their cash flow comes under threat, even in the most minor way, they go ballistic.

Take, for example, the case of Susan G. Komen for the Cure. Komen is a breast cancer foundation, pure and simple. That's all they care about: fighting breast cancer. They had a long-standing deal with Planned Parenthood whereby they gave a few hundred thousand dollars to Planned Parenthood so that the clinics could refer women to mammogram centers. In 2011, Komen decided that this wasn't the best use of grant money—after all, they could just give the grants directly to mammography centers, which would provide the mammograms directly. "Wherever possible," said Nancy Brinker, who founded the organization after losing her sister, Susan G. Komen, to breast cancer, "we want to grant to the provider that is actually providing the lifesaving mammogram." There was another factor, of course—Planned Parenthood was the source of major controversy for Komen due to Planned Parenthood's support of abortion.[23] Komen reportedly informed Planned Parenthood at that time that they'd be ending their grants program.

In late January 2012, the news hit the presses. And Planned Parenthood launched one of the great coordinated public campaigns of the last century. They did it in conjunction with the Obama administration, the media, and a bevy of other leftist nonprofit organizations.

To understand why the Komen bullying case was so critical, we have to recognize a fundamental truth: President Obama needed the women's vote to win reelection in 2012. We also have to recognize a second fundamental truth: Obama is a big fan of the late Saul Alinsky. Alinsky's strategy was basic and immensely effective: pick a target, freeze it, personalize it, polarize it.

So Obama needed a target—particularly in light of the fact that his economic policies had disproportionately impacted women negatively. As Mitt Romney pointed out in April 2012, "92.3 percent of the job losses during the Obama years have been women who lost those jobs."[24]

The easiest target, as it turned out, was Komen.

As we'll explore, that wasn't President Obama's only target—he decided to attack religious institutions, too, as enemies of women. But Komen was a more convenient target, since it didn't carry the risk of alienating Catholics.

And so when Komen, a *private organization*, decided to cut off grants to Planned Parenthood—grants amounting to less than 1 percent of Planned Parenthood's total budget—the Obama administration got active. When Coke pulled its cash from the American Legislative Exchange Council, the left cheered; when Komen pulled its cash from Planned Parenthood, it merited White House attention and horror.

Obama and company had deep ties to Planned Parenthood. Not only did the Planned Parenthood 501(c)4 provide consistent political cover to Democrats, but the head of Planned Parenthood, Cecile Richards, was an Obama advisor. Actually, Richards advised Obama that he ought to force Catholic organizations to provide contraception under Obamacare.[25]

It's no coincidence that in May 2012 she actually posted a video on behalf of Obama. "I think when women look at the positions of Mr. Romney, who really wants to take women back to the 1950s," she said, "and the record of President Obama and all that he has done for women and American families, there's a clear choice."[26] This is typical bully rhetoric—Romney had no intention of sending women back to the "concentration camps" of Betty Friedan. But Richards is a pro-Obama political hack.

And Obama is a pro–Planned Parenthood political hack. No wonder in June 2012, President Obama chose to stump for high school support by backing Planned Parenthood. "You can decide that instead of restricting access to birth control or defunding Planned Parenthood, we should make sure that in this country, women control their own health care choices," Obama told a bunch of high school students in New Hampshire, few of whom had ever engaged with Planned Parenthood. It wasn't the only time he'd cited Planned Parenthood as an inestimable good under assault from cruel Republicans. "We don't need another political fight about ending a woman's right to choose, or getting rid of Planned Parenthood," he said in May. He said the same thing in California and Denver. It's a regular part of his stump speech.[27] Because if there's a crowd that desperately needs taxpayer-provided abortions, it's sixteen-year-old girls, God knows.

So, given the fact that the Obama administration is as cozy as a fetus in a womb with Planned Parenthood—pre-abortion, of course—there's little doubt that when Komen defunded Planned Parenthood, the Obama administration was the first to know about it. And there's little doubt that they coordinated the assault on Komen—an institution that takes precisely zero tax dollars.

The timing of the assault on Komen was peculiar. It happened the week after the anniversary of *Roe v. Wade* and within just days of the Obama administration decision to apply Obamacare mandates on contraception to Catholic organizations. As *Politico*, one of Obama's favorite media outlets, later pointed out, "It deflected at least some of the attention away from the contraception controversy, and allowed reproductive rights groups—the administration's allies on the contraception rule—to remind Washington that the anti-abortion forces aren't the only ones that matter in politics."[28]

The media campaign against Komen started with a leak from somewhere, not a public announcement by Komen. And the first piece came from the Obama outlet *Huffington Post*, which blamed Komen's new strategy on evil right-winger Karen Handel, a staffer at Komen and a former Georgia gubernatorial candidate who wasn't too fond of Planned Parenthood—and who had been endorsed, saints preserve us, by Sarah Palin.[29] That same day, the Associated Press ran a hit piece against Komen, too.[30] Within days, Jeffrey Goldberg of the *Atlantic* had somehow been handed a copy of internal Komen documents about their granting procedures, and had inside sources at Komen who were willing to give him information to help Planned Parenthood.[31]

Soon it was all over the Internet. Planned Parenthood sent out a nasty email ripping Komen for its decision, stating that they had put anti-abortion ideology "over women's health and lives"—and, of course, Planned Parenthood asked for donations.[32] Other organizations, in a coordinated assault, began piling on: MoveOn.org, NARAL, Media Matters.

And the Democrats got active, too. The bullying campaign kicked into high gear. Twenty-two Democratic senators sent a letter to Komen pushing them to reverse themselves. "It would be tragic if any woman, let alone thousands of women, lost access to these potentially life-saving screenings because of a politically-motivated attack," the letter stated. This was the height of irony, since the letter itself was a politically motivated attack on a *fully private organization*. Besides which, Planned Parenthood *doesn't provide mammograms*.[33]

The coup de grâce, though, was provided by MSNBC "reporter" Andrea Mitchell, who did an absolute hatchet job of an interview on Komen founder Nancy Brinker. She pulled out every stop in an effort to press Komen to get back into bed with Planned Parenthood. She led off with a heartrending story about an obnoxious sweaty woman at her gym (who may or may not have been named Andrea Mitchell). As Mitchell told it, "I want to give you a chance to answer—let me just tell you what I was confronted with at the gym this morning. A woman came over to me, I had not met her before, gray-haired woman, probably in her 60s, she was wearing a gray T-shirt, and she said, 'Look at my T-shirt. It's inside out. I put it on by accident today. I'm not going to wear it anymore. I've torn the label out. It's a Komen T-shirt.'" Now, what this had to do with a *breast cancer institution* deciding to cut grants to an *abortion clinic* was beyond human logic. But it did tug at the heartstrings. The rest of the interview resembled an enraged hippopotamus attacking a baby zebra. It was ugly, and it was painful, and it didn't stop. And, naturally, Mitchell called in two of her friends—Senator Barbara Boxer (D-CA) and Senator Patty Murray (D-WA) to complain about Komen.[34]

The next day, Komen backed down. Karen Handel, the Palin-backed former Georgia gubernatorial candidate, was thrown under the bus. And the Democrat-media complex celebrated. House Minority Leader Nancy Pelosi led the cheerleading section: "It was an unfortunate situation but it was dealt with in a short period of time, [and] I commend the Susan G. Komen foundation for seeing the light on this," she said. "[It] just goes to show you, when women speak out, women win. Women's health has a big victory this morning." Suddenly Pelosi was all sweetness and light, acting as though her allies had never accused Komen of political game-playing with women's lives: "I can only take [Komen] at its word." Of course, she couldn't help adding a tacit threat that Komen had best keep in line from now on: "We certainly will be able to support them as we have in the past . . . [but there is] a question of what other people in the country think about it."[35] So stay in line, Komen—or face the wrath of the Botoxed Army!

The bullying worked. The astroturfed outrage had its effect. And Obama had his double whammy: a "war on women" he could exploit, and a distraction from his own assault on the Catholic Church.

The truth is that of all the liberal positions, the liberal position on abortion is the most inherently coercive and bullying. Feminists may think that they're standing up for women, but they don't give a damn about unborn women, who are the prime targets of abortion. In fact, liberals will even admit that they don't care about unborn girls. When Lila Rose of Live Action released a series of videos demonstrating that Planned Parenthood was okaying sex-selective abortions—abortions in which women said they wanted to abort their prospective babies because the babies would be female[36]—the feminist left came to the defense of Planned Parenthood. Democrats in Congress said they'd never even consider legislation to stop women from having sex-selective abortions.

So the feminist bully logic is simple: if you don't pay for the abortions of others, even if you're a private organization, you must be destroyed; if you abort a female fetus *specifically because it's female*, you're on solid feminist ground.

ANTI-MOM BULLIES

In April 2012, the Obama campaign realized that it had a bit of a problem. The Obama administration had been a disastrous failure on domestic and foreign policy; their "war on women" bullying rhetoric wasn't working. And, worst of all, Mitt Romney had a secret weapon: his wife, Ann.

While Mitt wasn't personally popular, thanks to his generally bland image, Ann had high positive ratings with the American public. She was tough, a survivor; she'd raised five boys, all the while fighting off multiple sclerosis and breast cancer.

Ann had to be stopped.

So the Obama administration trotted out its resident feminist spokeswoman, Hilary Rosen, to talk about Ann Romney.

Rosen is a militant lesbian. She made her name in politics as interim director of the Human Rights Campaign, an LGBT advocacy organization; her partner at the time, Elizabeth Birch, was the executive director of the same organization. Together, they adopted twins. Later on, Rosen dumped Birch and moved in with the head of the American Federation of Teachers, Randi Weingarten. Who takes care of the kids? The Guatemalan nanny, undoubtedly. All of this may have something to do with Rosen's less than traditional view of marriage and family.

At the time she decided to speak up about Ann Romney, she was being paid by the Democratic National Committee to help Debbie Wasserman Schultz shave off the rough edges.[37] Rosen was a frequent visitor to the White House, too. As a public relations executive at SKDKnickerbocker, her specialty was messaging.

And message she did. She appeared on CNN, where she told the American public that Ann Romney wasn't a real woman—she'd "never worked a day in her life."[38]

The blowback was immediate and harsh. President Obama sprinted to a microphone as fast as his skinny legs could carry him. He defended Ann Romney, stating, "[T]here's no tougher job than being a mom. . . . Anybody who would argue otherwise, I think, probably needs to rethink their statement."[39] He was followed by Michelle Obama, The Most Beautiful Woman In The World™, who tweeted, "Every mother works hard, and every woman deserves to be respected." This was a massive overstatement—the Octomom does not deserve to be respected. But point taken. David Axelrod and Obama campaign manager Jim Messina came out of the woodwork to express their disapproval, too[40]—though if the new media hadn't picked up on Rosen's comments, these same folks likely would have been nodding vigorously throughout Rosen's nasty monologue. The Obamas condemned the remarks. But they didn't disassociate from her.

And Rosen wasn't backing down. "This isn't about whether Ann Romney or I or other women of some means can afford to make a choice to stay home and raise kids," she said. "Most women in America, let's face it, don't have that choice. They have to be working moms and home moms. And that's the piece that I am not hearing from the Romney camp."[41] In other words, if you're a stay-at-home mom, you must be rich, so shut up.

The only problem is that it's not true. Stay-at-home moms are disproportionately poor and minority. So when Rosen argued that Ann couldn't identify with other women, she was simply blowing smoke. In all likelihood, a lesbian with a six-figure job, two adopted children, and regular access to the White House probably isn't in a position to talk about what the typical American woman is looking for out of life.

Unfortunately, though, Rosen's feminist bullying reflects the liberal perspective better than President Obama's supposed respect for stay-at-home moms (remember, Hilary Rosen was his surrogate). It goes all the way back to Friedan, she of the Holocaust-victim-stay-at-home-mom mentality.

The left ardently believes that a fulfilled woman works, that stay-at-home moms are less valuable to society, and that women who choose not to work have slighted their sex. Hilary Rosen was just echoing another Hillary—Clinton—who famously remarked back in 1992, "I could have stayed home and baked cookies and had teas, but what I decided to do was fulfill my profession."[42] Teresa Heinz Kerry, who'd never spent a day in her adult life not being married to a super-rich guy, said that First Lady Laura Bush had never "had a real job."

The main driver in this cultural crusade against stay-at-home moms is Hollywood, which used to uphold traditional family values but now mocks the *Leave It to Beaver* mentality. *Pleasantville* (1998) was cribbed straight from the Friedan playbook: the stay-at-home mom is sexually repressed, confined by her drab little life. *The Stepford Wives* has been made twice—and both times, it championed the Friedan notion that men who wanted women who played traditional wifely and motherly roles actually wanted women who were robots. *Desperate Housewives*, of course, provided one end of the spectrum for women—the miserable end; *Sex and the City* provided the other, more glamorous, end. And then there's the *Real Housewives* reality series, which portrays housewives as self-obsessed, pathetic freaks.

Of course, all that disrespect for stay-at-home moms goes out the window as soon as a conservative woman decides to enter the workplace. When Sarah Palin's daughter Bristol got pregnant out of wedlock, the media quickly suggested that Sarah get back to the kitchen and take off her shoes—she was a bad mommy! ABC News ran a story in September 2008 questioning Palin's "parenting choices" and caustically suggesting that she had "morphed into America's new conservative feminist."[43] Obama Campaign National Finance Committee member Howard Gutman said that she couldn't be a good parent if she was going to campaign. "Your responsibility is to put your family first," said Gutman on Laura Ingraham's radio show. John Roberts of CNN echoed the slur, stating, "Children with Down's syndrome require an awful lot of attention. The role of Vice President, it seems to me, would take up an awful lot of her time, and it raises the issue of how much time will she have to dedicate to her newborn child?" Brian Williams of NBC News questioned whether "she should be doing this." Michelle Malkin, another working mom who clearly makes her kids her first priority—I'm not sure I've ever met a more involved mother—sums up: "We're damned if we do stay home and we're damned if we don't. We're damned because we conservative moms drive the Left and its feminist shills mad with our mere existence, our exercise of free will, our fierce belief in protecting our families from the Nanny State, our embrace of free-market principles, and our rejection of the perpetual victim/grievance mentality."[44]

Malkin's right. But as a general matter, the feminist bullies *particularly* hate stay-at-home moms. And the feminist war on stay-at-home moms has wrought tremendous hell on the family structure. It's certainly possible for women to work and for them to be great mothers—my wife hopes to practice medicine and be a mom, too. But to pretend that there's no trade-off in time or effort—and to excoriate women for choosing family over career—is simply bullying. And that bullying results in real-world effects for society. With more and more women abandoning their families to work, children engage in more and more destructive behavior; the rest of us are supposed to pick up the slack via educational programs and babysitting projects paid for by the government. It's all fun and games to talk about how terrible stay-at-home moms are. But the myth of the mom who can have it all has bred an even worse myth, one that has largely destroyed America's inner cities: the myth of the supremely competent single mom. In the feminist world, men aren't necessary. They must be cowed into submission.

ANTI-BOY BULLIES

The ultimate goal of the feminist bullies is to create a sexless society. Or, more specifically, a maleless society. Feminists want to paper over differences between men and women in favor of a bizarre sort of gender androgyny; if there are real differences between the sexes, then women might need men and men might need women. And that would destroy any semblance of pure equality.

To achieve that sexual leveling requires more than just changing women into workhorses and "freeing their sexuality." It requires changing the very nature of men, too. And so the feminist left has set about their most important project of all: bullying men.

It starts within the educational system, where the feminist

bullies informed teachers that they need to be sure to bend over backward to overcome the patriarchal bias of the existing teaching tools. As Christina Hoff Sommers points out, this perspective "has given rise to an array of laws and policies intended to curtail the advantage boys have and to redress the harm done to girls." When teachers point out that girls generally perform better than boys do in school, they are dressed down. To level the system, the feminist thought goes, boys must be feminized.

Carol Gilligan, the first Harvard University professor of gender studies (aka the BS course you take to look good for your armpit-hair-growing lesbian cousin) and now at New York University, says that we need to transform "the fundamental structure of authority" by teaching little boys to be more sensitive. Or, in the words of famed empty-headed feminist Gloria Steinem, "Raise boys like we raise girls." As Sommers says, "In practice, getting boys to be more like girls means getting them to stop segregating themselves into all-male groups. That's the darker, coercive side of the project to 'free' boys from their masculine straitjackets."[45]

But that coercive project—we might even call it bullying—has become a cause célèbre for the feminist left. Just take a look at the *Sesame Street* website, which informs parents that they ought to "[t]ry to use gender-neutral language. Use plural pronouns such as 'they' and 'them,' instead of masculine pronouns such as 'he' and 'him.' Use words such as firefighter, flight attendant, garbage collector, and humankind to replace the use of 'man' as a generic noun or ending."[46] And as for those toys for the kiddies—why not try mixing up the gender toys in order to "break stereotypes about men and women, for example, dolls for boys and building toys and puzzles for girls."[47] Sure, the science isn't there for this idiocy. But it *feels* right!

As boys grow up, they're told not to engage in chivalrous action with regard to women, lest they infringe on women's independence. The male instinct to protect women is considered cliché and patriarchal. Why, the science is in, and it turns out that holding doors for women leads directly to the burqa. At least that's the conclusion of the Society for the Psychology of Women, which conducted a study of workers in America and Germany and found that women thought it was sexist for men to hold doors, call people "guys," or even make romantic comments about how they can't live without women. The study decided: "Women endorse sexist beliefs, at least in part, because they do not attend to subtle, aggregate forms of sexism in their personal lives. . . . Many men not only lack attention to such incidents but also are less likely to perceive sexist incidents as being discriminatory and potentially harmful for women." To boil that down, if you offer to carry your girlfriend's purse, you're harming her self-esteem. So let her take out the garbage once in a while.[48]

It gets even worse. Andrea Dworkin, so radical among feminist bullies that even they distance themselves from her, wrote, "*Violation* is a synonym for intercourse. . . . Intercourse as an act often expresses the power men have over women. Without being what the society recognizes as rape, it is what the society—when pushed to admit it—recognizes as dominance."[49] All penetrative sex, in other words, is dominant, and may be rape. This sounds like a philosophy bound to create sexual happiness.

GAY BULLIES

If the goal of the feminist left was to level the sexes, the goal of the gay bullies was to take the next step: if every person of every sex is exactly the same, there's no difference between men sleeping with men, men sleeping with women, women sleeping with women, or transvestites sleeping with transsexual hookers. Everybody's one big happy family. Or a big *Modern Family*, as Hollywood would have it. (Great show. Bizarre moral compass.)

Now, in and of itself, there's nothing bullying about this perspective. After all, what you do in the privacy of your bedroom is your business, no matter how distasteful anybody else finds it.

Where this perspective lends itself to bullying is in the insistence that sex lives be made *public*.

The sexual left insists, bizarrely enough, that the argument for the right to private sexual behavior is identical to the argument for the right to *benefits* predicated on such behavior. This is inane. Just because two men enjoy wearing assless chaps in the privacy of their bedroom doesn't mean that society should be forced to allow them to wear assless chaps down Santa Monica Boulevard at taxpayer expense. Nor does it mean that Americans should have to reeducate their children to accept the presence of assless chaps in the public square.

The same holds true of relationships. The state does have an interest in monogamous heterosexual relationships that produce children. That interest is greater than the interest it holds in monogamous homosexual relationships. That's because men and women are inherently different, a child needs a mother and a father, and society needs children.

Needless to say, however, there are good arguments for and against gay marriage. But for some reason, that's a point that the gay left refuses to accept. Instead, they bully.

For whatever reason, the gay bullies make the feminist bullies look like pikers when it comes to actual bully tactics. And as the group of people who cry the most about bullying, they're also the biggest hypocrites.

Take, for example, Dan Savage.

Savage is a gay sex columnist who, aside from writing pieces that would make Kim Kardashian blush, runs an organization called the It Gets Better Project. The It Gets Better Project was designed to protect children, particularly lesbian, gay, bisexual, and transgender children and teens, from bullying. Its suggested pledge states, "Everyone deserves to be respected for who they are. I pledge to spread this message to my friends, family and neighbors. I'll speak up against hate and intolerance whenever I see it, at school and at work. I'll provide hope for lesbian, gay, bi, trans and other bullied teens by letting them know that 'It Gets Better.'"

This is a good message. Nobody is for bullying, particularly of children and teens.

It's such a good message that President Obama cut a video on behalf of It Gets Better. He decried the suicide of several young teens who had been bullied. He said that it broke his heart, which is undoubtedly true. He explained how he had been alienated, and knew what it was like to feel left out: "I don't know what it's like to be picked on for being gay. But I do know what it's like to grow up feeling that sometimes you don't belong. It's tough. . . . [As you get older] you'll be more likely to understand personally and deeply why it's so important that as adults we set an example in our own lives and that we treat everybody with respect."

Obama liked the It Gets Better Project so much that he decided to force his entire administration to support it. He had major members of his administration cut videos on behalf of It Gets Better: Secretary of State Hillary Clinton, Vice President Joe Biden, Secretary of Health and Human Services Kathleen Sebelius, Secretary of Labor Hilda Solis, Secretary of Agriculture Tom Vilsack, the Justice Department, senior advisor Valerie Jarrett. They all stood up for treating everybody with respect. His administration even started a website, StopBullying.gov, complete with helpful tips for parents and kids.

This was wonderful. It was meaningful. It was touching.

There was only one problem.

Dan Savage is the world's most egregious bully.

You may not have heard of Savage; he's not a household name, thank God. But you've certainly seen his work. If you Google Rick Santorum's name, you'll get a disgusting definition: "The frothy mix of lube and fecal matter that is sometimes the byproduct of anal sex." That's because Savage coined the definition and Google-bombed it in order to slander Santorum for Santorum's opposition to gay marriage. The campaign was so successful that Savage threatened to change the definition of "Rick" to something similarly disgusting. As if that weren't enough, Savage also appeared on *Real Time with Bill Maher* stating that he wanted to "f— the shit out of [Santorum]."

This would probably violate the It Gets Better pledge.

But it doesn't stop there.

Back in 2000, Savage was hired by Salon.com to infiltrate the Gary Bauer presidential campaign. He became so frustrated with Bauer's religiosity that after contracting the flu, he decided to go around the office *licking doorknobs* in order to infect the other staffers. He even handed Bauer a saliva-coated pen, hoping to infect him with the flu. He then proceeded to vote in the Iowa caucuses, although he wasn't registered in the state. This isn't bullying. It's biological warfare. Beyond that, it's gross—no doorknob deserves to be licked by Dan Savage.

But wait, there's more. When 2012 Republican presidential candidate Herman Cain stated that he thought that homosexual activity was a choice, Savage responded by telling Cain to "show us how a man can choose to be gay. Suck my dick, Herman." This was not only bullying, it was bad logic—why would any sentient being want to put their mouth on Dan Savage's genitals?

The bullying goes on. Savage tried to coin the term "Saddlebacking" in order to target pro–Proposition 8 pastor Rick Warren and his Saddleback Church; he defined the term as "the phenomenon of Christian teens engaging in unprotected anal sex in order to preserve their virginities." Savage also said, "F— you, Utah," since Mormons largely backed Proposition 8. In 2006, Savage said that Green Party U.S. Senate candidate Carl Romanelli, who was running against Democrat Bob Casey (the eventual winner) in Pennsylvania, "should be dragged behind a pickup truck until there's nothing left but the rope." In 2011, Savage said on Bill Maher's show, "I wish the Republicans were all f—ing dead."

This is the founder of the project Obama chose—and

chooses—to honor with a leadership role on the bullying problem. The world's sickest bully. The Vasco da Gama of bodily orifices and vulgar insult.

Now, it's not as though the White House was ignorant of the fact that the It Gets Better Project is run by Savage. On the contrary—search the White House website for Savage's name, and two It Gets Better links come up. Not just that—in June 2011, Savage himself visited the White House and hung out with administration officials. There are pictures. Thankfully, they don't include Dan Savage's favorite sex practices.

But the point is this: Gay bullies are allowed to run roughshod over every decent standard of behavior. And the White House will lend its blessing.

THE GAY MARRIAGE BULLIES

Actually, that's not entirely true. The White House won't just lend its blessing to the gay bullies. It'll *become* a big gay bully itself.

For years, President Barack Obama had maintained that he was for civil unions and against the notion of same-sex marriage. In 2008, while he was running for president and wanted to appear a moderate on social policy, Obama told Americans that marriage was "between a man and a woman. I am not in favor of gay marriage."[50] Then, when Obama discovered that his fund-raising numbers were down in early 2012, he decided to tap into the gay community's collective bank account. Glory, hallelujah, and pass the collections plate! "I've been going through an evolution on this issue," said Obama, apparently ignoring that the notion of evolution generally includes a component of natural selection. "I have to tell you that over the course of several years, as I talk to friends and family and neighbors, when I think about it—members of my own staff who are incredibly committed, in monogamous relationships, same-sex relationships, who are raising kids together, when I think about those soldiers or airmen or marines or sailors who are out there fighting on my behalf and yet, feel constrained, even now that Don't Ask, Don't Tell is gone, because they're not able to commit themselves in a marriage, at a certain point, I've just concluded that for me personally, it is important for me to go ahead and affirm that I think same-sex couples should be able to get married."[51]

Aside from setting the record for the single longest sentence ever recorded, President Obama had now stepped into brave new territory: he was leading the charge on behalf of gays and lesbians. Within hours of his announcement, Obama's campaign was sending out missives to his supporters asking for cash. And it worked. He raked in the dough, especially when he headed out to Hollywood that same week to have a party at George Clooney's house.

Obama was standing up for gays and lesbians.

And bullying everybody else. Because think about that language for a second—he had "evolved." The implication was obvious: the Americans who opposed same-sex marriage were unevolved. Neanderthals. You might even call them bitter clingers.

Lest you miss that point, Obama released an ad the very next day ripping Mitt Romney's position on same-sex marriage—a position Obama had held about five minutes prior to cutting the ad. "President Obama Is Moving Us Forward," said the ad. "Mitt Romney Would Take Us Back."[52]

Or, perhaps, they just disagree about the proper policy.

More accurately, they don't even disagree about policy—both Romney and Obama have suggested that definitions of marriage ought to be a state matter.

But where the gay bullies come from—and, as First Gay President according to *Time*, Obama falls into this category—there is no proper disagreement on this issue. There is only the right way (wave the rainbow flag!) and the wrong way (kids need a mom and a dad).

This bullying position quickly bore poisonous fruit. When

Chick-Fil-A president Dan Cathy did an interview in which he supported traditional marriage, the left quickly leaped into action against this egregious threat. They started by boycotting Chick-Fil-A, even though the restaurant had never discriminated against gays and lesbians. Savage immediately took to Twitter to redefine the term "Chick-Fil-A" to mean an especially bizarre form of anal sex. Gays and lesbians decided to hold a "Kiss In" at Chick-Fil-A—because having two dudes making out in front of customers and employees would show those crazy Christians a thing or two!

Then things got really nasty.

It wasn't enough for the left to boycott Chick-Fil-A, which they have every right to do, even if they're missing out on a dynamite sandwich. They had to shut down Chick-Fil-A.

Two of Barack Obama's closest political allies, Mayor Thomas Menino of Boston and Mayor Rahm Emanuel of Chicago, decided to ban Chick-Fil-A from their cities. "Chick-Fil-A's values are not Chicago's values," Emanuel declared—even though "Chicago values" didn't prevent him from inviting in absolute homophobe Louis Farrakhan to help stop gang crime. As for Menino, he wrote to Cathy, "I was angry to learn on the heels of your prejudiced statements about your search for a site to locate in Boston. There is no place for your discrimination on Boston's Freedom Trail and no place for your company alongside it."

Neither Emanuel nor Menino had the right to ban Chick-Fil-A from their cities. But they tried to do so anyway—not because Chick-Fil-A actually discriminated against gays, but because they opposed gay marriage.

But that wasn't the end of the story. As the hubbub grew, a gay activist painted an anti-Chick-Fil-A mural on the side of a Chick-Fil-A restaurant; the left had nothing to say about it. Then, on August 16, 2012, an LGBT activist named Floyd Corkins stormed into the headquarters of the pro–traditional marriage Family Research Council. He was carrying a Chick-Fil-A bag filled with sandwiches. He was also carrying a handgun and fifty rounds of ammo. When confronted by a security guard, he shouted, "I don't like your politics!," then shot the guard in the arm. The guard heroically subdued him.

And the media ignored it. For hours, they didn't report the story. When they finally did, they tried to downplay Corkins's political views. They had been only too happy to blame Sarah Palin for Jared Lee Loughner's shooting of Gabby Giffords, but now they were intent on protecting the gay rights movement from any association with Corkins. When Tony Perkins, head of the FRC, blamed the Southern Poverty Law Center, an extreme liberal nonprofit that had labeled FRC a "hate group," for creating the environment for shooters like Corkins, the press went ballistic. How dare Perkins mirror what the left had said about Sarah Palin and the Tea Party?! Gays couldn't be bullies, and pro-gay forces couldn't create an environment of hate!

Same-sex marriage advocates and LGBT groups weren't responsible for Corkins. But the media's double standard on bullying was breathtaking. Had a Christian shot up an LGBT center while wielding copies of a Jerry Falwell book, the left would have called it Christian terrorism. When a gay man shot up a Christian group, the left called him a lone nut.

But disproportionate rage against those who believe in traditional marriage has become a hallmark of the left. The leaders in this respect are the elites of Hollywood, who have been pushing same-sex marriage for decades.

And nobody bullies like Hollywood.

If only President Obama had listened to the wisdom of noted thinker Perez Hilton, he might have evolved to the Correct Moral Decision sooner. Between posting pictures of celebrities with semen painted on their face, this moral sophisticate Hilton had time to judge the Miss USA contest in 2009. He asked Miss California, Carrie Prejean, if she believed that gay marriage ought to be made the law of the land. She answered respectfully: "Well, I think it's great that Americans are able to choose one way or the other. We live in a land where you can choose same-sex marriage or opposite marriage. And, you know what, in my country, in my family, I think that, I believe that marriage should be between a man and a woman, no offense to anybody out there. But that's how I was raised and I believe that it should be between a man and a woman."

Hilton went insane on Prejean, to put it mildly. He called her a "dumb bitch." Repeatedly. He scored her low in the contest, throwing the win to Miss North Carolina. And he said he would have ripped the tiara off her head had she won the contest.[53]

This was rude. But it wasn't rare.

Just prior to Perez Hilton's hissy fit, California had passed by popular vote Proposition 8, which enshrined in the state constitution the notion that marriage is between a man and a woman. This certainly ticked off the Hollywood crowd, which promptly cut a video starring Jack Black, Neil Patrick Harris, John C. Reilly, Andy Richter, Maya Rudolph, and Rashida Jones, among others. Marc Shaiman, Tony Award–winning gay composer of *Hairspray*, penned the piece.

The point of the video: Opponents of Proposition 8 were stupid and evil. And, of course, Obama is awesome. The video opens with a bunch of liberals singing, "It's a brand-new bright Obama day!" (Never mind that at this point, Obama was unevolved just like the rest of us. In Hollywood, that never mattered.) Then we get John C. Reilly popping up to proclaim that he's here to "spread some hate" via "Proposition 8." Reilly and his gaggle of religious friends then get into an argument with the gay population . . . until Jesus, played by Jack Black, shows up to teach Americans that they've just been misinterpreting scripture for the last couple of thousand years. He then goes into the typical liberal litany of biblical misinterpretations: "Well, you can sell your wife, or stone your daughter!"[54]

Dumbasses.

How did the video come about? From another case of gay bullying. As a general matter, the most radical gay bullies have decided to financially ruin their enemies. More careers have been destroyed by members of the radical gay community than by any other political or lifestyle community in America. Ask Scott Eckern, artistic director of the California Musical Theater. Eckern quietly contributed a thousand dollars to the Proposition 8 effort—he's a Mormon, and the Church of Latter-day Saints heavily supported Proposition 8. Gay bullies online revealed his donation. That's when Shaiman—the *Prop 8: The Musical* composer—called him up. He told him he wouldn't let *Hairspray* be performed in the California Musical Theater so long as Eckern worked there.

"I was uncomfortable with money made off my work being used to put discrimination in the Constitution," Shaiman told the *New York Times*. He said that he was afraid, however, that by pressuring Eckern, he'd be lending credence to the support of . . . well . . . people like yours truly, who would point out that he's a massive bully. "It will not help our cause because we will be branded exactly as what we were trying to fight," said Shaiman. But, of course, that didn't stop him from wrecking Eckern's career and forcing his resignation.

Shaiman was joined in his outrage against Eckern by Jeffrey Seller, a producer of the Tony-winning musical *Avenue Q*. "That a man who makes his living exclusively through the musical theater could do something so hurtful to the community that forms his livelihood is a punch in the stomach," said Seller.[55] As a musical theater lover myself, I can guarantee that the vast majority of folks who attend the musical theater are not gay. They're little old ladies who love cats, which is why Andrew Lloyd Webber's abysmal *Cats* ran for years. But even if most patrons *were* gay, why should that equate to support for gay marriage? If most of the patrons were Jewish, would Seller have to quit Mormonism because it tries to convert Jews?

What did Shaiman feel about forcing Eckern out of his livelihood? "[I]t felt fantastic," he told the *Times*.[56] Somehow, one doubts Shaiman would feel the same about a school firing a gay teacher.

After Eckern resigned his job, Shaiman decided he wanted to take the next step. So he sent around a mass email targeting Eckern; one of his friends suggested he make a viral video. Thus bullying leads to bullying.

Even businesses that aren't directly related to the entertainment industry have been targeted by the gay bullies. El Coyote Restaurant, a terrific place in Los Angeles, found itself under boycott and march by gay bullies after a manager gave a hundred dollars to the Proposition 8 campaign. The manager is a daughter of the owner, Margie Christoffersen, who is Mormon; the owner met with protesters and at one point broke down in tears. Crowds of hundreds of people showed up to the restaurant, chanting and screaming. "We're just kind of dealing with it, and we're hoping it will blow over," said another manager. "We're hoping this will ease things, but it seems like they want a personal apology or a donation made by Margie to kind of equal what she made . . . and she has refused because it's her own personal belief." Under pressure, other members of the restaurant staff then gave five hundred dollars to the group leveling a legal challenge against Proposition 8.[57]

When you can't even serve tacos without kowtowing to the gay agenda, you know the gay bullies have gone too far.

The sad fact is this: you cannot expect to work in Hollywood if you are anti–gay marriage these days. And Hollywood uses its political power to forward the gay agenda regularly. Most major shows are screened before the Gay and Lesbian Alliance Against Defamation (GLAAD) to ensure that they don't offend gay sensibilities. Hollywood's been pushing gay marriage for years in its shows and movies—they actually see it as one of their great moral causes. The co-creator of *Friends*, Marta Kauffman, told me that during their Season 1 lesbian wedding, they purposefully cast Newt Gingrich's half sister as the pastor as a "f— you . . . to the right wing directly." And that's the typical feeling in Hollywood—the rest of America deserves a big f— you.

Unfortunately, it's not just Hollywood. It's large swaths of the gay left.

And when they have power to change policy, they use it to slap Americans in the face. Just ask Judge Vaughn Walker, a gay man, who struck down Proposition 8 as violative of the California state constitution. Why? Because, said Walker, only morons would vote for Proposition 8. There was, he said, no "rational basis" for upholding traditional marriage. As it turns out, this one gay judge had discovered the utter irrationality of thousands of years of human history, every major religious leader, the vast majority of Western philosophers, all the founders, and the majority of the people of California. Or, he was just using the power of his gavel to justify his sex life.

GAY EDUCATIONAL BULLIES

It's one thing to bully adults, who at least have the capacity to fight back. It's another to use the educational system to indoctrinate children. And while the idiotic actors of "Prop 8: The Musical" said that gay bullies would never—*never!*—try to ram the gay agenda down the throats of students, that's precisely what they've done.

In the state of California, liberals forced through a bill that would require all state schools to teach gay and lesbian history—whatever that means. "We are failing our students when we don't teach them about the broad diversity of human experience," said gay bully state senator Mark Leno, a Democrat. What was the excuse for forcing students to learn about the sexual lifestyles of historic figures? To make way for gay students so that they wouldn't be bullied.[58]

So 98 percent of students should be bullied into thinking one way so that the other 2 percent don't face quite as much of a possibility of being called names. Even though it's already punishable to call gay kids names. And bullying more generally is already punished in schools. Got it.

But it's more than that. Not only does gay history have to be taught in schools, it's now forbidden to teach any material that reflects poorly on homosexuality, bisexuality, or transgenderism . . . and you *cannot remove your child from the classroom* over the material.[59]

Normally, it's not bullying to force through legislation—legislation is generally legitimized by the democratic process that put representatives in place. But in this case, there's no way to call this statute anything *other* than bullying. Parents aren't allowed to pull their kids out over the teaching of values inimical to their own values. This is thought control, pure and simple. When it comes to kids, politics should not be a factor in education.

But they are, of course, because the gay bullies say they should be. Thus President Obama appointed as his "safe schools czar" one Kevin Jennings, former head of the Gay, Lesbian and Straight Education Network (GLSEN—emphasis on the Gay and Lesbian, less emphasis on the Straight). At a GLSEN event in conjunction with the Massachusetts Department of Education, held at Tufts University in 2000, Jennings was the keynote speaker. What did he and others speak about? Among other perverse sexual practices, they discussed fisting—the practice of inserting your hand up somebody's rectum or vagina. Who attended? Two hundred young teens and three hundred adults. Homosexual sex techniques were widely discussed, as were sadomasochistic ones. Jennings never disowned the event. GLSEN is still funded by the state of Massachusetts.[60] GLSEN also handed out apparent fisting kits (including plastic gloves and lubricant) to students.[61] As for Jennings's reading list at GLSEN, it included episodes of children playing "sex therapist" with each other and incestuous relationships; GLSEN even sponsored a gay Santa play in 2009.[62] When the conservative blogosphere exposed the fact that Jennings once failed to report a high school student having random sexual encounters with a child predator in a public bathroom, the gay bullies promptly labeled them "anti-gay."[63]

As mandatory gay education becomes a larger and larger issue across the country, so does transgenderism. The Department of Justice has given in to the gay bullies, accepting a ruling from the Equal Employment Opportunity Commission that claims that so-called gender identity discrimination is illegal. So if Jim Bob shows up to the construction site tomorrow in a two-piece bikini and a Cher wig, you're a bigot if you fire him.[64]

If that sounds ridiculous, wait until you hear this one: the DOJ actually forced the University of Arkansas at Fort Smith to allow a fully male transgender student to use the women's bathrooms on campus. He'd been married twice and had a biological daughter. But he wanted to use the little girls' room. So the DOJ said he should be able to, even though there are unisex bathrooms on campus. "In the eyes of the law," said Mark Horn, vice president of university relations, "this individual is entitled to use the bathroom that she identifies with."[65]

The losers of this cultural battle will most certainly be Americans, who are no longer free to keep dudes out of ladies restrooms, or to protect their children from learning about sodomy at age seven.

CONCLUSION

With President Obama's newfound support of gay marriage, his allies in the press decided to launch a concerted offensive against Mitt Romney on the issue. That offensive started the day after Obama's announcement, in obvious coordination with the Obama campaign, with a *Washington Post* piece accusing Romney of bullying a gay kid . . . fifty years ago. "John Lauber, a soft-spoken new student one year behind Romney [at Cranbrook School], was perpetually teased for his nonconformity and presumed homosexuality," wrote Jason Horowitz in the *Post*. "Now he was walking around the all-boys school with bleached-blond hair that draped over one eye, and Romney wasn't having it."[66]

As it turned out, there was little or no evidence that Romney had bullied the kid because he was gay. In fact, the kid didn't come out as gay until later in life to his family. In reality, it was far more likely that Romney had been empowered by the administration to enforce the dress code, which likely banned long hair (remember, this was 1965). The family of the supposedly bullied kid said the story was "factually incorrect and we are aggrieved that he would be used to further a political agenda."[67] And the *Post* story itself was greatly exaggerated—one of the supposed witnesses to the story was quoted as saying that he was "long bothered" by the incident, but told the press that he hadn't even remembered the incident.[68]

But the damage was done. Romney was anti-gay, a bigot; Obama was pro-gay, a haloed angel (he was actually portrayed that way on the cover of *Time*). Former CNBC host Donny Deutsch appeared on *The Tonight Show*, where he explained that Romney was "the guy beating up the weaker kid growing up. . . . I think that's really going to hurt him."[69] Never mind that Obama admitted in his own autobiography to bullying a girl: "I ran up to Coretta [a little black girl] and gave her a slight shove; she staggered back and looked up at me, but still said nothing. 'Leave me alone!' I shouted again. And suddenly Coretta was running, faster and faster, until she disappeared from sight."[70] All that mattered was that Romney had to be portrayed as a thug. As Dr. Peggy Drexler, an Obama sycophant, put it at *Huffington Post*, "So to a generation of current and future voters, Obama has deftly offered a choice: a respectful and inclusive voice of the future; versus a schoolyard tormenter aligned with the intolerant voices of the past."[71]

So, who's the real bully here? The guy slandered with he-said, she-said experiences from five decades ago? Or the guy slandering that guy by using his lackeys in the press to push out half-century-old smears?

The answer's obvious. The real bully here wasn't Mitt Romney—who, by all accounts, treats gays and lesbians with immense respect—but Barack Obama and his allies in the press.

But that's how the left works its magic.

Feminists bully both men and women who disagree with them while simultaneously claiming to be victimized by the patriarchal structure. Radicals like Andrea Dworkin maliciously state that "right-wing women agitate for their own subordination"—they're sellouts. And they seek to change society to reflect their nonscientific view of the world, in which men and women are precisely the same—except for the ding-dongs and vajingoes, of course. If reality doesn't comply with their vision of the universe, society must change to accommodate them. Men must be trained to stop acting like men; women must be cowed into submission, or forced to comply with feminist demands.

The same holds true for the gay bullies. Not only are traditional marriage advocates supposed to sit down and shut up, but gays who dare defy them are rhetorically beaten to death. Says Michael Musto, columnist for the *Village Voice*, the gays of GOProud, the Republican gay group, are "like Jewish Nazis! Black Klan members! Women who campaign for Rush Limbaugh. Mexican Republicans! Roaches who moonlight as exterminators!"[72] Joe Jervis, a gay blogger who refers to GOProud as "kapo bootlickers"—a reference to Jews who helped the Nazis during World War II—has received awards from GLAAD.[73] And Dan Savage, whose mouth also doubles as a biological weapon of mass destruction, calls gays who disagree with him "house faggots" who "grab their ankles."[74] It is considered a mortal sin in the gay community not to comply with their thug tactics.

Of course, if a gay Republican decides *not* to come out, for fear of being bullied, the gay bullies simply bully him or her anyway. They out him.

Now, gay bullies never out leftists. That would be inconsiderate. After all, leftists don't deserve to be bullied, since they agree with the militant gay agenda first and foremost.

But right-wing gays? They must be outed and destroyed.

Now, this should violate gays' basic sense of morality. That morality is based on two notions: consent and privacy. And the gay bullies have to violate both essential principles in order to accomplish their goals.

Fortunately, the morality of the gay bullies is quite malleable, so they have no problem with that.

The chief architect of the outing phenomenon is Michelangelo Signorile. Signorile founded the magazine *Outweek;* his preferred strategy was targeting those who in any way disagreed with them, then making their sex lives public. Randy Shilts, a gay man who wrote for the *Advocate* and the *San Francisco Chronicle* and penned the massive bestseller *And the Band Played On*, thought outing was abominable. As he wrote, "No matter how high-sounding the rhetoric, outing makes some of the most august gay journalists and leaders look like a lot of bitchy queens on the set of *Boys in the Band*, bent not on helping each other but on clawing each other. It's not a pretty sight. As for the nastiness of outing, whether outing is done to Army privates by Pentagon policy or to prominent officials by the gay press, it's still a dirty business that hurts people." Shilts rightly called outers "lavender fascists" and compared them to "a third-grader stomping his foot and yelling, 'Do what I want you to or I'll tell on you!'" Signorile responded in typical Alinsky fashion: Shilts's remarks, he said, "reeked of self-loathing."[75] He wasn't a true gay man, because he was against fascist tactics like outing.

Gay bullying works. Even Shilts eventually backed down and decided that "selective outing" was fine. Shilts backed this new consensus in a piece he wrote in 1990 for the *New York Times*. Politicians who "engaged in rabidly anti-gay politicking" should be outed, he wrote, because "the politicians themselves would have already asserted that homosexuality was an issue that demanded intense public scrutiny."[76] If someone opposes the gay rights movement, that doesn't mean he's suggesting that homosexuality itself demands intense public scrutiny, of course. Far from it. But gay bullying needs no logic. It just needs hatred and rage to motivate it.

The sex bullies have taken over the social sphere. Now you're considered intolerant if you simply want to protect the innocence of a child in the classroom, or think that you ought to be able to teach your kids about the advantages of traditional marriage, or believe that men and women are different from each other. You must be cured of your thought crimes. And the sex bullies are there, bullhorns in hand, ready to apply that cure at a moment's notice.

6.

GREEN BULLIES

Meet Mike and Chantell Sackett. The couple decided to buy a $25,000 parcel of land, approximately 0.63 acres, near scenic Priest Lake in northern Idaho. Priest Lake is surrounded by a beautiful greenery; its wildlife includes bear, deer, and moose. It also has terrific trout fishing. It's a tourist hot spot.

In 2007, Mike and Chantell decided to build on their land. This wasn't rare—their own tract was separated from the lake by several large man-made structures. So they did what people do when building: they brought in dirt and rock, and filled in part of the lot to create a foundation for their dream home.

A few months later, they opened their mail to find a letter from the friendly neighborhood U.S. Environmental Protection Agency (EPA). To the Sacketts' surprise, they were informed that the property "contains wetlands . . . adjacent to Priest Lake." Further, they were told that they had caused "fill material to enter waters of the

United States" and had therefore polluted under the Clean Water Act (CWA). Never mind that their land contained no water.[1]

Not only were the Sacketts barred from building on their own land, the EPA said; they also had to "repair" the land they had damaged. It would cost them $27,000 to do so—more than they'd paid for the tract in the first place.[2] The EPA also threatened millions of dollars in fines—up to $75,000 per day for failure to comply. That's $9 million per year. Because you never know when fish will need to spawn in the middle of dry land—and you never know when they'll need a Scrooge McDuck money vault to swim in.

So the Sacketts asked for a hearing on the issue.

And the EPA denied it.

So the Sacketts sued. The case went all the way to the Supreme Court, which sided with the Sacketts. As Justice Samuel Alito wrote, concurring with the opinion of the Court, "The position taken in this case by the Federal Government—a position that the Court now squarely rejects—would have put the property rights of ordinary Americans entirely at the mercy of Environmental Protection Agency (EPA) employees." This, in short, was bullying.

What made the bullying worse, Alito noted, was the fact that the CWA is "notoriously unclear. Any piece of land that is wet at least part of the year is in danger of being classified by EPA employees as wetlands covered by the Act, and according to the Federal Government, if property owners begin to construct a home on a lot that the agency thinks possesses the requisite wetness, the property owners are at the agency's mercy."[3]

It was a victory for Americans, who could challenge the EPA's hegemony now—they'd have a way to yell and scream if the EPA suddenly designated the puddle near their broken garden hose a "wetland." But the case didn't stop the growth of the EPA. The agency, which sprang full-formed into being in 1970, was never fully approved by Congress—but it started with a budget in excess of $1 billion (about $6 billion in terms of today's purchasing power) and well over 4,000 employees. All that just to ensure that Americans didn't befoul Gaia.

Today, the EPA has a budget of $8.3 billion and a working staff of more than 17,000. The earth is the same as it was then. Same dirt. Same trees. Same rocks. In fact, the environment is cleaner than it was in 1970. Government is the only organization in which you solve a problem, then put more people on the problem in order to solve it even better.

And these regulators know that idle hands were the capitalistic devil's playground. So they began regulating. And regulating. And regulating. Within the first few years of its existence, the EPA was placing 1,500 rules in the Federal Register. *Annually*.[4]

And now, President Obama wants to use the EPA to regulate climate change. After all, this is the president who said in 2008, upon winning the Democratic nomination, that "this was the moment when the rise of the oceans began to slow and our planet began to heal."[5] This is the president who campaigned in 2011 on the notion that Republicans wanted "dirtier air, dirtier water."[6] This is the "green energy" president who handed billions in subsidies to idiotic green boondoggles, and who insisted that green cars like the Chevy Volt would drive the American economy back to the top of the world stage. Sadly, the Chevy Volt's engine burst into flame on the way up that hill. America's economic future was burned alive.

Nobody wants dirty air and dirty water. Nobody wants to live in an old British industrial town where everybody's dying of the black lung, *Zoolander*-style. But by the same token, most Americans like the notion of working for a living. They like being able to buy nice things. They like being able to afford air-conditioning—and they like being able to use air-conditioning without express written consent from the government. Americans like to build houses near lakes, especially when they're not killing endangered duck-billed platypuses to do it.

Americans like balance. We're conservationists. Teddy Roosevelt recognized the balance we wanted to establish between economic growth and a pristine natural environment. He especially advocated carving out particular areas in which natural beauty would be left to its own devices. But he wasn't for cutting off American industry.

Today's environmentalists are obsessed with cutting off American industry. They set America's economic growth in stark contrast to environmental stewardship, as though every time a cash register rings, an endangered woodpecker loses its wings. They are Luddites who oppose economic progress, and who generally seek wealth redistribution. Many of them are watermelon environmentalists: green on the outside, red on the inside.

Others, like President Obama, lie. They pretend that spending taxpayer cash on windmill farms that make landscapes ugly and chop birds into delicious puree is a wonderful idea, and creates jobs. They suggest that new auto emissions standards, written and applied unilaterally by executive branch agencies, somehow stimulate the economy. It's a lie, and it's a waste of taxpayer resources.

When those policies fail, the environmental bullies turn from business to individual citizens. They make Americans feel guilty for enjoying climate-controlled bedrooms and liking luxury vehicles. Instead, we're supposed to act morally enlightened only if we drive a Prius. Sure, there may be a dead priest in the trunk. But at least we're cutting down on our carbon footprint.

For these environmentalists, worship of the environment is like any other religion: if you abide by the antihuman code, sacrificing your own wants and needs to those of the dandelions, you're a better person by definition. A study from the journal *Social Psychological & Personality Science* says that people who are exposed to organic foods immediately become jerks. Seriously. People shown comfort foods like cookies volunteered to spend more time to help strangers; people who were shown pictures of organic vegetables were more judgmental. "There's something about being exposed to organic food that made them feel better about themselves," said one of the scientists. "And that made them kind of jerks a little bit, I guess."[7]

Hence Michelle Obama, The Most Beautiful Woman In The World™.

But the Jerk Effect is not limited to organic food. Another study shows that people who buy so-called green products don't share money with others; cheat more often; and lie more easily.[8] These holier-than-thou cretins think that because their apples aren't spiked with hormones, they get to steal from the rest of us. Which is probably why they're Democrats.

And they get to lecture us at the same time. According to one survey, the number-one reason people buy the hideous and expensive Toyota Prius is that "it makes a statement about me." Overall, 57 percent of Prius owners attributed their love of dumb cars that accelerate from 0 to 60 in eight years to wanting people to know they care about the environment. They're special![9] In the words of *New Yorker* columnist and Prius owner Bruce McCall, "As morally superior citizens of planet Earth, we Prius owners consider it our duty to keep finding new ways to enlighten those eco-heathens who are still floundering in the eco-darkness, even as our cars sometimes fail to decelerate when the brake pedal is depressed, a violation of Newton's third law of motion, caused by global warming."[10]

Environmentalists are so much better than the rest of us that they can tell us what to do while ignoring their own restrictions. Al Gore can fly around in his super-giant jet airplane while telling us that we're wasting gas for driving our old Honda. Barbra Streisand can complain about our environmental impact while trying to block off public beaches for her own use. That's because these are *good* people. Even if they do occasionally ask masseuses to touch their fifth chakras.

These environmentalists would be nothing but laughs were it not for their unfortunate tendency to bully the hell out of their opponents. They falsify science, and attempt to destroy the careers of those who disagree with their results. They tell Americans that they shouldn't dare to enjoy high living standards—there are trees in China that are dying! And they build up a massive, nondemocratic regulatory state to tell you how much water should flush through your toilet, how much electricity you should use, and why you need to separate your garbage into separate piles before the state takes those piles in separate trucks to separate gates in the same dump.

ORIGINS OF THE ENVIRONMENTAL BULLIES

Environmentalism, more than any other bullying philosophy, relies on scare tactics. You know that guy with the long beard walking around in the comics carrying a sign reading THE END IS NEAR? That guy is an environmentalist, and he's worried that soon Dennis Quaid and Jake Gyllenhaal will be surfing waves down Fifth Avenue.

Leftists like to look back to Henry David Thoreau and Walden Pond as the origins of environmentalism. But real environmentalism goes back further, to Thomas Malthus, the philosopher and economist who suggested that man and nature are in constant tension, and that if we don't restrict our use of nature, we'll all end up dead. In Malthus's words, "[I]n every age and in every State in which man has existed, or does now exist . . . the increase of population is necessarily limited by the means of subsistence. . . . [P]opulation does invariably increase when the means of subsistence increase, and . . . the superior power of population is repressed, and the actual population kept equal to the means of subsistence, by misery and vice." Think of the world as a giant lifeboat. And there are three people on it. They're running out of food. And Johnny's just fat enough to feed two. Soon, says Malthus, there will be two people left on that lifeboat. Then one. Then none.

Malthusian economics is the basis for today's environmental movement. We live in a world of scarce resources, say the environmentalists. If we use those resources too fast, we'll deplete the resources. Then we'll all assume room temperature.

Malthus's thought process was echoed by ecologist Garrett Hardin in 1968, in a highly popular article called "The Tragedy of the Commons." It's a real barn burner. In it, Hardin talks about the riveting case of a cattle commons—a grazing area for all the herds in an area. As it turns out, all the farmers bring their cattle to graze. Soon the area has no more grass. The cows starve. And die. The end.

What was needed? Sustainable development—a system by which the farmers would be restricted so that the grass remained green, the cows remained moderately fat, and sprinkler costs weren't too high.

Sounds great, right? But the question is this: What restrictions should be placed on the farmers? And what happens when we're not talking about cows but about human beings? And are the world's resources really being depleted to such an extent that we have to drastically reduce our consumption to prevent mass extinction?

These questions may sound exaggerated, but they're precisely what the radical environmentalists have been asking for decades. Back in 1968, Professor Paul Ehrlich of Stanford University penned one of the dumbest books of all time: *The Population Bomb*. He posited, in full watermelon fashion (green on the outside, red on the inside), that mankind had eleven inalienable rights, including the "right to eat well," the "right to drink pure water," the "right to freedom from thermonuclear war," and the "right to decent, uncrowded shelter." How would all of this be accomplished? By limiting consumption, particularly in First World countries. While Ehrlich said that mankind had a right "to avoid regimentation," he didn't really mean it—he wanted mankind regimented down to the barest bones. And that would start with the biggest problem of all: more people.

Overpopulation, he said, was the crisis. "Too many cars, too many factories, too much detergent, too much pesticide, multiplying contrails, inadequate sewage treatment plants, too little water, too much carbon dioxide—all can be traced easily to *too many people*," he wrote. He actually suggested that over the course of the decade, hundreds of millions of people would starve to death thanks to overpopulation.[11]

So what should we do? Stop having babies. And stop buying and consuming things. Embrace the primitive. Remember your great-great-great-great-great-great-grandfather walking the prairies of the West in nought but a loincloth? Wasn't that great? "The key to the whole business, in my opinion, is held by the United States. We are the most influential superpower; we are the richest nation in the world. . . . We, of course, cannot remain affluent and isolated. At the moment the United States uses well over half of all the raw materials consumed each year."[12]

If this sounds familiar, it should. It's a meme constantly trotted out by the left, including by President Obama: we consume far more than we should of the world's resources. Usually, Obama's talking about oil. You filling up your car means that some poor shlub in Sudan is getting murdered. "As a country that has 2 percent of the world's oil reserves, but uses 20 percent of the world's oil—I'm going to repeat that—we've got 2 percent of the world oil reserves; we use 20 percent," said Obama in March 2012. He repeated the same fact over and over in many of his speeches. Because we're nasty and greedy![13]

Ehrlich identified some solutions to problems like this: forcibly sterilize the American population via drugs in the water supply or food supply. So much for that right to pure water. Unfortunately, said Ehrlich, the technical abilities weren't available. So they'd have to find other means.[14]

There's only one problem: The crisis never materialized. Millions didn't starve. Resources didn't deplete. Humanity's population exploded. And we're all still here.

Ehrlich wasn't the first environmentalist scare bully. Rachel Carson, author of *Silent Spring* (1962), suggested that DDT, a pesticide used to kill malarial mosquitos, thinned the eggs of bald eagles and therefore should be banned. Frightened for the precious bird population, the EPA restricted the use of DDT on American soil. International governmental agencies did the same. Thanks to Carson, 30–60 million people have died from malaria. But Carson did get her own postage stamp.

Overall, though, it's the panic-creating watermelon Malthusianism of Ehrlich that has left its mark on the environmental movement. They create a crisis; they promote the crisis; they lie and falsify evidence to convince people of the crisis; and then they bully Americans into giving up their standard of living. Because, after all, *Oh my God otherwise we're all gonna die!*

CLIMATE CHANGE BULLIES

Today's great environmentalist bullies are the climate change bullies. The evidence that man's production of greenhouse gases causes climate change is questionable at best; there is no question that man suddenly ceasing to produce greenhouse gases would bring down the global temperature in any case. Lest we forget, the climate change protagonists were global warming protagonists originally; when the earth got cooler, they simply changed their mantra to "climate change" so that they wouldn't have to be pegged down to predictions of hotter temperatures. Now, as the ultimate scare tactic, environmentalists peg wild weather events like tornados and hurricanes to climate change. Thus, your Range Rover or F-150 is responsible for Katrina. Are you happy yet, you capitalist racist pig?!

So, how do the environmentalist bullies prove all of this? They don't. The truth is that the planet hasn't warmed for fifteen years. According to new estimates, we might even be looking at an ice age rather than a warming period. Who admitted this? The University of East Anglia Climate Research Unit (CRU), one of the world's leading anthropogenic global warming proponents (and a far less interesting place than CTU, the Jack Bauer–led Counter-Terrorism Unit). As Henrik Svensmark, director of the Center for Sun-Climate Research at Denmark's National Space Institute—and a guy we should listen to because he sounds European—said, "World temperatures may end up a lot cooler than now for 50 years or more. It will take a long battle to convince some climate scientists that the sun is important. It may well be that the sun is going to demonstrate this on its own, without the need for their help." When you have to tell climate scientists that the sun—the giant ball of fire and gas that heats the earth—is important, you may have a problem.[15]

So if they can't prove it, how do the climate change extremists make their case? They destroy those who disagree.

In 2009, a hacker broke into the CRU. What the emails showed is that the climate change left had involved itself in a concerted attempt to stifle opposing research and manipulate data.

"The fact is that we can't account for the lack of warming at the moment and it is a travesty that we can't," read one weepy email. Emails between scientists asked each other to delete prior emails to cover the trail of evidence. Some emails fantasized about physical violence against those who disagreed: "Next time I see [climatologist] Pat Michaels at a scientific meeting, I'll be tempted to beat the crap out of him. Very tempted."

Worst of all were the emails explicitly attempting to destroy the careers of those who disagreed. "I think we have to stop considering 'Climate Research' as a legitimate peer-reviewed journal," read one email. "Perhaps we should encourage our colleagues in the climate research community to no longer submit to, or cite papers in, this journal." Another email: "I will be emailing the journal to tell them I'm having nothing more to do with it until they rid themselves of this troublesome editor."[16] Now *that's* bullying.

And it's not rare for environmentalists. The libertarian Heartland Institute has spent tremendous resources exposing climate change fraud and manipulation. That's made it the target of the radical left. In February 2012, leftists allegedly got hold of inside documents from the institute. Those documents supposedly said that the institute would spend $100,000 to fund schools to tell students that "the topic of climate change is controversial and uncertain—two key points that are effective at dissuading teachers from teaching science." The documents also included references to the Koch brothers. Greenpeace celebrated the supposed stolen document release. So did DeSmogBlog, an ardent Heartland Institute opponent, which released the documents.[17]

The leftist media was jubilant. "The Heartland Institute Self Destructs," celebrated a *Huffington Post* blogger. The incident was a "huge public fiasco."[18] "It costs a pretty penny to question the findings of scientific research. Just ask the Heartland Institute and the Koch brothers," gloated *Slate*.[19] The *New York Times* ran an article promoting the documents and ripping the Koch brothers.

Only one problem: some of the crucial documents were fake, and others were altered. "We cannot authenticate any of the documents," said Jim Lakely, communications director for Heartland. The institute filed legal action in the case. As it turned out, the documents had been stolen and some believe falsified by global warming leftist Peter Gleick.

But that didn't stop the *New York Times*. Even after the Koch brothers informed them that the documents linking them to Heartland were forged, the *Times* refused to pull the story. Tonya Mullins, director of communications for the Koch Foundation, wrote in fully justified disgust, "One might expect the Times to have some chagrin about its reporting that was based on material obtained by fraud, motivated by an ulterior ideological agenda, and suspect in its authenticity. Yet even though that source lied, cheated, and stole—and refuses to answer any further question from the Times or anyone—reporter Andrew Revkin nonetheless found room to praise him, writing, 'It's enormously creditable that Peter Gleick has owned up to his terrible error in judgment.'"[20]

That's how the climate change bullies work. They're not interested in truth. They have an agenda. And that agenda includes ripping the Koch brothers, destroying the Heartland Institute, and lying about both in order to do it.

Academic bullying and manipulation bleed down to the general population. All the lies of CRU were rehashed in Al Gore's soporific *An Inconvenient Truth*. Truth be told, I'm grateful to Al for that film—my wife and I were dating when it came out, and she was forced to watch it for her class. She didn't make it through the movie, and instead went out on a great date with me. So thanks, Mr. Vice President!

Nonetheless, *An Inconvenient Truth* was filled with the same sort of bunk as the CRU research. It had dozens of errors, some big, some small. It manipulated data. And it won an Oscar, and Gore won a Nobel Prize, because we're just supposed to accept that Gore knew what he was talking about. Of course, we were also supposed to accept that Al and Tipper were so in love that he just couldn't keep his tongue out of her throat during the 2000 presidential campaign.

Despite the errors, omissions, and scientific malfeasance, the environmentalist bullies pull out their brass knuckles when anyone questions the veracity of anthropogenic climate change. First, Gore pulls out the scare tactics: we're all gonna die! "Are we destined to destroy this place that we call home, planet earth? I can't believe that that's our destiny. It is not our destiny. But we have to awaken to the moral duty that we have to do the right thing and get out of this silly political game-playing about it. This is about survival." Says CBS News, Gore is "the popular prophet of global warming, and has helped change the way the country thinks about the issue."[21] Or not.

But if you disagree, Gore bullies you. People who don't believe Al Gore, says Al Gore, are like racists. At one point in time, said

Gore, "people said, 'Hey man, why do you talk that way? That's wrong, I don't go for that, so don't talk that way around me. I just don't believe that.' That happened in millions of conversations, and slowly the conversation was won. And we still have racism, God knows, but it's so different now and so much better. And we have to win the conversation on climate."[22] It's so true. You never know when one of those flat-earther global warming opponents is going to string somebody to a tree. If they haven't cut down all the trees by then.

Many of the environmentalist bullies on the left simply call their opponents stupid if they disagree. Because the essence of the scientific process is noncritical thinking, of course. Peter Raven, a former advisor to President Clinton, says it's "foolishness" to deny anthropogenic global warming. Thanks to the foolish crowd, Raven continues, the world has "pretty well given up" on the United States as a global leader. "It's not a matter of conjecture anymore," Raven explains. "Climate change is the most serious challenge probably that the human race has ever confronted."[23] Really? More serious than Hitler? Or the Black Plague? Or the rise of Hannah Montana?

This sort of alarmism is incredibly common on the environmentalist left. That's because shouting fire in a crowded theater is effective bullying. As Al Gore put it, "The planet has a fever. If your baby has a fever, you go to the doctor. If the doctor says you need to intervene here, you don't say, 'Well, I read a science fiction novel that told me it's not a problem.' If the crib's on fire, you don't speculate that the baby is flame retardant. You take action."[24] Don't you see? If you do nothing, your baby *will* be on fire! And you know what you do with a burning baby? You put it out! In the ocean! Which will have risen to cover your house, you sick bastard!

Thank God Pat Buchanan was on that butterfly ballot.

But Gore's just the ringmaster of this three-ring circus of bullying and stupidity. Finnish philosopher Pentti Linkola says that we should send global warming deniers to eco-gulags, deny people the freedom to have kids, get rid of fossil fuels altogether, end international trade, stop air travel, destroy suburbs, and plant parking lots with trees. "The sole glimmer of hope," says this insane person, "lies in a centralized government and the tireless control of citizens." Glad we have that glimmer of hope. Otherwise, sounds like things would get *really* nasty.

Or try James Lovelock, the British scientist who created the "Gaia" theory of earth, positing that the planet was a single organism. He said in 2006, "[B]efore this century is over billions of us will die and the few breeding pairs of people that survive will be in the Arctic where the climate remains tolerable." This may make a good pickup line in academic bars—"Hey, baby, are you ready for the climate apocalypse? I've got a nice futon where you can explore my North Pole"—but it's also ridiculous. He declared in September 2010, "I have a feeling that climate change may be an issue as severe as a war. It may be necessary to put democracy on hold for a while."[25] Because as we all know, an extraordinarily hot day means you shouldn't vote. (A couple of years later, even Lifelock acknowledged he was being a douche. "The climate is doing its usual tricks. There's nothing much really happening yet. We were supposed to be halfway toward a frying world now," he said in 2012, undoubtedly disappointed that his plans for an Arctic harem had gone awry. Oops.)[26]

Steve Zwick, another climate change guru, writes that deniers should be hunted down. "Let's start keeping track of them now, and when the famines come, let's make them pay. Let's let their houses burn. Let's swap their safe land for submerged islands. Let's force them to bear the cost of rising food prices," Zwick suggests. "They broke the climate. Why should the rest of us have to pay for it?"[27] If that's not extreme enough for you, check out columnist Richard Glover: "Surely it's time for climate-change deniers to have their opinions forcibly tattooed on their bodies. . . . On second thought, maybe the tattooing along the arm is a bit Nazi-creepy. So how about they are forced to buy property on low-lying islands, the sort of property that will become worthless with a few more centimetres of ocean rise, so they are bankrupted by their own bloody-mindedness? Or what about their signed agreement to stand, in the year 2040, lashed to a pole at a certain point in the shallows off Manly?"[28]

Or how about we all agree that Richard Glover has just enough brain power to toast a piece of organic bread . . . lightly?

These are the extremists. But even the moderates ain't so moderate. Micah White of the British newspaper the *Guardian* says that the only way to avoid global meltdown, Wicked Witch of the West–style, lies in "liberating humanity from the compulsion to consume. . . . Democratic, anti-fascist environmentalism means marshaling the strength of humanity to suppress corporations. Only by silencing the consumerist forces will both climate catastrophe and ecological tyranny be averted. Yes, western consumption will be substantially reduced. But it will be done voluntarily and joyously."[29]

Really? Will it? Because there were almost riots when people couldn't get the iPad fast enough. Communism, which had zero corporations, didn't breed a new race of humans who didn't want stuff. Turns out, stuff is pretty great. We like it. And we're not going to give it up just because pointy-headed academics threaten global extinction based on faulty science.

Professor Kari Norgaard of the University of Oregon goes even further, stating that denying anthropogenic global warming is a "sickness," and that you—yes, you—have to be "treated" for it. "This kind of cultural resistance to very significant social threat is something that we would expect in any society facing a massive threat," she wrote. Then, echoing Al Gore, she explained that denying global warming was akin to denying the evils of slavery in the American South. All these folks needed some reeducation. "If you have to push a heavy weight, it doesn't mean it can't be moved, but in order to push it you had better know that you have something heavy and figure out how to move it—where to put the lever to shift the weight," she explained.[30]

And what better way to move that weight than with some good old-fashioned bullying? With the help of President Obama, of course. Norgaard penned an open letter to President Obama calling for him to suspend the Constitution and do what was necessary to curb the dramatic threat of global warming. Democracy be damned, this is a crisis of epic proportions! Send Bruce Willis to that asteroid! "Public opinion does matter in a democracy, but this is a time when following it would be a serious mistake. . . . [A] primary recommendation of my report commissioned by the World Bank on climate denial is that policymakers should not wait for public opinion to take necessary action." She asked Obama to "eliminate coal," throw out the notion of "clean coal," and toss out nuclear power. As for oil, she's against that, too. So I guess we're down to animal feces.[31]

It appears that Obama was listening.

President Obama has used the EPA to implement his global warming goals. In 2009, Obama's EPA did something unprecedented: they declared that under the Clean Air Act, they had the authority to regulate greenhouse gases—particularly carbon dioxide—as an "air pollutant." Now, this makes no sense, and for a very simple reason: the Clean Air Act was designed to fight actual pollutants, not the stuff that you breathe out. No city has ever been polluted by too much carbon dioxide. Nonetheless, the courts upheld the unbelievably idiotic construction. And Obama was free to regulate, without having to go back to Congress for authorization for this thuggery.

After utilizing UN studies to back his case, Obama authorized the EPA to put into place regulations that, according to Senator James Inhofe (R-OK), would "cost American consumers $300 to $400 billion a year, significantly raise energy prices, and destroy hundreds of thousands of jobs. This is not to mention the 'absurd result' that the EPA will need to hire 230,000 additional employees and spend an additional $21 billion to implement its [greenhouse gas] regime."[32]

Obama has leveraged the entire administration to back the climate change play. "The area of climate change has a dramatic impact on national security," said Secretary of Defense Leon Panetta, when he wasn't too busy covering Obama while Obama personally capped Osama bin Laden.[33] Secretary of Health and Human Services Kathleen Sebelius told an international conference, "President Obama and I understand that we cannot wait any longer to act. President Obama has made it clear that he's committed to passing comprehensive energy and climate legislation that will create millions of new jobs and secure clean energy sources that are made in America and work for America."[34] Because fighting cancer just isn't good enough anymore. The department must focus on the dramatic shortage of sunscreen. Even the Department of Labor has gotten in on the act, committing the agency to "addressing the impacts climate change may have on our operations and assets through adaptation planning."[35]

Remember, this wasn't done through legislation. It was done unilaterally by the executive branch, prep work and press done by the environmentalist thugs. And it was that toxic combination that would truly bring its weight to bear on the issue of oil.

THE WAR ON OIL

Oil is the cheapest, most efficient fuel source on the planet.

And it's yucky.

According to the environmentalist bullies, we all have to beat our cars into plowshares. Oil companies have to divest themselves of profit and hobble on bended knee to Washington, D.C., to proffer their loyalty to the left.

Now, nobody has yet come up with a viable alternative to oil. Nobody. Green technology does not yet relieve the oil burden; short of green technology becoming significantly more affordable and effective, it's not slated to replace black gold anytime soon.

But that doesn't stop the left. "What we can be scientifically certain of is that our continued use of fossil fuels is pushing us to a point of no return," says Barack Obama. "And unless we free ourselves from a dependence on these fossil fuels and chart a new course on energy in this country, we are condemning future generations to global catastrophe."[36]

Well, no. What we *can* be scientifically certain of is that if we cut off our own oil supply, we'll cripple our own economy. Not only does the oil industry directly provide jobs to hundreds of thousands of employees, it provides the energy that drives our economy. Theorists believe that the September 2008 economic crash occurred thanks to the sharp oil spike earlier that year. When the Arab nations shut off their spigots, America enters an economic downturn—every single time.

Obama's goal from the beginning was to raise the price of oil on the American public to serve his environmentalist buddies. Secretary of Energy Steven Chu told Congress in February 2012, with gas prices at $3.65 per gallon, that the Obama administration wasn't concerned with high prices at the pump. That was for those rednecks in their SUVs to worry about. When asked whether it was the administration's goal to lower oil prices, Chu quickly replied, "No, the overall goal is to decrease our dependency on oil, to build and strengthen our economy." That was perfectly consistent. Back in 2008, Chu said, "Somehow we have to figure out how to boost the price of gasoline to the levels in Europe."[37]

But the Obama administration needed a pretext.

Obama got his greatest wish—and the environmentalists' ultimate fantasy—when a massive deepwater well owned by British Petroleum (BP) in the Gulf of Mexico burst in April 2010, filling the Gulf with oil and precipitating an environmental catastrophe. "Never let a good crisis go to waste," urged CNN. Obama and his allies agreed. As CNN reported, "The energy policy favored by . . . many Democrats in Congress, and most renewable energy advocates, involves making fossil fuels more expensive either by adding some type of tax or putting a price on carbon emissions." Now was the time to go cold turkey on oil!

But Obama had a problem. As badly as people felt for the storks wading around in goo in the Gulf, they still had to get to work. So Obama hit upon a solution. He wouldn't be cracking down on oil drilling to protect the sea lions. He'd be doing it to get BP.

It was a brilliant tactic. Instead of doing the bidding of the environmental left, Obama could claim he was doing the bidding of the class bullies. He was just standing up for the little guy. How? Well, by sticking it to the Oil Man! But didn't the little guy need oil? Shut up, you!

And so, a few weeks after the spill began, Obama released the hounds. First, Interior Secretary Salazar said, "[O]ur job basically is to keep the boot on the neck of British Petroleum."[38] It was a line he repeated over and over on the media. The next day, White House Press Secretary Robert Gibbs echoed Salazar: "We will keep our, as Secretary Salazar said, our boot on the throat of BP to ensure that they're doing all that they—all that is necessary, while we do all that is humanly possible to deal with this incident." When asked by the press pool just what he meant by that, Gibbs backed down . . . sort of. Instead he suggested that he just wanted to hold BP's "feet to the fire."[39] Yeah, right.

Of course, even as the Obama administration did little or nothing to actually stop the leak, forcing Governor Bobby Jindal of Louisiana to essentially take charge of the crisis, they did plan a response: a response that targeted the oil industry. "If we find they're not doing what they're supposed to be doing, we'll push them out of the way appropriately," said Salazar, knowing full well that the feds had no capacity to fix the issue.[40] The bullying got so bad that in June 2010, Prime Minister of Britain David Cameron called up Obama to tell him to stop bullying BP, especially given the fact that thousands of British pensioners relied on BP's financial success.[41]

But Obama's bullying wasn't just for show. He had a plan.

Obama did what only great actors are capable of doing: he hid his glee beneath a veneer of moral outrage. Then he acted. In May 2010, he announced a six-month deepwater drilling moratorium. He also decided that there wouldn't be any more lease sales in the western Gulf of Mexico; he canceled a lease sale off the coast of Virginia; he stopped drilling off the coast of Alaska. As the *New York Times* reported, "The White House also will propose more rigorous oil development regulations and oversight as part of an effort to boost its response to the disaster as criticism has mounted of its handling of the worsening crisis." Said Interior Secretary Salazar, "We simply will not allow any more deepwater drilling until we can ensure it is done safely."[42]

Unfortunately for him, a court soon levied an injunction against the moratorium, given that it was completely uncalled for. There had been one major accident, and no evidence whatsoever that another was imminent. It was the equivalent of one multiple-fatality shooting taking place in downtown Los Angeles and Obama immediately declaring a nationwide moratorium on gun sales. The judges called Obama's action "arbitrary and capricious."

But that sort of thing—the rule of law and that stuff—couldn't stop the Obama bully machine. In July 2010, he announced a revised moratorium on deepwater drilling.[43] Then he proceeded to slow offshore oil and gas drilling permits for months at a time, prompting noted non-oil-lobbyist Bill Clinton to acknowledge "ridiculous delays in permitting when our economy doesn't need it."[44]

But that sort of stuff wouldn't stop Obama from putting his boot on the neck of the oil industry. In November 2011, President Obama announced that he'd be killing the Keystone XL pipeline, which would carry oil from Canada down to Texas for refinement. That would have increased American oil supply and provided Americans with jobs. But Obama wasn't interested in that. He was interested in the Anti-Oil Crusade. It didn't matter that all the environmental concerns expressed by the left were hooey. As Charles Krauthammer pointed out, "[T]he State Department had subjected Keystone to *three years* of review—the most exhaustive study of any oil pipeline in U.S. history—and twice concluded in voluminous studies that there would be no significant environmental harm." And environmentalists were ecstatic—so ecstatic that they began talking about their need to reelect President Obama. Which, of course, was the whole point.[45]

As Obama launched his reelection campaign, it was time for him to disown his bullying. Suddenly he announced that gas prices were the fault of "speculators"—he had apparently been reading his FDR again.[46] He even said, obviously without exercising his neurons, that drilling "every inch" of the United States would not affect gas prices—which is like saying that buying and milking a thousand cows will not lower the price you pay for moo juice.

Obama now brags that he has opened more land for drilling, and that he "quadrupled the number of operating rigs to a record high . . . added enough new oil and gas pipeline to encircle the Earth and then some . . . we are drilling all over the place right now. That's not the challenge. That's not the problem."[47] Except that Obama was not a drill, baby, drill president. He was a kill, baby, kill president. As in, he killed drilling off the mid-Atlantic coast, the Florida Gulf coast, the Gulf of Mexico, the Arctic National Wildlife Refuge, the Rockies, Keystone XL.[48] Drilling on state lands—land that he didn't control—went up. Drilling on federal land went down to a nine-year low. In 2011 alone, oil and gas production on federal land decreased 14 percent.[49]

Obama wants to have his cake and eat it, too. And the way he achieves that is to bully the oil companies into submission, bully Americans at the pump, and hope that the American public doesn't catch on.

CONCLUSION

The environmentalist bullies have a singular goal—and it's been their goal since the days of Malthus. They want you—yes, you—to stop living so high on the hog. If you don't, they warn, we'll all die. And it'll be your fault.

It just so happens that this catastrophic worldview crosses paths politically with the class bullies, who also want Americans to stop consuming so many resources. They don't care that it's our consumption of resources that enriches other nations—if we don't buy things, they don't make money. All they see is an unjust world where we live in our cozy air-conditioned houses and people in Afghanistan live in mud huts. The best solution, for both environmentalists and class bullies, is for us all to live in mud huts. That's equality. And what's more, mud is green . . . well, brown, but you know what they mean.

And if you don't, just ask President Obama. Campaigning in Oregon back in 2008, then-senator Obama had some harsh words for America's environmentally unconscious consumers. Clearly, they didn't drive Priuses. And that, said Obama, made Americans bad people. Obama told his crowd that Americans had to "lead by example" on global warming. What would that mean? "We can't drive our SUVs and eat as much as we want and keep our homes on 72 degrees at all times . . . and then just expect that other countries are going to say OK. That's not leadership. That's not going to happen."[50]

As a matter of fact, basic economics says that other countries should be fine with us keeping our homes at 72 degrees, considering we're buying our parts for the air conditioners from them. And those in Rwanda are likely too busy running from machetes to worry about President Obama's Marxist injunctions.

In fact, not even President Obama listens to President Obama. As soon as he entered the Oval Office, cameras caught him in his shirtsleeves—generally, a presidential no-no. What would prompt him to shed his coat? Reported the *New York Times:* "Mr. Obama, who hates the cold, had cranked up the thermostat. 'He's from Hawaii, O.K.?' said Mr. Obama's senior adviser, David Axelrod, who occupies the small but strategically located office next door to his boss. 'He likes it warm. You could grow orchids in there.'"[51]

Guess when the Potomac overruns its banks and swamps the White House, we'll know whom to blame.

And thanks to the environmentalist bullies, even the youngest among us will look at President Obama with the stricken eyes of the betrayed. Hollywood has spent the last two decades indoctrinating kids with pap like *Captain Planet*, in which the honorable Captain battled the likes of Hoggish Greedily (Ed Asner), a pig-man who can't stop consuming and presumably keeps his thermostat at 72 degrees; Duke Nukem (Dean Stockwell), a doctor who shows the evils of nuclear power; Looten Plunder (James Coburn), an unrestrained capitalist; Sly Sludge (Martin Sheen), who just won't recycle; and the rest of the crew, all of whom presumably sit in the Republican caucus on their days off. If you aren't a *Captain Planet* fan—and let's face it, who is?—you can always rent *Wall-E*, in which humans have so polluted the earth with trash that they've decided to float around in space for generations. (Though *Wall-E* never explains why, if humans were able to shoot themselves into space, they didn't just shoot the trash there.) For older audiences, Hollywood provides *Avatar*, also known as *Ferngully on the Moon* and *Dances with Marxist Aliens*, James Cameron's revolutionary re-enactment of Pocahontas with large blue people and awkward sex scenes.

The goal of all of this is to make you feel bad for consuming. Of course, as soon as you stop consuming, the economy tanks—at which point the environmentalist bullies and class bullies begin complaining about the ills of capitalism. If only we'd all listened to Sheryl Crow and started using one square of toilet paper, how much better off the world would have been! And smellier!

The bullying from the environmentalist left extends to all of our lives. If you decide you don't feel like picking through your trash for dried-out orange peels and grease-soaked pizza boxes for composting in San Francisco, you could find yourself facing a hefty fine.[52] In Portland, it's too bad for you if you like your trash picked up more often than bimonthly. Those dirty diapers will just have to rot on the curb for two weeks.[53] Nobody likes pollution. But nobody except Susan Sarandon likes the smell of dirty diapers pervading the house.

The environmental bullies have convinced Americans to spend their time micromanaging their garbage. What's worse, they have pushed for the handing over of U.S. sovereignty to foreign nations, since Americans can't be trusted not to be fat slobs. So prior to the Rio+20 Conference in June 2012, the Earth System Governance Project, an international consortium of environmentalist academics, proposed that in order to stop the world from imploding, the UN should institute a new form of voting so that the United States couldn't veto anything.[54] Surely our global citizen president wouldn't mind—after all, we're supposed to ask other nations permission before flushing twice.

Americans are right to worry about the loss of a clean and healthy environment. Who wouldn't truly worry if the earth were about to turn into a giant smokestack spewing garbage into the air, transforming our climate into Dante's inferno?

But it isn't. And if it is, Americans deserve to make that judgment themselves, not to be bullied into it by a bunch of thugs slated to make money off their alarmism. In the years that Al Gore has been hawking his green energy Brooklyn Bridges, including "carbon credits"—fictional measures of carbon emissions that can be bought and sold to avoid regulation—Gore positioned himself to make hundreds of millions of dollars. Which means that for this Elmer Gantry of environmentalism, global warming is a Very Convenient Untruth.[55]

Bullying is a profitable business for the environmentalists. Their entire game is shouting fire in a crowded theater—or rather, burning baby in a crowded theater. And they stifle the truth to prevent people from fighting back.

7.

★

SECULAR BULLIES

On June 28, 2012, Michelle Obama, The Most Beautiful Woman In The World™, spoke at the African Methodist Episcopal Church's General Conference. There, in her own charming style, she urged church leaders to get politically active. Not Jeremiah Wright active, mind you, but active enough to get out the vote for Barack Hussein Obama, who made America a country Michelle could be proud of.

"To anyone who says that church is no place to talk about these issues," said Michelle, "you tell them there is no place better—no place better. Because ultimately, these are not just political issues—they are moral issues. They're issues that have to do with human dignity and human potential, and the future we want for our kids and grandkids."[1] The crowd went wild, reacting almost as if they'd heard pastor Jeremiah Wright term the United States the "US of KKKA."

Michelle was exactly right. Politics and religion are two sides of the same coin; both are expressions of our ethics. Trying to remove politics from religion and religion from politics is a fruitless task, and one our founding fathers would have abhorred. The Constitution designed the separation of church and state to prevent people from imposing their particular religions on others, not to stop people from allowing their religious beliefs to influence their views on public policy.

But, of course, Michelle wasn't serious. She *meant* to say that liberal churchgoers should talk until their faces turn blue. Conservative churchgoers, however, are religious bigots, and should shut their pieholes until Jesus makes his big comeback in *The Passion II: He Won't Be Crossed Again*.

How do we know that? Because Michelle's husband said so back in 2006, in his single most comprehensive speech about religion. There, he said that progressives should hijack religious imagery and language to argue for their positions. But he also argued that the religiously motivated had to "translate their concerns into universal, rather than religion-specific, values. . . . I may be opposed to abortion for religious reasons, but if I seek to pass a law banning the practice, I cannot simply point to the teachings of my church or evoke God's will. I have to explain why abortion violates some principle that is accessible to people of all faiths, including those with no faith at all."

Now, this all sounds very reasonable. But it is a fundamental denial of the role of religion in people's lives when you argue that they have to use the language of secularism to justify the laws for which they vote.

Think of religion, especially Judeo-Christian religion, as a language—Italian, perhaps.

And think of secularism as its own language—German.

What Obama is saying is that everyone should speak German, even if their natural language is Italian. Actually, they shouldn't even be allowed to have a ballot in Italian. They should speak German, act German, and vote German. And then Obama has the temerity to tell us that he's pro-Italian.

Why should religious people have to justify their votes or policies on secular grounds? So long as the policies themselves are not establishing a particular religion, they shouldn't. If a Mormon votes for Proposition 8 because scripture tells him that he ought to, he doesn't owe an explanation to anybody. The fact that Proposition 8 doesn't force anybody to join the Tabernacle Choir is a good indicator that it's not establishing religion. You don't have to be a Mormon to vote for Proposition 8. And if a gay person wants to know why you voted for the proposition, you don't *have* to explain why in terms of social science data.

But Obama doesn't think this is true. He believes people should vote only for the reasons he thinks are valid. He says so himself in the speech. He says that he, Barack Obama, should be able to choose for everyone which biblical principles are most important—namely, those that are apolitical—and which can simply be discarded. A belief in "Christ's divinity," said Obama back in 2006, is "central to Christian faith," but the practical values for which Christ stood . . . well, not so much. Which is why, Obama explained, "some of those opposed to gay marriage nevertheless are opposed to a Constitutional amendment to ban it. Religious leadership need not accept such wisdom in counseling their flocks, but they should recognize this wisdom in their politics."

Obama gets even clearer. He's willing to accept people mentioning God in the Pledge of Allegiance. But he's not okay with people invoking God when they talk about their most cherished beliefs. That's because people argue about biblical interpretation, says Obama. Obama actually paraphrased a famous 2000 email in which he supposedly pointed out biblical inconsistencies: "And even if we did have only Christians in our midst, if we expelled every non-Christian from the United States of America, whose Christianity would we teach in the schools? Would we go with James Dobson's, or Al Sharpton's? Which passages of Scripture should guide our public policy? Should we go with Leviticus, which suggests slavery is ok and that eating shellfish is abomination? How about Deuteronomy, which suggests stoning your child if he strays from the faith? Or should we just stick to the Sermon on the Mount—a passage that is so radical that it's doubtful that our own Defense Department would survive its application? So before we get carried away, let's read our bibles. Folks haven't been reading their bibles."[2]

To put it mildly, Obama knows nothing about religion. To put it less mildly, this is moronic.

First, this is scripturally incorrect—religious Jews still don't eat shellfish, the Talmud clearly says that the injunction about the rebellious child has never been invoked, and Obama's interpretation of the Sermon on the Mount is more in line with Karl Marx than with Jesus. Actually, this is just cribbing from a popular 2000 email that purports to debunk the Bible by saying some of it has been reinterpreted. The email's stupid, too.

Second, and more importantly, even if there is a dispute about religious interpretation, why should that invalidate religion as a means of deciding voter values? People disagree about secular rationales for policy all the time—well, until Obama's glowing visage strikes their brain, and they're rendered dumb by the brilliance of his countenance.

Here's the bottom line. Obama seems to believe that if we must all start without a set of values—we must start with a secular tabula rasa. Judeo-Christian believers think that we should begin with a common set of biblical values—and then we can discuss whether those beliefs are subject to new interpretation.

This is an absolutely stark difference—especially because those of the Judeo-Christian worldview generally don't begrudge others when it comes to their voting justification. Only secularists think that religious people have no right to discuss their politics.

Take, for example, Proposition 8 again. Now take a look at the judicial ruling by Judge Vaughn Walker, the federal judge who decided that Proposition 8 violated the federal constitution. To understand just how insane this is, you have to recognize that according to Walker, the Constitution of the United States, ratified in 1789, was meant to stop states from exclusively recognizing male-female marriages. In 1789, Thomas Jefferson was recommending castration for homosexuals. That was actually the *liberal* position—the Virginia legislature prescribed death. So it's fairly safe to say that the founders would not have been fans of *Glee*.

Nonetheless, Walker said that the Constitution barred traditional marriage amendments. Why? Well, said Walker, there was no rational basis for such legislation. Proposition 8, wrote Walker, was "premised on the belief that same-sex couples simply are not as good as opposite-sex couples." This, of course, is true in certain respects. For example, same-sex couples are not as good at creating children, for obvious biological reasons—no matter what beautiful babies Anderson Cooper and the straight man Tom Cruise would have, they'll have some obstacles getting there. Same-sex couples are not as good at providing a stable male-female home for a child, by definition. But Walker said that such a belief simply had no basis in rationality whatsoever. Why? Simply because Walker disagreed with it—and in particular, disagreed with religious people.

Actually, Walker went full-scale fan mail crazy, with CAPSLOCK glued down to the keyboard. Here's what he wrote—yes, including the capitalization: "A PRIVATE MORAL VIEW THAT SAME-SEX COUPLES ARE INFERIOR TO OPPOSITE-SEX COUPLES IS NOT A PROPER BASIS FOR LEGISLATION." Just to ensure we got the point, Walker went after religious people directly: "The evidence shows conclusively that moral and religious views form the only basis for a belief that same-sex couples are different from opposite-sex couples. . . . [R]eligious beliefs that gay and lesbian relationships are sinful or inferior to heterosexual relationships harm gays and lesbians."

This is complete and utter antireligious bullying. There are excellent reasons why same-sex marriage should not be enshrined in state law. Traditional marriage is built around the needs of children. Children need a mother and a father. Men and women are inherently different; they bring different qualities to the raising of children. The biological parents of a child, especially, bring unique qualities to the raising of their own children. Just because Vaughn Walker disagrees with those reasons, and just because many of the people who happen to agree with those reasons are religious, does *not* mean that such legislation should be ruled off-limits by a judge duty-bound to implement the Constitution.

But Walker is a secularist bully. So is Obama.

The left's view of religion requires a jihad on it in the public square. If you sense somebody voting because of their religious worldview, smack them in the face—they're betraying the basic liberal notion that only secularism matters. If you think a Christian is judging you, tell that Christian to stop being un-American. Religion is fine, so long as it doesn't impact your vote on gay marriage, abortion, contraception, welfare, food stamps, universal health care, or foreign policy.

OBAMA'S WAR ON RELIGION

President Obama's secular bullying serves a dual purpose for him. First, it provides him the personal satisfaction of supplanting God with himself. Second, it gives him a convenient enemy to target in order to garner the female vote.

See, President Obama knows that women have never had it better in this country. And he knows that Republicans are not only fine with women working, they're making a heavy play for women by running charismatic female politicians like Sarah Palin, Michele Bachmann, Kristi Noem, and dozens more. As it turns out, married women are especially apt to vote Republican, since the Republican Party is heavy on traditional family values. And even among women, sentiment surrounding abortion is incredibly mixed—and thanks to *Roe v. Wade*, the abortion issue is off the table for the most part anyway.

But somehow, Obama needed to grab a higher percentage of the female vote. And if the Republicans weren't going to paint themselves into a corner, Obama would have to fence them in another way: he'd have to target religious institutions with more controversial views on sexual issues.

And so, on January 7, 2012, during a Republican debate, Obama media lackey George Stephanopoulos of ABC News asked Mitt Romney a very specific question. "Governor Romney," the Keebler Elf giggled, "do you believe that states have the right to ban contraception? Or is that trumped by a constitutional right to privacy?" It would be hard to imagine a less relevant question. Nobody in the Republican Party has proposed banning contraception. No state has considered banning contraception for nearly fifty years. So what was this all about?

Republicans found out—and so did religious people. On January 20, 2012, Secretary of Health and Human Services Kathleen Sebelius announced that under the new Obamacare program, religious employers would be forced to provide health insurance including contraception.

This was obviously an attempt to start a war with religious institutions. It's one thing to ask religious institutions to stay out of the political limelight; it's another thing to specifically ask them to overrule their own beliefs and provide coverage for what they consider to be sinful activity. The Obama administration had made its choice: Religious liberty didn't matter. Only the collective secularist ideology did. "This decision was made after very careful consideration, including the important concerns some have raised about religious liberty," Sebelius lied. "I believe this proposal strikes the appropriate balance between respecting religious freedom and increasing access to important preventive services."[3] Where exactly was the balance? Forcing the Catholic Church to provide condoms wasn't balancing religious liberty against health needs—it was balancing secularism against religion, and finding religion wanting. After some blowback, the Democrats made a small exemption for churches, but continued to force religious business owners and institutions like charities, hospitals, and schools to provide contraception.

The strategy was obvious: attack religious institutions; force Republicans to side with religious institutions; imply that Republicans are siding with religious institutions not because they believe in religious liberty, but because they secretly want to ban contraceptives altogether. It was now crystal clear just why George Stephanopoulos had mentioned birth control back on January 7. He was softening the ground for the Obama administration blitzkrieg on religion. As Mitt Romney pointed out, "You recall, back in the debate we had George Stephanopoulos talking all about birth control. We wondered why in the world that contraception—it's like, 'why's he going there?' Well, we found out when Barack Obama continued his attack on religious conscience."[4]

When Republicans tried to force a bill through the Senate that would have stripped the contraceptive mandate from Obamacare, Democratic bullies denounced them. "The closeness of this vote shows how high the stakes are for women in this country," said Senator Chuck Schumer (D-NY). "A Republican-led Senate might pass this bill. A Republican president like Mitt Romney would definitely sign it." And the Obama administration chimed in, too: "The Obama administration," said Sebelius, "believes that decisions about medical care should be made by a woman and her doctor, not a woman and her boss. We encourage the Senate to reject this cynical attempt to roll back decades of progress in women's health."[5]

This wasn't progress in women's health. Sebelius and all other women were still free to go down to CVS and pick up Yaz themselves. They were also free to choose jobs with nonreligious employers. In fact, this wasn't even a "women's health" issue at all. Choosing birth control is just that . . . a choice. It isn't healthy or unhealthy.

But the Obama administration wasn't interested in honesty. They were interested in fighting a war on religion. House Minority Leader Nancy Pelosi took the lead in that war. Pelosi, who purports to be a Catholic, said that this was a "women's health issue" rather than a religious issue. Then she called Catholics hypocrites. "Ninety percent of Catholic women of childbearing age use birth control," she spouted. "It's a matter of conscience for each woman, her doctor, her husband, her family and her God to make their own decisions. And as a Catholic, I support the right of a woman to make that decision."[6] As a Catholic, she apparently also supported Thomas Cromwell–type terrorism aimed at the Catholic Church. If Pelosi stood up as a Catholic, she was also standing against every bishop in the United States. Literally.[7]

The battle between religion and secularism truly took center stage when congressional Democrats brought forth one Sandra Fluke, a radical feminist activist who had enrolled at Georgetown Law School, a Catholic institution, planning to protest their health-care coverage. Fluke played the poor, downtrodden student, even though she and her boyfriend somehow scraped together the cash to take vacations to Europe. Called before a congressional committee, Fluke told her sob story: "When I look around my campus, I see the faces of the women affected, and I have heard more and more of their stories." Sandra was apparently under the grave misimpression that she went to school in Rwanda. She told horror story after horror story—an anonymous lesbian who had to have an ovary removed because the school wouldn't cover her birth control pills, an anonymous girl who didn't go for an STD test after being raped. All anonymous. How strange. But she continued, "Women [whose contraception isn't covered by the school] have no choice but to go without contraception. . . . We refuse to pick between a quality education and our health, and we resent that, in the 21st century, anyone thinks it's acceptable to ask us to make this choice simply because we are women." Fluke put the cost of contraception at about $3,000 annually.[8]

It was typical secularist bullying—anonymous sob story nonsense mixed with fact, a political diatribe against the Catholic Church. Essentially, Fluke was saying that if a girl wants to have sex and work for the Vatican, the pope should have an obligation to hand over the Trojans. And since Fluke wanted to have sex and go to a Catholic school, they should pay for it.

It was absurd.

When Rush Limbaugh called Fluke a "slut" on air for essentially asking a Catholic university to subsidize her sex life—an inappropriate response that Rush quickly apologized for—the left went berserk. Suddenly the world's leading radio entertainer found himself the center of an Obama-orchestrated assault. Obama pivoted off the war on religion and suggested instead that conservatives were starting a "war on women." President Obama immediately activated his "I'm a sympathetic fellow" face (and hid his gleeful "I get to bash Rush Limbaugh!" face) and called up Fluke to offer his support. As Rachel Maddow body double and White House press secretary Jay Carney said, Obama wanted to "express his disappointment, that she was the subject of an inappropriate personal attack and thank her for exercising her rights as a citizen to speak out on public policy." Carney said they talked for "several minutes . . . [Obama] said the personal attacks directed her way are inappropriate. The fact that political discourse has become debased in many ways is bad enough. It's worse when directed at a private citizen simply expressing her views on a matter of public policy."[9]

Obama did not call Sarah Palin to offer his condolences for Bill Maher calling her a "c—," long after Palin was a private citizen. He didn't call Michelle Malkin after Keith Olbermann labeled her a "big, mashed up bag of meat with lipstick on it."

It was a perverse political ploy, designed to cow everyone

into submission about the contraception mandate. And the bullies weren't done. Media Matters launched an astroturfed boycott campaign against Rush's advertisers, trying to force them to pull their dollars from El Rushbo. It was a brilliant strategy. Media Matters wasn't going to get people to stop listening to Rush—he's too talented and popular. Instead, they focused on risk-averse advertisers, who simply want people to buy their product, and want to avoid controversy at all costs. Angelo Carusone, director of online strategy for the Obama outlet, admitted that Media Matters had dusted off an old "Stop Rush" campaign and activated allies to inundate advertisers. Carusone personally began contacting sponsors.[10]

Media Matters wasn't doing this on its own. The Democratic Congressional Campaign Committee fund-raised off the incident. When Limbaugh read their letter on the air, they played victim. And they quoted St. Sandra, the newly elevated pope of Anti-Religious Bigotry: "The millions of American women who have and will continue to speak out in support of women's health care and access to contraception prove that we will not be silenced."[11]

Meanwhile, the contraceptive mandate remained in place. It remains there to this day. The secularist bullies won. They usually do.

But not always. When the Hosanna-Tabor Evangelical Lutheran Church and School fired one of their teachers for acting against church teachings, the Obama Department of Justice sued the church. The DOJ argued that there shouldn't be any religious exception to employment laws—even though the First Amendment creates such an exception. It's called "freedom of religion." The Supreme Court justices found the government's argument incredible. When Leondra Kruger, Obama's lawyer in the case, tried to argue that there didn't need to be special treatment for religious institutions, Justice Scalia jumped down her throat: "That's extraordinary! There, black on white in the text of the Constitution, are special protections for religion. And you say it makes no difference?" The Court struck down the EEOC case 9–0. Even the Court's liberals found this bullying of religious institutions too blatant.[12]

President Obama isn't content with forcing religious institutions to abandon their principles in favor of secular morality. He wants people to stop giving cash to religious charities altogether. Every one of President Obama's proposed budgets has suggested that charitable donations from families making more than $250,000 and individuals making over $200,000 be taxed. According to Senator Orrin Hatch (R-UT), Obama's proposal would "cost charities as much as $5.6 billion per year. . . . The nonpartisan Congressional Budget Office found that other proposals to limit the charitable deduction could result in as much as a $10 billion drop in donations annually." A huge number of these charities are religious.[13]

"YOU'RE JUST LIKE THE TALIBAN"

America, President Obama is fond of repeating, "is not a Christian nation." He's said this over and over and over again. He did it in that speech in 2006. He did it again shortly after his inauguration, when he visited Turkey. "We have a very large Christian population," he told the Islamist regime. "We do not consider ourselves a Christian nation or a Jewish nation or a Muslim nation. We consider ourselves a nation of citizens who are bound by ideals and a set of values."[14]

But what are those ideals and values?

Obama would be loath to label them Judeo-Christian. That's because he's not a Christian. He's not a Muslim, either—although under Muslim law he's a Muslim, he certainly doesn't slap down a prayer rug and bow toward Mecca (he saves his bowing for foreign dictators, not Allah). Obama's an atheist, or at the very least an agnostic. His view on religion is pretty obvious: he's not one of those bitter Americans clinging to God.

So if, according to Obama, we're not a Judeo-Christian nation, what are we? Here, Obama is lost. What he *does* know is that no traditional religious justification for action is legitimate. He believes, as most leftists do, in the absolute separation of church and state.

And the leftist bullies use that nonconstitutional phrase as a baton with which to club their opponents into submission. Jefferson's "wall of separation between Church & State," a phrase from his 1802 letter to the Danbury Baptists, was meant not to prevent people from expressing religion in the public square but to prevent *government from infringing on religious freedom.* Here's the phrase in context: "Believing with you that religion is a matter which lies solely between Man & his God, that he owes account to none other for his faith or his worship, that the legitimate powers of government reach actions only, & not opinions, I contemplate with sovereign reverence that act of the whole American people which declared that their legislature should 'make no law respecting an establishment of religion, or prohibiting the free exercise thereof,' thus building a wall of separation between Church & State." In short, government shouldn't do what Obama has done with the Catholic Church. And Catholics aren't expected to shut up, as Obama would undoubtedly prefer.

But the left's interpretation of Jefferson's phraseology is less nuanced than this. It requires that religion never influence public policy, and that the government never fund any activities associated with religion. Jefferson would have been appalled by such a construction.

Unfortunately, that construction is gaining ground. The secular left has succeeded in bullying religious people into a sort of abashed silence. It's not merely through action; it's through attitude. The scorn in which atheists hold believers is almost incredible—if atheists had the power to do so, they'd ban religion forthwith. As linguistics professor turned crappy commie philosopher (and owner of multiple homes) Noam Chomsky reportedly put it, "Take any country that has laws against hate crimes, inspiring hatred and genocide and so on. The first thing they would do is ban the Old Testament. There's nothing like it in the literary canon that exalts genocide, to that extent. And it's not a joke either. Like where I live, New England, the people who liberated it from the native scourge were religious fundamentalist lunatics, who came waving the holy book, declaring themselves to be the children of Israel who are killing the Amalekites, like God told them."[15]

Not coincidentally, there are other groups that want to ban the Bible to avoid conflict. One group wants the Supreme Court to ban the Bible to prevent certain sections from being used to insult others. That group is the radical clerics in Pakistan, who want their Supreme Court to step in and censor the Bible for political reasons.[16] So, who's the real Taliban here?

According to the left, religious people are. Even though secular people haven't generally been bullied in this country for their secularism, the secular bullies like to play the victim. Their latest label for religious people is "American Taliban." The left loves it. It's meant to denigrate Christians as potential threats to world peace (although the greatest threats of the last century, Nazism and communism, were both secular). It's meant to paint the right as a bunch of whackos ready to hop on their nags, grab some torches, and go looking for the nearest woman to wrap in a burlap sack.

And thus *Daily Kos* runs posts explaining that the religious right isn't interested in religious freedom (false), wants a national religion established (false), wants to "dominate women and tell them how to act" (false), doesn't care about freedom of speech (false), and thinks homosexuality is a sin (true).[17] They're just like the Taliban! Except of course, for how the Taliban want to do all those things—and still like to shag each other in the hills of Tora Bora.

It's not just random posters on *Daily Kos*. It's Markos Moulitsas, the website's creepy founder. He wrote an entire book called *American Taliban*, which posited that "war, sex, sin and power bind jihadists and the religious right." Sadly, the book sold three copies, all reportedly to Osama bin Laden. And even he used them as doorstops.

Bill Maher, whose drug use has clearly affected his sense of humor first and foremost, says that 2012 presidential candidate Rick Santorum is "anti-knowledge." He said that while Muslims just want to go back to the eighth century, Christians want to go back before the Tree of Knowledge. The three scariest words to religious people, says Maher, are "here's an idea."[18] He's wrong. The three scariest words are "let's watch *Religulous*."

Or "now on *Hardball*." Chris Matthews echoes Maher when he says, "[T]he group in this country that most resembles the Taliban, ironically, is the religious right."[19]

Hollywood, too, paints Christians as an incipient Torquemadas. As it happens, liberals are the only folks who expect the Spanish Inquisition. The actual Spanish Inquisition. Every movie pastor is John Lithgow in *Footloose;* every religious Christian is a prude or a simpleton or a serial killer. Every small Christian town is just waiting to unleash their inner witch-burning cretin (who, it should be noted, was technically Jewish). Hollywood lives in constant fear of the cross-waving, pitchfork-wielding mobs. "There are a lot of people who really have medieval minds in all sorts of ways," Susan Harris, creator of the hit liberal TV show *Soap*, told me. "Who aren't open to anything new. Aren't open to anything reasonable. Think science is a matter of belief. And that's who you're dealing with. . . . It's not an audience, I think, I could ever speak to."[20] Back in the 1980s, Thomas Wyman, a top executive at CBS, actually labeled Christian conservatives a "constitutionally immoral minority."

But we're the intolerant ones.

Who are the real Taliban? Ask the ubiquitous Dan Savage. Actually, you don't even have to ask—he'll tell you. And if you don't want to listen, he'll yell it at you. For some reason beyond human comprehension, the administration behind the National High School Journalism Conference decided to ask Savage to speak—presumably not about butt plugs. Instead, he launched into an anti-Bible rant, telling students that religious people hate gays. "We can learn to ignore the bullshit in the Bible about gay people . . . the same way we have learned to ignore the bullshit in the Bible about shellfish, about slavery, about dinner, about farming, about menstruation, about virginity, about masturbation," spouted the doorknob-licking Mensa member. "We ignore bullshit in the Bible about all sorts of things."

This was that same old 2000 email again, listing all the supposedly obsolete parts of the Bible. And Christian students weren't tremendously interested in this brainless screed. So they got up and walked out. As they did, he berated them from a giant, *1984*-style screen: "It's funny, as someone who's been on the receiving end of beatings that are justified by the Bible, how pansy-assed some people react when you push back."

Now, Savage may be unfamiliar with basic standards of polite behavior, but what the students did was polite. Instead of rushing the stage and beating him up, as the Taliban would do, they walked out. But this made Savage insane. He quasi-apologized: "I didn't call anyone's religion bullshit. I did say that there is bullshit—'Untrue words or ideas'—in the Bible. . . . I would like to apologize for describing that walkout as a pansy-assed move. I wasn't calling the handful of students who left pansies (2,800+ students, most of them Christian, stayed and listened), just the walkout itself."[21] He added, "I did not attack *Christianity*. I attacked *hypocrisy*."[22]

Well, no. He attacked Christianity. And Christians.

He bullied. If he could blow up statues of Jesus, he'd do it. And he'd replace them with bathhouses, pure Taliban style.

THE "PRO-SCIENCE" BULLIES

The secular bullies believe they have an exclusive patent on scientific knowledge. Of all the antireligious slander perpetrated by the secularists, the most common and the most damaging is the self-flattering leftist notion that only the left is interested in science. Barack Obama himself is a lead purveyor of this myth. In one of his first acts as president, Obama signed an executive order granting federal funding for embryonic stem cell research.

President Bush had stopped federal funding of embryonic stem cell research based on the notion that a balance had to be drawn between the dictates of science and the dictates of morality—creating human life to destroy it for the purpose of saving other human life was not an acceptable pursuit, in President Bush's belief. Charles Krauthammer rightly called Bush's address on the subject "the most morally serious address on medical ethics ever given by an American president"—and Krauthammer disagreed with Bush on stem cell research.[23]

But Obama saw no such complexity. Instead he ripped President Bush's decision to stop federal funding of certain lines of embryonic stem cell research as little more than benighted Dark Ages superstition. "[I]n recent years, when it comes to stem cell research, rather than furthering discovery, our government has forced what I believe is a false choice between sound science and moral values. In this case, I believe the two are not inconsistent. As a person of faith, I believe we are called to care for each other and work to ease human suffering. I believe we have been given the capacity and will to pursue this research—and the humanity and conscience to do so responsibly. . . . [T]he proper course has become clear . . . [we must] develop a strategy for restoring scientific integrity to government decision making."[24]

This was asinine. Bush had never stripped scientific integrity. He had merely done what all moral people must do on questions of science: he had measured the ends of science against the means used to get there. Perhaps his measurements were off; that was open to debate. What was *not* open to debate was the fact that Bush did the right thing in attempting the moral question.

But the left is not interested in such moral questions. To them, the religious right is waging a "war on science." Chris Mooney, a journalist for the *Washington Post*, the *Washington Monthly*, and *Mother Jones*, penned an entire book called *The Republican War on Science*. Katrina vanden Heuvel, publisher and owner of the *Nation*, says that "Republicans have become proudly and unquestionably anti-science. (It is their litmus test, though they would probably reject the science behind litmus paper.)"[25] *Slate* says, "The Republican war on science is un-American."[26] Hillary Clinton said that the Bush administration had declared "open season on open inquiry."[27]

This type of rhetoric is all too common among secularists on the left. They paint a false dichotomy between religion and science. They say that religious people are anti-science, because science makes God irrelevant—therefore, religious people want to stop scientific progress. They point to the fact that many religious people are skeptical about the theory of evolution—as though skepticism of a scientific finding were in and of itself unscientific. The left likes to say that religious people who have questions about evolution are like people who oppose the theory of gravity. They seem to miss the irony that if Einstein hadn't been skeptical of Newton's theory of gravity, there would be no General Theory of Relativity. That's not to say that the theory of evolution is wrong—I believe strongly in the punctuated equilibrium theory of evolution. And, as a religious believer, I believe that God acted through the natural world in creating such a system.

The truth is that it is the *left* that consistently wages a war on science. As a general matter, the right is far less worried about scientific results than it is the means by which those results were obtained. So, for example, in the embryonic stem cell context, religious people are worried about the morality of destroying a potential human life to save a human life. But they don't argue with the results of the scientific research.

The left, by contrast, is far less interested in scientific means than it is in scientific ends. They'll do anything to obtain a scientific result . . . but if the result doesn't meet their expectations, they'll attack the science. So, for example, the left is fine with research that uses fetuses. But they reject, ignore, and demonize anyone who says that new scientific findings about the development of the fetus show the barbarity of abortion. If the scientific results show that abortion is the murder of an unborn child, the left screams bloody murder. That's why Planned Parenthood and its allies dislike 4-D ultrasounds and oppose legislation to use them—they don't want potential mothers seeing that their unborn children aren't actually random blobs of tissue. The left isn't interested in the science. They hate the results, so they silence them.

The same holds true with regard to homosexuality. Scientific studies tend to show that homosexuality is not entirely genetic—studies show that identical twins are not both gay a solid 50 percent of the time. But the left ignores such studies. Instead it simply announces, sans evidence, that homosexuality is entirely genetic and has no environmental component. When there are any efforts made to delve into the actual *science* behind homosexuality, the left goes berserk.

In Oregon, scientist Charles Roselli started a study researching why 8 percent of rams were gay. The goal of the study: to find the brain differences between gay rams and straight rams, and to cure gay rams. As it turns out, gay rams are not nearly as useful to society as straight rams, for obvious reasons: they don't procreate.

And unlike gay human beings, rams have a few specified purposes on the planet, first and foremost of which is procreation.

A relatively harmless study. About rams. Being gay.

Not according to the left. "Information has been brought to light about ridiculous 'gay sheep' experiments that are being conducted at the school," said People for the Ethical Treatment of Animals. The university received twenty thousand letters astroturfed from the leftist community. Martina Navratilova, a lesbian woman apparently frightened that she would magically transform into a lesbian sheep and thus be subject to experimentation, issued a statement: "[F]or the many gays and lesbians who stand to be deeply offended by the social implications of these tests, I ask that you please end these studies at once." One of the PETA associates said that the problem was the oft-cited slippery slope: "[O]nce you've figured out what makes gay sheep gay, it's an obvious implication that you can then turn off or change the hormone that can make them straight. [The researcher is] not taking responsibility for that."

The university backed down. They said that the purpose of the study was no longer to cure gay rams, but to understand "important relationships between physiology and behavior." Because it would be homophobic to cure gay rams so they can create little rams. You never know when you might be curing the ram version of Leonardo da Vinci—and God knows, according to the secular left, Leonardo would never have been a great thinker had he not liked men.[28]

The liberal war on science isn't restricted to abortion and homosexuality. When it comes to teenagers, the left doesn't want to hear that teen brains are not fully developed and are therefore incapable of making fully rational decisions. They don't care that the prefrontal cortex, which inhibits risky behavior, is underdeveloped. All they care about is that they be allowed to hand out condoms in school and tell kids how much fun sex is.

The same holds true for the feminist crowd, which seeks to

obliterate any distinction between men and women. Sure, men and women are different according to science—"In mammalian species numerous sex differences in brain structure and function have now been documented," writes Judy L. Cameron of the University of Pittsburgh Departments of Psychiatry, Neuroscience, and Cell Biology & Physiology. "Behaviors showing documented sex difference include behaviors associated with reproduction (mating and maternal behaviors), aggression, activity, and various cognitive functions including spatial cognition, verbal skills, and various aspects of learning and memory." But when any scientist dares to suggest fundamental and legitimate differences between men and women, the feminists try to undermine the studies and destroy those who promoted them. Just ask Larry Summers.

The secularist bullies' implication that the religious are a bunch of witch-burning fanatics seeking to smash all test tubes and replace them with Bibles isn't just wrong—it's a reversal of the facts. The right cares deeply about whether scientific methods are moral. The left couldn't care less about the methodology, so long as the result meets their fancy. If it doesn't, there's hell to pay.

ANTI-SEMITIC BULLIES

The secular bullies aren't content with focusing on the Christian half of Judeo-Christian values. They hate Judaism just as much—in some ways, even more—than Christianity, since Judaism forms the root of the Judeo-Christian tree. That hatred manifests itself in vast hatred of the state of Israel, the Jewish state. To the secular bullies, the concept of a Jewish state violates secular notions, despite Israel's own largely secular values; it smacks of intolerance for other religions. More than that, it doesn't acknowledge the supremacy of areligious nonjudgmentalism—Israel's very claim to existence is biblically and historically based. Thus Israel's claims are illegitimate. And Israel must be destroyed.

That's why the secular bullies don't seem to care that Israel is significantly more pro–gay rights than any other nation in the region; instead, they accuse Israel of "pinkwashing" when Israel points that out. (Max Blumenthal, son of Clinton hit man Sidney Blumenthal, and self-hating Jew, leads the anti-Israel crew on this score.[29] Blumenthal is such an Israel-hater that he suggested in an interview with Al Jazeera that any black person who supported Israel had to be brainwashed to do so—a deeply racist sentiment that didn't seem to bother this serial liar.) The secular bullies don't care that Israel's record on human rights is absolutely stellar next to every other country in the region; they don't care that Israel's record on women's rights is better than or equal to any nation on the planet; they don't care that Israel allows freedom of religion, up to and including handing over the holiest site in Judaism, the Temple Mount, to the tender caresses of the artifact-destroying Muslim Waqf. All that matters to the secular left is that Israel be endlessly criticized, labeled a colonialist outpost, and undermined in every way.

Now, it's not anti-Semitic to criticize Israel's actions. Every country does things worthy of criticism. But it *is* anti-Semitic to hold Israel to a higher standard than any other nation; to ignore all of its good points in favor of its flaws; to ignore the historic Jewish tie to the land of Israel; to associate with anti-Semites; to engage in activities that dramatically undermine Israel's security. The Obama administration has done all of this.

President Obama is on the leading edge of the anti-Semitic secularist thug crowd. If he's not an anti-Semite, he's certainly quite comfortable with them. Jeremiah Wright, his longtime pastor, is a massive anti-Semite, a man whose newsletter included quotes from Hamas and Louis Farrakhan. Obama's ideological mentor, Professor Derrick Bell of Harvard Law School, was an anti-Semite, too, a man who denounced "Jewish neoconservative racists who are undermining blacks in every way they can," and said that the black community should celebrate Farrakhan and his deputy, Khalid Muhammad, who maintained that Jews were "bloodsuckers" whose "father was the devil."[30]

During the 1990s, Obama spoke at Palestinian fund-raisers. His friend Ali Abunimah, founder of the anti-Israel website Electronic Intifada, said, "I knew Barack Obama for many years as my state senator—when he used to attend events in the Palestinian community in Chicago all the time. . . . Barack Obama used to be very comfortable speaking up for and being associated with Palestinian rights and opposing the Israeli occupation. . . . He was very supportive of US pressure on Israel." According to Abunimah, Obama told him in 2004 that he'd be more anti-Israel after he got elected; at the time, he was in a tough primary fight.[31]

In 2003, Obama attended a dinner for his good friend, former PLO spokesman Rashid Khalidi, at which attendees delivered addresses comparing "Zionist settlers on the West Bank" to Osama bin Laden and suggesting that Israel "will never see a day of peace." Hussein Ibish, a defender of terrorist professor Sami Al-Arian and an anti-Israel extremist, called Obama "more sympathetic to the position of ending the occupation than either [Hillary Clinton or John Edwards]." And Obama himself praised Khalidi thus: "[My talks with Khalidi are] consistent reminders to me of my own blind spots and my own biases. . . . It's for that reason that I'm hoping that, for many years to come, we continue that conversation."[32]

And Obama *has* continued that conversation. During his campaign, one of his surrogates, Robert Malley, was caught communicating with the terrorist group Hamas. No wonder Hamas, which now controls the Gaza Strip, endorsed Obama for president in 2008, claiming "he is like John Kennedy, great man with great principles." For his part, David Axelrod, Obama's campaign honcho, said the words were "flattering."[33] During the 2008 cycle, Obama also allegedly raked in illegal campaign cash from the Palestinian territories.[34] Obama's campaign staff was chockablock with anti-Semites—Merrill McPeak, who suggested that American Jews were controlling politicians (a common anti-Semitic slur); Zbigniew Brzezinski, one of Obama's foreign policy advisors and a former Jimmy Carter national security advisor, who agrees with McPeak that Jews control American politics; Al Sharpton, who has called New York Jews "bloodsuckers" and "white interlopers"; Samantha Power, his current special assistant, who suggested that America place troops on the ground *in Israel* to stop the Jews from engaging in anti-Palestinian human rights violations.

Worst of all is Obama's association with Media Matters, a deeply anti-Semitic organization filled to the gills with anti-Israel bigots. M. J. Rosenberg, Media Matters' senior foreign policy fellow, routinely used the white supremacist anti-Semitic slur "Israel Firster" to describe any Jew who was hawkish on Israel. Only after Alan Dershowitz pointed out the nastiness of Obama's association with Media Matters did Obama pressure Media Matters to throw Rosenberg under the bus.

But that didn't solve Media Matters' little anti-Semitism problem. Eric Boehlert, senior fellow at Media Matters, wrote a piece on September 11, 2001, for Salon.com in which he quoted a Muslim stating, "We won't rest until all the Jews are dead." Boehlert lamented, "In the wake of the WTC attacks, however, those brash sentiments were muted." It's a good indicator you're an anti-Semite when you think "kill the Jews" is no more than a "brash sentiment." And Boehlert didn't stop there. He defended Professor Sami Al-Arian ("God cursed those who are sons of Israel. . . . Those people, God made monkeys and pigs") as an "innocent." He thinks that media coverage of Israel isn't anti-Israel enough, and suggests that Jewish pressure affects journalism.[35]

And there's Oliver Willis, too. Willis is a prominent research fellow at Media Matters; he once referred to Paul Wolfowitz as "filthy" and Joe Lieberman as "fascistic." He accused Israel of "Playing Games With American Lives," and he said he wanted to tell both Israel and the Palestinians "to go to hell." He wanted the Democratic Party to "marginalize" pro-Israel liberals. He defended the "Israel Firsters'" anti-Semitic nastiness.[36]

This is Obama's favorite group.

So, what does Obama himself think about Israel? His actions speak louder than his words—but his words, too, speak rather loudly. When he visited Cairo to speak to the Muslim world in February 2009, Obama sent a subtle message about the legitimacy of the state of Israel. And it wasn't good. "[T]he aspiration for a Jewish homeland is rooted in a tragic history that cannot be denied," said Obama. "Around the world, the Jewish people were persecuted for centuries, and anti-Semitism in Europe culminated in an unprecedented Holocaust."

This is a massively problematic reading of Israel's raison d'être. It suggests that Israel exists only due to anti-Semitic persecution. It ignores Israel's historic ties to the land. It ignores Israel's religious ties to the land. It reduces Israel to a colonialist outpost thrust in the midst of Muslim land. Obama doesn't have to believe the Pentateuch. But if he's going to quote the Koran when talking about what Muslims think, he ought to quote the Bible when talking about the basis for the state of Israel.

Obama's actions have been worse than his words. He has held the Palestinians to no standard at all with regard to their anti-Semitism—in fact, in April 2012, Obama unilaterally disregarded Congress's call to cut off aid to the Palestinians after Mahmoud Abbas tried to declare Palestinian statehood at the UN. Instead Obama handed them $192 million of U.S. taxpayer dollars. His spokesperson lied and stated, "[T]he PA [Palestinian Authority] had fulfilled all its major obligations, such as recognizing Israel's right to exist, renouncing violence and accepting the Road Map for Peace."[37] Which is somewhat like saying that the Taliban have renounced violence, accepted the presence of secularism in Afghanistan, and declared their willingness to engage in the political process. Or pretending that the Egyptian Muslim Brotherhood is a worthy anti-violence organization without anti-Semitic aspirations—and then cutting them an enormous foreign aid check. Oh, wait. Obama did all that, too.

Leaving aside Obama's shoddy treatment of Israeli prime minister Benjamin Netanyahu—Obama has repeatedly snubbed Bibi behind the scenes,[38] and agreed with then–French president Nicolas Sarkozy on an open mic that Bibi was a liar—Obama's policies on Israel have been consistently anti-Israel. Back in 2008, after he said that he wanted Jerusalem to remain undivided, he quickly backtracked—he couldn't state that the capital of the Jewish state should remain Jewish.[39] A couple of years later, Obama called on Israel to return to its suicidal pre-1967 borders[40]—borders so indefensible that inside Israel they're often referred to as the Auschwitz borders. In fact, his State Department later refused to say whether Jerusalem was even a part of Israel. At all.[41]

And then there's Obama's treatment of Israel with regard to Iran. This alone shows the Obama administration to be the biggest anti-Israel bully administration in American history. In April 2009, Secretary of State Hillary Clinton warned Israel that if it didn't make concessions to the Palestinians, the Arab world might not lend it support in its fight against Iran going nuclear. This was a tacit threat. That threat became explicit the next month when supposed pro-Israel thugmaster Rahm "Dead Fish" Emanuel visited the American Israel Public Affairs Committee, where he told major AIPAC donors that "thwarting Iran's nuclear program is conditional on progress in peace negotiations between Israel and the Palestinians." In other words, the United States would let Iran go nuclear unless Israel ponied up to the Palestinian terror regime.[42]

The Obama administration was so desperate to protect Iran's burgeoning nuclear anti-Semitic genocidal regime that it has routinely leaked Israeli security secrets, sinking any Israeli attempt to strike at Iran's nuclear facilities. In June 2010, the *Times* of London reported that the Saudis had cut a deal with the Israelis to allow Israel to use their airspace for a strike on Iran. According to the *Jerusalem Post*, the report was sourced to a "US defense source."[43]

In February 2012, Defense Secretary Leon Panetta announced in the *Washington Post* that Israel might strike Iran in April, May, or June. Why would Panetta do that? Explained the *Post*, "President Obama and Panetta are said to have cautioned the Israelis that the United States opposes an attack, believing that it would derail an increasingly successful international economic sanctions program and other non-military efforts to stop Iran from crossing the threshold."[44]

Then, in March 2012, another leak—this one absolutely devastating for Israel's attempts to defend herself. *Foreign Policy* magazine reported that Israel had created ties with Azerbaijan that would allow Israel to use that country's airbases as a stopover point for an aerial attack on Iran's facilities. Who leaked it? According to *Foreign Policy*, "four senior diplomats and military intelligence officers."[45]

And then another. In June 2012, the Obama administration leaked that the Stuxnet computer virus, which devastated Iran's nuclear production capabilities for well over a year, was a joint U.S.-Israel project.[46]

So it's safe to say that the Obama administration is far less concerned with Israel's security than Iran's. And this is the worst form of bullying—revealing the secrets of another sovereign ally in order to undermine their national security.

Obama knows he's vulnerable with the Jewish community. To shore up his collapsing support in the Jewish community, he's teamed up with the anti-Semitic bully front group J Street. J Street, for those who haven't heard of it, is the Jewish equivalent of Media Matters—it's a nonprofit organized to do the bidding of the secular bullies in the Obama administration. Its entire business model is predicated on finding self-hating Jews willing to criticize Israel ceaselessly. And its chief funder is self-hating Jew George Soros, who says that Israel is essentially the sole rationale for resurgent world anti-Semitism. A militant secularist, Soros says, "I don't deny the Jews their right to a national existence—but I don't want to be a part of it."[47] Except that he *does* deny that right, by denying Israel's legitimacy.

And he's the man behind J Street, which acts out his vision. When M. J. Rosenberg of Media Matters came under fire for his "Israel Firster" garbage, J Street—purportedly a pro-Israel organization, remember—*defended him*. "If the charge is that you're putting the interests of another country before the interests of the United States in the way you would advocate that, it's a legitimate question," self-hating Jew Jeremy Ben Ami, president of J Street, said. Why would J Street defend such a piece of human *dreck*? Because one of J Street's biggest funders is—no coincidence—one of Media Matters' biggest funders.[48]

J Street has even sided with a group of radical leftists who propose boycotting Israel—a tactic only the worst anti-Semites would use. J Street hosted the book launch party of Peter Beinart, a newfound anti-Israel poseur who suggests that the way to help promote Israel among young Jews is to tear it limb from limb in the press.[49] They ushered Richard Goldstone, author of the virulently anti-Semitic *Goldstone Report*, around Capitol Hill;[50] the report, which falsely labeled Israel a massive human rights violator, was so nasty that even Goldstone later apologized for it. J Street acted in concert with the National Iranian American Council, suggesting that Iran not be subject to new sanctions. The J Street PAC took cash from one of the producers of the virulently anti-Semitic film *Valley of the Wolves*, in which Jewish doctors steal Muslim organs.[51]

Were the Obama administration not anti-Semitic, this would seem like the last group with which they'd want to associate.

Not so much.

Early in the administration, the Israeli newspaper *Haaretz* reported, "The Obama administration appears to be welcoming the efforts of the left-leaning Jewish lobby in Washington, J Street.

"While Israel's ambassador to the U.S. will probably not be attending the group's October 25 conference, senior U.S. administration officials who have confirmed their participation include James Jones, national security adviser in the Obama administration. . . . Senior members of J Street have had close ties to senior figures in the Obama campaign, and since he was elected, they have been consulted by the administration."[52]

That warmth has only increased. J Street honchos have held fund-raisers for Obama.[53] Valerie Jarrett spoke at J Street to push the Obama reelection campaign.[54] In May, J Street published—then scrubbed—a video showing Carinne Luck, J Street's vice president for campaigns, stating that "the administration" and people "on the Hill" want J Street to push American Jews to the left, and to "provide [the left] with cover."[55] This sort of coordination between the Obama administration and an organization specifically dedicated to bullying Israel and Jewish advocates isn't just despicable, it's downright vomit-inducing—especially considering that Obama lies to Jews that he has Israel's back.

Secularism underlies all of this. It's no coincidence that the anti-Israel agenda is led by secular leftists, many of whom are ethnically Jewish (or, as I call them, Jews In Name Only). Karl Marx was the first such self-hating Jew—and he hated his own Jewishness because he was a secular bully. "What is the Jew's foundation in this world? Usury. What is his worldly god? Money," wrote Marx. "Money is the zealous one God of Israel, beside which no other God may stand. . . . The bill of exchange is the Jew's real God. . . . Only then could Jewry become universally dominant. . . . The social emancipation of Jewry is the emancipation of society from Jewry."

This sort of rhetoric isn't exactly popular nowadays. But the secularist anti-Semitic bullies haven't changed much. They simply substitute Israel for Jewry and they're good to go. Tony Kushner, writer of the anti-Israel travesty *Munich*, which makes excuses for the murder of eleven Israeli athletes at the 1972 Olympics by Palestinians, says that "the founding of the State of Israel was for the Jewish people a historical, moral, political calamity." Not coincidentally, he feels that religion generally, and Judaism in particular, are invested with "a tremendous amount of prejudice."[56] Noam Chomsky hates Israel—and, not coincidentally, thinks that religion is "irrational." Chomsky also hates the "Christian fundamentalist right" and therefore despises their support for Israel. He suggests that Israel be dissolved and a binational state take its place.

This is anti-Semitic bullying. It fundamentally denies the legitimacy of another point of view; it suggests that Judaism should not have the same right to respect as other religions, and that Jews do not deserve their own state—a unique proposition that the anti-Semitic bullies never aim at the nearly fifty Muslim countries dotting the globe. And it all springs not from honest appraisal of Israel's flaws or strengths, but from a secular dislike of the Bible, the Jewish role in the world, and the very concept of a separate Jewish way of life.

CONCLUSION

The secular bullies do not like religion. What's more, they don't want religious values expressed in nondenominational legislation. They want religion removed from the public square—and they scorn religious believers with the hatred of a Karl Marx. They don't like Christians. They don't like Jews. They don't like Mormons. They don't like anyone who has the temerity to base their value system on anything like a Judeo-Christian scriptural system.

Just check the polling data. When it comes to Jews, 70 percent of Republicans have a positive evaluation of Jews; just 51 percent of Democrats do. Catholics? Republicans are warmer, 68 to 51. Methodists? Republicans like them better, by a 67–51 margin. Mormons? Republicans are friendlier by a 12-point margin. Evangelical Christians: 32 points. Unbelievably, Republicans and Democrats are actually dead even when it comes to positive evaluation of Muslims—even though liberals like to pretend that conservatives are anti-Semites and Islamophobes. As it turns out, Democrats are *way* bigger anti-Semites, and neither group really likes Muslims all that much. The only areas of religious thought in which Democrats outpace Republicans: atheism and Scientology.[57] So at least Tom Cruise and John Travolta can sign their checks to Barack Obama and sleep easy between massage therapies.

The secular bully media, of course, plays it as though evangelical Christians aren't just bigoted Taliban types when it comes to atheism, an ever-present theocracy lurking in the wings—they act as though conservative Christians are also the people who won't vote Mormon. This meme has grabbed center stage with the nomination of Mitt Romney as the Republican candidate for president. Martin Bashir of MSNBC, who seems more intelligent because he has a British accent, said that "the vast majority of evangelicals . . . believe Mormonism is a cult . . . [and] they share Mark Twain's view of the Book of Mormon, which in 1861, as you probably know, he described it as 'chloroform in print.' And that's what many of these people believe."[58] Dennis Wagner wrote in *USA Today*, "[R]eligious discrimination remains an obstacle for Mormon political candidates for president and a vexation for members of the church."[59] Michelangelo Signorile, who spends most of his days staking out people's bedrooms so he can out them, says that Mormons are the new gays: "Mitt Romney is very much like a gay Republican. . . . No matter how much Romney joins in the bullying of gays, he continues to get bullied himself by the same gang of thugs for being a Mormon."[60]

Sure, there are Christians who won't vote for Romney thanks to his religious beliefs. But there are *way* more secular bigots who won't vote for Romney for the same reason—and they'll make fun of his religious practices to boot. The polls show that anti-Mormon bias has skyrocketed among liberals ever since Mormons became politically involved. Since 2007, anti-Mormon bias among secularists has jumped from 21 percent to 41 percent; among liberals, that number has jumped from 28 percent to 43 percent. As for evangelicals, the numbers have actually *dropped*, from 36 percent in 2007 to 33 percent in 2012.[61]

If you don't believe the stats, just take a look at secularist hatred for Mormons. Mormons were nice folks when they were leaving the Folger's on the supermarket shelves and avoiding the Coke machines. But when they got all uppity and started wanting to influence American politics according to Judeo-Christian values, then they were worthy of mockery. Thus the gorgeous and brilliant Joy Behar of Al Gore's Current TV (current viewership: Keith Olbermann's cats) ranted, "I'd like to see his house burn, one of his millions of houses burning down. Who's he going to call, the Mormon fire patrol?"[62] Cher, who is not a transvestite, called Romney "Uncaring Richie Rich! The whitest man in MAGIC UNDERWEAR in the WH."[63] And intellectual giant Charles Blow of the *New York Times* tweeted, "Let me just tell you this Mitt 'Muddle Mouth': I'm a single parent and my kids are 'amazing'! Stick that in your magic underwear."[64] Blow still works for the *Times;* the *Times* still blows. Coincidence?

As soon as Mormons had the temerity to start acting out traditional values on the national stage, the targets were painted on their backs by the secular bullies. The moment Mormons stood up for traditional marriage in California, they found themselves relentlessly mocked. They were told to sit down and shut up. If that sort of open hatred had been directed at Muslims, the press would have gone nuts. It was directed at Mormons, so the press picked up a bat and started whacking that piñata.

But that's how it works for the secular bullies. Religion is never to be part of the political conversation, unless it's being blamed for bombings or bigotry. America, say the secular bullies, has no roots in the Judeo-Christian tradition. Because the secular bullies have taken over our major cultural institutions, they've been able to implement their vision of society, despite the opposition of the vast majority of Americans, who still believe in Judeo-Christian values. Undoubtedly, the Supreme Court will soon rule that same-sex marriage is mandated by the Constitution of the United States—and religious people will be told that they must allow public schools to instruct their kids in gay history, as they already do in California.

The true threat to American values isn't the Christian going door to door with a Bible. It's the secular bullies going network to network, school to school, and church to church with legal and rhetorical clubs.

CONCLUSION

★

I hate bullies.

I entered high school at the age of thirteen—and I entered as a sophomore, skipping freshman year. Since I didn't hit my major growth spurt until I was sixteen, the year I graduated, I wasn't just younger than the rest of my class, I was significantly shorter. As in five foot two and 110 pounds throughout most of high school.

This meant that bullies targeted me regularly. I spent my share of time on the receiving end of both fists and belts; I learned to keep my head down and my grades up. I went to the administration, but they did nothing about it. After all, I was at a private school, and these were rich kids, and the school cared more about their parents' cash than about preventing physical abuse on campus.

And then one day, I decided I'd had enough.

One of the bigger bullies considered himself a terrific athlete, and had visions of playing baseball on scholarship in college. As it turned out, his opinion of his own athletic ability was approximately as accurate as his perception of his intelligence (he was a moron).

On this particular day, he started picking on me just as he always did. Only this time, I talked back to him. He threatened to beat me up. I told him to go ahead and try.

Now, I wasn't bulky. I wasn't muscular. But I was relatively quick, and so I was able to slip through his grasp. I scampered around the room avoiding him, until I finally undercut his legs. He went down, and I proceeded to hold him down. The other kids cheered in disbelief and mockery for this now-unfortunate thug.

Well, they cheered for a moment.

Then a couple of his friends pulled me off him. He regained his feet, then proceeded to thrash me. Once I was on the floor again, he placed a desk on top of me—one of those chair-desk all-in-one deals—and then sat on the chair for the rest of the class. The teachers did nothing.

So I lost. But he didn't bother me as much anymore.

Here's the takeaway: bullies don't stop bullying until somebody fights them. In today's political world—and for the last few decades—the biggest bullies have been almost universally on the left. It is the left that uses thug tactics to silence voices rather than celebrating the grand panoply that makes up American politics. It is the left that tells Americans that political unity is more important than freedom of speech. It is the left that uses the clubs of race and class to attack those on the right; it is the left that labels religious people and traditional values people rubes and simpletons, and tells them that their perspective has no place in the public square; it is the left that creates environmental crises out of whole cloth, then rams remunerative measures down our collective throats. It is the left that tells us that it is unpatriotic to be patriotic. And most of all, it is the left that uses our most powerful institutions—the institutions through which we connect with each other and build common bonds—to tear us apart.

So we have to fight the left.

In the days leading up to Andrew Breitbart's death, Andrew was increasingly concerned with a new phenomenon dreamt up by the radical leftist bullies: SWATting. In his last broadcast radio interview, on Hugh Hewitt's show, Andrew talked about this new and sickening phenomenon: "[O]ne of the things they've done to people who have worked with me in the past, including an L.A. prosecutor, is to 'SWAT.'. . . It's happened twice: once in New Jersey, once in Los Angeles, with an L.A. County . . . prosecutor who [is] associated with me."

Here's what SWATting was. Anonymous leftists would target conservatives. They would then imitate the phone numbers of conservatives and call 911. They would tell the operators that they had murdered a loved one; the SWAT team would then show up, guns blazing. The risk of death was tremendous.

The Los Angeles County prosecutor to whom Breitbart referred was Patrick Frey, also known in the blogosphere as Patterico. And here's what happened to him: "At 12:35 a.m. on July 1, 2011, sheriff's deputies pounded on my front door and rang my doorbell. They shouted for me to open the door and come out with my hands up. When I opened the door, deputies pointed guns at me and ordered me to put my hands in the air. I had a cell phone in my hand. Fortunately, they did not mistake it for a gun. They ordered me to turn around and put my hands behind my back. They handcuffed me. They shouted questions at me: IS THERE ANYONE ELSE IN THE HOUSE? and WHERE ARE THEY? and ARE THEY ALIVE? I told them: *Yes, my wife and my children are in the house. They're upstairs in their bedrooms, sleeping. Of* course *they're alive. . . .* Meanwhile, police rushed into my home. They woke up my wife, led her downstairs and to the front porch, frisked her, and asked her where the children were. Then police ordered her to stand on the front porch with her hands against the wall while they entered my children's bedrooms to make sure they were alive. The call that sent deputies to my home was a hoax. Someone had pretended to be me. They called the police to say I had shot my wife."[1]

It didn't happen just to Frey. It also happened to Red State founder and CNN contributor Erick Erickson; luckily, Erickson had already warned the cops that somebody might try such a tactic.[2]

Who was behind the SWATtings? The evidence is still unclear.

But there were many on the right who speculated that the circumstances point to the involvement of Brett Kimberlin. Kimberlin is the cofounder of Velvet Revolution, a far-left site devoted to calling for the arrest and prosecution of nonliberals. But there's more to Kimberlin than involvement with a little-known thug website. He's a convicted domestic terrorist also known as the Speedway Bomber. In 1981, Kimberlin planted a series of bombs throughout Indianapolis; he blew up a police cruiser and maimed one Carl DeLong so badly that DeLong had to have a leg amputated. DeLong later committed suicide; his wife won a $1.6 million civil suit against Kimberlin. Kimberlin has also been involved with drug running, impersonation of federal officials, and receipt of explosives. Kimberlin claimed publicly that he had sold pot to former vice president Dan Quayle.

These days, Kimberlin's organization receives cash from the George Soros–funded Tides Foundation.[3] He has bragged on court tape that he speaks regularly with congressmen—undoubtedly Democrats.[4] In Kimberlin's spare time, he files frivolous lawsuits against conservatives.[5] Columnist Robert Stacy McCain says that Kimberlin harasses conservatives with the most brutal of thug tactics—tactics so egregious that McCain himself was forced to flee the state of Maryland "to ensure the safety of my family and others who might be endangered if Kimberlin resorts to violence to accomplish his malicious purposes."[6]

Not every leftist is like Kimberlin. Most aren't. But Kimberlin represents the political theology of the left: the ends justify the means. The right disowns Timothy McVeigh. The left funds Brett Kimberlin. Deep down, they are thugs, and they will not stop until they are stopped.

"I'm a soldier in this war," Andrew told me hours before he died. "And I'm not going to back down against these people. Because if they win, they will not stop until they have destroyed the country I love. F— them."

I got the call about Andrew's death the next morning from

Alex Marlow, Andrew's right hand and first employee at Big Hollywood. Like everyone else, I was stunned. Andrew was a life force. Unflinchingly honest, unvaryingly uncompromising in the face of thuggery, Andrew—as his lifelong friend and Breitbart News business partner Larry Solov said—was willing to take slings and arrows on behalf of others. His instinct was to protect. When a leftist bully launched an attack, Andrew would spring into action. His jaw would jut out. He'd smile—but behind his eyes, there was no smile. He'd enter battle mode. Game on.

And now he was gone.

And the revisionist history began.

Now Andrew wasn't a bully-fighter. He was a bully himself, according to the left. "Provocateur, website founder and collector of America's largest wads of spittle Andrew Breitbart died last Thursday morning, when some sentient shred of his cardiac organ kamikazed out of an exhausted sense of justice," wrote one columnist at Gawker. "Like any good bully, Breitbart picked his targets well."[7] This is sick stuff, but it wasn't an atypical feeling from members of the left, who were still sore from Andrew's destruction of ACORN and exposing of Anthony Weiner. Every element of the leftist bullies' arsenal came out against Andrew's memory. He was a racist; he was a sexist; he was a homophobe; he was a bigot. Commentators like Howard Kurtz of CNN said Andrew left a "mixed legacy." Touré—whom Andrew had once jokingly suggested should host a show called "That Broccoli Is Racist," because to Touré, everything is racist—promptly said that Andrew had been "dangerous" and "offensive."[8] David Frum, columnist for the *Daily Beast* and a supposed Republican always eager to attack other conservatives, said that Andrew's "impact upon American media and American politics . . . [was] poisonous."[9] *Slate*'s Matthew Yglesias, a man whose neural circuitry could power an Easy-Bake-Oven—said, "The world outlook is slightly improved with @AndrewBreitbart dead."[10]

The torch had been dropped; the vultures were circling.

But Andrew was always about more than just Andrew. He was

about creating a movement of people who would be emboldened to speak their minds and join the debate. And as the torch fell, a million hands reached to hold it aloft. Those were the hands Andrew had trained; they were Americans Andrew had inspired. Across Twitter, the hashtags #IAmBreitbart and #BreitbartIsHere began trending. Posters of Andrew's face began appearing at events across the country.

It wasn't because Andrew was a folk hero, though he was. It was because Andrew empowered everyone else to stand up to the bullies. He wasn't just a shield. He was a testament that you could—to use his phrase—walk toward the fire, and have a wonderful time doing it. As he once told me, "Walk toward the fire. Don't worry about what they call you. All those things are said against you because they want to stop you in your tracks. But if you keep going, you're sending a message to people who are rooting for you, who are agreeing with you. The message is that they can do it, too."

But it took guts to do that. It took bravery. Andrew was brave.

So are the American people.

We've spent decades being cowed by the jackboots of the politically correct: the race-baiters, class warriors, secularist and scaremongering thugs. We have bowed to their whims. We've tried to be polite; they've spit in our faces, then blamed us for debasing the level of our national discourse. They've tried to minimize the number of voices in the political arena. And we've gone along with it because we pine for a time when Americans can all share their hopes and dreams together, rather than quarreling over what separates us. We want *E Pluribus Unum*—"from many, one"; they want the opposite, "from one, many."

We were willing to stay quiet if we could have our *E Pluribus Unum*. But it hasn't worked. We haven't been left in peace. For every inch we've given to the left, they've sought to bully us into handing over a mile.

That must end now.

"My goal," Andrew told me, "is to try and teach as many people as possible *not* to be fearful of sending a message to these people: we reject your worldview the same way you reject ours. I want to bottle that. I want to teach everyone that I know that they don't have to fear anymore, that there's strength in numbers. My entire business model is trying to accumulate an army that takes that mind-set and says, 'Not only can you take the assaults from the bullies, they'll make you stronger. Not only will they make you stronger, you'll have the power to punch back. You can go on the offensive.' These people have spent so many years on the offense with people not punching back, they don't know what it's like to be on defense, and when you come after them hard, they are defenseless."

There is only one way to stop a bully: to punch back. We've seen who the bullies are and what they've done. Now it's time to fight them.

NOTES

★

INTRODUCTION

1. Nick Gillespie, "Stop Panicking About Bullies," *Wall Street Journal*, April 2, 2012, http://online.wsj.com/article/SB10001424052702303404704577311664105746848.html, accessed June 2012.

2. "Remarks by the President and First Lady at the White House Conference on Bullying Prevention," WhiteHouse.gov, March 10, 2011, http://www.whitehouse.gov/the-press-office/2011/03/10/remarks-president-and-first-lady-white-house-conference-bullying-prevent, accessed June 2012.

3. Gillespie, "Stop Panicking About Bullies."

4. Jonathan Capehart, "Bullying is not a rite of passage," *Washington Post*, March 10, 2011, http://www.washingtonpost.com/blogs/post-partisan/post/bullying-is-not-a-rite-of-passage/2011/03/04/ABBpIrQ_blog.html, accessed June 2012.

5. Amie Parnes, "Obama puts the bully in bully pulpit," TheHill.com, April 14, 2012, http://thehill.com/homenews/administration/221469-obama-puts-bully-in-bully-pulpit, accessed June 2012.

1: INSTITUTIONAL BULLIES

1. Howard Kurtz, "The Press, Turning Up Its Nose at Lame Duck," *Washington Post*, February 5, 2007, http://www.washingtonpost.com/wp-dyn/content/article/2007/02/04/AR2007020401280_pf.html, accessed June 2012.

2. KC Johnson, "March Madness, II," Durham-In-Wonderland, March 18, 2007, http://durhamwonderland.blogspot.com/2007/03/march-madness-ii.html, accessed July 2012.

3. "Transcripts: New Developments in Duke Rape Investigation," *Nancy Grace* (CNN), June 9, 2006, http://transcripts.cnn.com/TRANSCRIPTS/0606/09/ng.01.html, accessed July 2012.

4. Duff Wilson and Jonathan D. Glater, "Files From Duke Rape Case Give Details but No Answers," *New York Times*, September 18, 2006, http://today.duke.edu/showcase/mmedia/pdf/nytimes825.pdf, accessed July 2012.

5. Rachel Smolkin, "Justice Delayed," *American Journalism Review*, August/September 2007, http://www.ajr.org/article.asp?id=4379, accessed July 2012.

6. Scott Whitlock, "ABC Looks at Media Bias in Duke Rape Case; Ignores Example From Own Network," Newsbusters.org, September 4, 2007, http://newsbusters.org/blogs/scott-whitlock/2007/09/04/abc-looks-media-bias-duke-rape-case-ignores-example-own-network, accessed June 2012.

7. Smolkin, "Justice Delayed."

8. Michael Calderone, "JournoList: Inside the echo chamber," Politico.com, March 17, 2009, http://www.politico.com/news/stories/0309/20086.html, accessed July 2012.

9. Alex Pareene, "Breitbart's JournoList bounty and the secret Republican listserv leak," Salon.com, June 29, 2010, http://www.salon.com/2010/06/29/dc_listserv_scandal/, accessed July 2012.

10. Ezra Klein, "On JournoList, and Dave Weigel," *Washington Post*, June 25, 2010, http://voices.washingtonpost.com/ezra-klein/2010/06/on_journolist_and_dave_weigel.html, accessed July 2012.

11. Jonathan Strong, "E-mails reveal Post reporter savaging conservatives, rooting for Democrats," DailyCaller.com, June 25, 2010, http://dailycaller.com/2010/06/25/emails-reveal-post-reporter-savaging-conservatives-rooting-for-democrats/?print=1, accessed July 2012.

12. Michael O'Brien, "Obama open to newspaper bailout bill," TheHill.com, September 20, 2009, http://thehill.com/blogs/blog-briefing-room/news/59523-obama-open-to-newspaper-bailout-bill/, accessed July 2012.

13. Glenn Thrush, "Switching Allegiances," NewsDay.com, September 6, 2006, http://www.newsday.com/news/switching-allegiances-1.690641, accessed July 2012.

14. Chuck Todd, "Calling out Media Matters' bias," MSNBC.com, November 15, 2007, http://firstread.msnbc.msn.com/_news/2007/11/15/4429164-calling-out-media-matters-bias, accessed June 2012.

15. Ibid.

16. Jacques Steinberg, "An All-Out Attack on 'Conservative Misinformation,'" *New York Times*, October 31, 2008, http://www.nytimes.com/2008/11/01/washington/01media.html?_r=1, accessed July 2012.

17. Ibid.

18. Betsy Rothstein, "Fighting ire with fire," TheHill.com, November 3, 2008, http://thehill.com/capital-living/24113-fighting-ire-with-fire, accessed June 2012.

19. Jack Shafer, "Media Madders," Reuters.com, February 15, 2012, http://blogs.reuters.com/jackshafer/tag/david-brock/, accessed July 2012.

20. Tucker Carlson, Vince Coglianese, Alex Pappas, and Will Rahn, "Inside Media Matters: Sources, memos reveal erratic behavior, close coordination with White House and news organizations," DailyCaller.com, February 12, 2012, http://dailycaller.com/2012/02/12/inside-media-matters-sources-memos-reveal-erratic-behavior-close-coordination-with-white-house-and-news-organizations/?print=1, accessed July 2012.

21. Alan Dershowitz, "Media Matters Hurts Obama," FoxNation.com, February 28, 2012, http://nation.foxnews.com/media-matters/2012/02/28/alan-dershowitz-media-matters-hurts-obama, accessed July 2012.

22. Ben Shapiro, "Exodus: MJ Rosenberg Sacrificed For Media Matters' Sins," Breitbart News, April 6, 2012, http://www.breitbart.com/Big-Journalism/2012/04/06/Exodus-MJ-Rosenberg-Out-Media-Matters, accessed July 2012.

23. Will Rahn, "Media Matters tax-exempt status may face new scrutiny from Congress," DailyCaller.com, February 15, 2012, http://dailycaller.com/2012/02/15/media-matters-tax-exempt-status-may-face-new-scrutiny-from-congress/, accessed July 2012.

24. "What are my Kids Learning? Poll Shows Professors Fail Presidential History," Townhall.com, February 21, 2012, http://townhall.com/columnists/townhallcomstaff/2012/02/21/what_are_my_kids_learning_poll_shows_professors_fail_presidential_history/page/full/, accessed July 2012.

25. Howard Kurtz, "College Faculties A Most Liberal Lot, Study Finds," *Washington Post*, March 29, 2005, http://www.washingtonpost.com/wp-dyn/articles/A8427-2005Mar28.html, accessed July 2012.

26. "What are my Kids Learning? Poll Shows Professors Fail Presidential History."

27. Kurtz, "College Faculties A Most Liberal Lot, Study Finds."

28. Paul Johnson, *Modern Times* (New York: Harper Perennial, 1992), 643–44

29. Jill Laster, "College Makes Students More Liberal, but Not Smarter About Civics," *Chronicle of Higher Education*, February 5, 2010, http://chronicle.com/article/College-Makes-Students-More/64040/, accessed July 2012.

30. Peter Wood, "College for All: Obama's Higher-Education Agenda, Part 3 of 8," *Chronicle of Higher Education*, March 6, 2012, http://chronicle.com/blogs/innovations/college-for-all-obamas-higher-education-agenda-part-3-of-8/31832, accessed July 2012.

31. John Cook, "Bloodthirsty Bully Harvey Weinstein Releases Movie About Bullies," Gawker.com, March 30, 2012, http://gawker.com/5897885/bloodthirsty-bully-harvey-weinstein-releases-movie-about-bullies, accessed August 2012.

32. Jonah Goldberg, "Funny Girl," NationalReview.com, December 7, 2005, http://old.nationalreview.com/goldberg/goldberg200512071123.asp, accessed July 2012.

33. "Barbra Streisand's bed demands," FemaleFirst.co.uk, December 4, 2008, http://www.femalefirst.co.uk/celebrity/Barbara+Streisand-23862.html, accessed July 2012.

34. "Carey's Gum-Chum," ContactMusic.com, November 5, 2005, http://www.contactmusic.com/news-article/careys-gumchum, accessed July 2012.

35. Garance Franke-Ruta, "Mitt Romney criticizes Obama for focusing on health care, instead of jobs," *Washington Post*, March 5, 2010, http://voices.washingtonpost.com/44/2010/03/mitt-romney-criticizes-obama-f.html, accessed July 2012.

36. Robert Pear, "Obama's Health Plan, Ambitious in Any Economy, Is Tougher in This One," *New York Times*, March 1, 2009, http://www.nytimes.com/2009/03/02/us/politics/02health.html?pagewanted=all, accessed July 2012.

37. Ben Shapiro, "President Bush's Roberts pick disappoints," Creators Syndicate, July 20, 2005, available at http://townhall.com/columnists/benshapiro/2005/07/20/president_bushs_roberts_pick_disappoints/page/full/, accessed July 2012.

38. Jan Crawford, "Roberts switched views to uphold health care law," CBSNews.com, July 1, 2012, http://www.cbsnews.com/8301-3460_162-57464549/roberts-switched-views-to-uphold-health-care-law/, accessed July 2012.

39. Corbett B. Daly, "Obama: Supreme Court overturning health care would be 'unprecedented,'" CBSNews.com, April 2, 2012, http://www.cbsnews.com/8301-503544_162-57408181-503544/obama-supreme-court-overturning-health-care-would-be-unprecedented/, accessed July 2012.

2: ANTI-PATRIOTIC BULLIES

1. Scott Macleod, "How al-Arabiya Got the Obama Interview," Time.com, January 28, 2009, http://www.time.com/time/world/article/0,8599,1874379,00.html, accessed June 2012.

2. "[TRANSCRIPT] Obama's interview with Al Arabiya," AlArabiya.net, January 27, 2009, http://www.alarabiya.net/articles/2009/01/27/65096.html, accessed June 2012.

3. "Remarks By President Obama To The Turkish Parliament," WhiteHouse.gov, April 6, 2009, http://www.whitehouse.gov/the_press_office/Remarks-By-President-Obama-To-The-Turkish-Parliament/, accessed June 2012.

4. "Remarks By President Obama At Strasbourg Town Hall," WhiteHouse.gov, April 3, 2009, http://www.whitehouse.gov/the_press_office/Remarks-by-President-Obama-at-Strasbourg-Town-Hall/, accessed June 2012.

5. "Remarks By The President At The Summit Of The Americas Opening

Ceremony," WhiteHouse.gov, April 17, 2009, http://www.whitehouse.gov/the_press_office/Remarks-by-the-President-at-the-Summit-of-the-Americas-Opening-Ceremony/, accessed June 2012.

6. Jake Tapper, "Chavez Gifts Obama With Book That Assails U.S. for Exploiting Latin America," ABCNews.com, April 18, 2009, http://abcnews.go.com/blogs/politics/2009/04/chavez-gifts-ob/, accessed June 2012.

7. Peter Nicholas, "Obama defends greeting Hugo Chavez," *Los Angeles Times*, April 20, 2009, http://articles.latimes.com/2009/apr/20/world/fg-obama-americas20, accessed June 2012.

8. "Remarks By The President To CIA Employees," WhiteHouse.gov, April 20, 2009, http://www.whitehouse.gov/the_press_office/Remarks-by-the-President-to-CIA-employees-at-CIA-Headquarters/, accessed June 2012.

9. "Remarks By The President On National Security," WhiteHouse.gov, May 21, 2009, http://www.whitehouse.gov/the_press_office/Remarks-by-the-President-On-National-Security-5-21-09, accessed June 2012.

10. "The President's News Conference in Strasbourg," April 4, 2009, in *Public Papers of the Presidents of the United States: Barack Obama, 2009, Book 1* (Washington, DC: U.S. Government Printing Office, 2010).

11. "Obama in Dover as fallen troops arrive home," WashingtonPost.com, October 29, 2009, http://voices.washingtonpost.com/44/2009/10/29/obama_in_dover_as_fallen_troop.html, accessed June 2012.

12. Philip Elliott, "Obama Gets Warning From Friendly Voter," Associated Press, August 14, 2007, http://www.washingtonpost.com/wp-dyn/content/article/2007/08/14/AR2007081400812.html, accessed June 2012.

13. Ken Thomas, "Obama praises Vietnam veterans' contributions," Associated Press, May 29, 2012, http://bostonglobe.com/news/nation/2012/05/28/president-obama-says-vietnam-veterans-too-often-denigrated/gcPDrcip9sb6WeIZefkccM/story.html, accessed June 2012.

14. Lee-Ann Goodman, "John Kerry acting as key Obama surrogate, fuelling secretary of state buzz," Associated Press, April 30, 2012, http://news.yahoo.com/john-kerry-acting-key-obama-surrogate-fuelling-secretary-202823487.html, accessed June 2012.

15. Barack Obama, *Dreams from My Father* (New York: Three Rivers Press, 2004), ix–x.

16. "Doug Feith: 'The President wants to cut America down to size,'" CNN.com, March 23, 2011, http://globalpublicsquare.blogs.cnn.com/2011/03/23/doug-feith-the-president-wants-to-cut-america-down-to-size/, accessed June 2012.

17. Jonah Goldberg, *The Tyranny of Clichés* (New York: Sentinel, 2012).

18. Matthew Shaffer, "Ten Liberal Perspectives on Manning," NationalReview.com, March 14, 2011, http://www.nationalreview.com/blogs/print/262108, accessed June 2012.

19. Maureen Dowd, "Why No Tea and Sympathy?,"*New York Times*, August 10, 2005, http://www.nytimes.com/2005/08/10/opinion/10dowd.html, accessed June 2012.

20. Jonah Goldberg, *Liberal Fascism: The Secret History of the American Left, from Mussolini to the Politics of Change* (New York: Broadway Books, 2009), 112–13.

21. Ibid., 154, 159.

22. Ibid., 176.

23. James Jones, *The Thin Red Line* (New York: Delta Trade Paperbacks, 1998).

24. Howard Zinn, "The Scourge of Nationalism," Progressive.org, June 2005, http://www.progressive.org/node/199/, accessed June 2012.

25. Kevin Gillies, "The Last Radical," *Vancouver*, November 1998, http://www.columbia.edu/cu/computinghistory/1968/radical.html, accessed June 2012.

26. Senate Judiciary Committee, *Report of the Subcommittee to Investigate the Administration of the Security Act and Other Internal Security Laws of the Committee of the Judiciary* (Washington, DC: U.S. Government Printing Office, 1975), 5, 8–9, 13, 18, 137–47.

27. Jonah Goldberg, "Peace Lovers All," NationalReview.com, October 7, 2008, http://www.nationalreview.com/corner/171406/peace-lovers-all/jonah-goldberg, accessed June 2012.

28. "Vietnam War Veteran John Kerry's Testimony Before The Senate Foreign Relations Committee," April 22, 1971, https://facultystaff.richmond.edu/~ebolt/history398/JohnKerryTestimony.html, accessed June 2012.

29. Bryant Jordan, "Obama Praises Vietnam Vets at Memorial Wall," Military.com, May 29, 2012, http://www.military.com/daily-news/2012/05/29/obama-praises-vietnam-vets-at-memorial-wall.html, accessed June 2012.

30. Sam Roberts, "The Port Huron Statement at 50," *New York Times*, March 3, 2012, http://www.nytimes.com/2012/03/04/sunday-review/the-port-huron-statement-at-50.html?pagewanted=all, accessed June 2012.

31. Tom Hayden, "The Port Huron Statement: A manifesto reconsidered," *Los Angeles Times*, May 6, 2012, http://articles.latimes.com/2012/may/06/opinion/la-oe-hayden-port-huron-statement-20120506, accessed June 2012.

32. "Tom Hayden," Discoverthenetworks.org, http://www.discoverthenetworks.org/individualProfile.asp?indid=1334, accessed June 2012.

33. Tom Hayden, "An Endorsement of the Movement Barack Obama Leads," Huffingtonpost.com, January 27, 2008, http://www.huffingtonpost.com/tom-hayden/an-endorsement-of-the-mov_b_83478.html, accessed June 2012.

34. Dinitia Smith, "No Regrets for a Love Of Explosives," *New York Times*, September 11, 2001, http://www.nytimes.com/2001/09/11/books/no-regrets-for-love-explosives-memoir-sorts-war-protester-talks-life-with.html?pagewanted=all, accessed June 2012.

35. Jonathon Seidl, "Calif. School Orders Boy To Remove American Flag From

Bike," TheBlaze.com, November 12, 2010, http://www.theblaze.com/stories/calif-school-orders-boy-to-remove-american-flag-from-bike/, accessed June 2012.

36. Jonathon M. Seidl, "School Responds: Boy Forced To Remove Flag For His Own 'Safety,' Can Fly It Again," TheBlaze.com, November 12, 2010, http://www.theblaze.com/stories/school-responds-boy-forced-to-remove-flag-for-his-own-safety/, accessed June 2012.

37. "National Furor Over California School's American Flag Ban," Thomas More Law Center, June 25, 2010, http://www.thomasmore.org/press-releases/2010/06/national-furor-over-california-school-s-american-flag-ban, accessed June 2012.

38. "Morgan Hill Students Lose Lawsuit Over Right To Wear Flag," SanFrancisco.cbslocal.com, November 11, 2011, http://sanfrancisco.cbslocal.com/2011/11/11/morgan-hill-students-lose-lawsuit-over-right-to-wear-flag/, accessed June 2012.

39. "Teacher Deems American Flag 'Offensive,'" FoxNews.com, May 10, 2010, http://nation.foxnews.com/american-flag/2010/05/10/teacher-deems-american-flag-offensive, accessed June 2012.

40. Melica Johnson, "Apartment residents told to take down U.S. flags," KATU.com, October 19, 2009, http://www.katu.com/news/local/64059697.html, accessed June 2012.

41. "Flag ban lifted at Oaks Apartments after outcry," KATU.com, October 14, 2009, http://www.katu.com/news/local/64262707.html, accessed June 2012.

42. Randy Streu, "Property and Patriotism: Army vet forced to remove flag on pain of eviction," RedState.com, May 26, 2012, http://www.redstate.com/rstreu/2010/05/26/property-and-patriotism-army-vet-forced-to-remove-flag-on-pain-of-eviction/, accessed June 2012.

43. Susan Edelman, "School pulls patriotic song at graduation, but Justin Bieber's 'Baby' is OK," *New York Post*, June 9, 2012, http://www.nypost.com/p/news/local/school_silences_patriotic_song_xdunXcLPbE8S2rAEcZoUiP?utm_medium=rss%26utm_content=Local, accessed June 2012.

44. *Real Time with Bill Maher*, June 8, 2012.

45. John Sexton, "Exclusive—The Vetting—Barack Obama, The First Tea Partier," Breitbart.com, May 23, 2012, http://www.breitbart.com/Big-Government/2012/05/23/Exclusive-The-Vetting-Barack-Obama-First-Tea-Partier, accessed June 2012.

46. Department of Homeland Security, "Rightwing Extremism: Current Economic and Political Climate Fueling Resurgence in Radicalization and Recruitment," MichelleMalkin.com, April 7, 2009, http://s.michellemalkin.com/wp/wp-content/uploads/2009/04/hsa-rightwing-extremism-09-04-07.pdf, accessed June 2012.

47. Jennifer Steinhauser, "Arizona Shooting Casts a Harsh Light on the State," NYTimes.com, January 9, 2011, http://www.nytimes.com/2011/01/10/us/10arizona.html?_r=2&src=twt&twt=nytimes, accessed June 2012.

48. Jack Mirkinson, "Megyn Kelly Debates Sheriff Clarence Dupnik About His Comments On Arizona Shooting," Huffingtonpost.com, January 9, 2011, http://www.huffingtonpost.com/2011/01/09/megyn-kelly-debates-clarence-dupnik_n_806521.html, accessed June 2012.

49. "Dupnik calls tea party members bigots," *Arizona Daily Star*, September 10, 2010, http://azstarnet.com/news/blogs/pueblo-politics/article_ea73f980-c4f4-11df-a52b-001cc4c03286.html, accessed June 2012.

50. Andrew Malcolm, "Have gun, Will talk: Arizona Sheriff Clarence Dupnik not speechless over Tucson shootings or much else," *Los Angeles Times*, January 11, 2011, http://latimesblogs.latimes.com/washington/2011/01/clarence-dupnik-tucson-shootings-gabrielle-giffords.html, accessed June 2012.

51. Paul Krugman, "Climate of Hate," *New York Times*, January 9, 2011, http://www.nytimes.com/2011/01/10/opinion/10krugman.html, accessed June 2012.

52. Adam Clark Estes, "Jon Stewart on shooting: No idea how to process this," Salon.com, January 11, 2011, http://www.salon.com/2011/01/11/jon_stewart_arizona_shooting/, accessed June 2012.

53. "Keith Olbermann Issues Special Comment On Arizona Shooting: 'Violence Has No Place In Democracy,'" HuffingtonPost.com, January 8, 2011, http://www.huffingtonpost.com/2011/01/08/keith-olbermann-arizona-shooting_n_806311.html, accessed June 2012.

54. Leslie Minora, "Keith Olbermann Calls Out Conservatives for Inciting Tucson Shooting, Includes Allen West, Repents," BrowardPalmBeach.com, January 9, 2011, http://blogs.browardpalmbeach.com/pulp/2011/01/tucson_shooting_gabrielle_giffords_olbermann.php, accessed June 2012.

55. Scott Whitlock, "The Worst of the Worst: A Look Back at Keith Olbermann's Most Outrageous Quotes," Newsbusters.org, January 24, 2011, http://newsbusters.org/blogs/scott-whitlock/2011/0½4/worst-worst-look-back-keith-olbermanns-most-outrageous-quotes, accessed June 2012.

56. James Piereson, *Camelot and the Cultural Revolution* (New York: Encounter Books, 2007), 88–97.

57. "Bush warns against Arab-American backlash," BBC News, September 13, 2001, http://news.bbc.co.uk/2/hi/americas/1540371.stm, accessed June 2012.

58. Howard Zinn, *A People's History of the United States: 1492–Present* (New York: Harper Perennial, 2005), 681.

59. "Just days after 9/11, Ron Paul blames America," TheRightScoop.com, December 26, 2011, http://www.therightscoop.com/just-days-after-911-ron-paul-blames-america/, accessed June 2012.

60. Michael Sheridan, "Tom Hanks attacked by conservatives over 'racism' in war remarks while promoting 'The Pacific,'" *New York Daily News*, March 17, 2010, http://articles.nydailynews.com/2010-03-17/news/27059287_1_racism-iraq-and-afghanistan-terror, accessed June 2012.

61. Michael Buchanan, "US Muslims fight 9/11 backlash," BBC News, September 11, 2003, http://news.bbc.co.uk/2/hi/americas/3098568.stm, accessed June 2012.

62. Associated Press, "For Muslims, backlash fear builds each 9/11," MSNBC.com, September 11, 2009, http://www.msnbc.msn.com/id/32782444/ns/us_news-9_11_eight_years_later/t/muslims-backlash-fear-builds-each/#.T9TAxGBsg1c, accessed June 2012.

63. Ahmed Rashid, "After 9/11, Hate Begat Hate," *New York Times*, September 11, 2011, http://www.nytimes.com/2011/09/11/opinion/sunday/and-hate-begat-hate.html?pagewanted=all, accessed June 2012.

64. "Durbin Apologizes for Nazi, Gulag, Pol Pot Remarks," FoxNews.com, June 22, 2005, http://www.foxnews.com/story/0,2933,160275,00.html, accessed June 2012.

65. Ben Shapiro, "Why the 'chickenhawk' argument is un-American: Part I," Creators Syndicate, August 17, 2005, available at http://townhall.com/columnists/benshapiro/2005/08/17/why_the_chickenhawk_argument_is_un-american_part_i/page/full/, accessed June 2012.

66. Paul Whitefield, "Mitt Romney, the pandering chicken hawk on Iran," *Los Angeles Times*, March 5, 2012, http://opinion.latimes.com/opinionla/2012/03/obama-aipac-speech-romney-iran-saber-rattling-enough.html, accessed June 2012.

67. James Joyner, "John Kerry: Get An Education or Get Stuck in Iraq," OutsideTheBeltway.com, October 31, 2006, http://www.outsidethebeltway.com/john_kerry_get_an_education_or_get_stuck_in_iraq/, accessed June 2012.

68. Tim Kane and James Jay Carafano, "Whither the Warrior—the Truth About Wartime Recruiting," *Army Magazine*, May 2006, http://www.army.mil/professionalWriting/volumes/volume4/june_2006/6_06_3.html, accessed June 2012.

69. Benedict Carey, Damien Cave, and Lizette Alvarez, "Painful Stories Take a Toll on Military Therapists," *New York Times*, November 8, 2009, http://www.nytimes.com/2009/11/08/us/08stress.html?partner=rss&emc=rss, accessed June 2012.

70. Tabassum Zakaria, "General Casey: Diversity shouldn't be casualty of Fort Hood," Reuters.com, November 8, 2009, http://blogs.reuters.com/talesfromthetrail/2009/11/08/general-casey-diversity-shouldnt-be-casualty-of-fort-hood/, accessed June 2012.

71. "Transcript: President Obama's Memorial Day remarks at Vietnam War Memorial," FoxNews.com, May 28, 2012, http://www.foxnews.com/politics/2012/05/28/transcript-president-obama-memorial-day-remarks-at-vietnam-war-memorial/, accessed June 2012.

72. "Text of Obama's Speech in Afghanistan," *New York Times*, May 1, 2012, http://www.nytimes.com/2012/05/02/world/asia/text-obamas-speech-in-afghanistan.html?pagewanted=all, accessed June 2012.

73. White House, "WEEKLY ADDRESS: A New Chapter in Afghanistan," WhiteHouse.gov, May 5, 2012, http://www.whitehouse.gov/the-press-office/2012/05/05/weekly-address-new-chapter-afghanistan, accessed June 2012.

76. Jacob Laskin, "The Truth About The Troops," FrontPageMag.com, November 26, 2007, http://archive.frontpagemag.com/readArticle.aspx?ARTID=28954, accessed June 2012.

77. "U.S. troops battle both Taliban and their own rules," WashingtonTimes.com, November 16, 2009, http://www.washingtontimes.com/news/2009/nov/16/us-troops-battle-taliban-afghan-rules/, accessed June 2012.

78. Gina Cavallaro, "Stephen Colbert: 'There's nothing more patriotic than a Marine fart,'" MilitaryTimes.com, September 23, 2011, http://militarytimes.com/blogs/battle-rattle/tag/farting/, accessed June 2012.

79. "July 4 Celebrations Make Children More Likely To Become Republican: Harvard Study," HuffingtonPost.com, August 31, 2011, http://www.huffingtonpost.com/2011/07/01/july-4-republicans-harvard_n_888659.html, accessed June 2012.

80. *Texas v. Johnson*, 491 U.S. 397 (1989), at 420–21.

3: RACE BULLIES

1. "Trayvon Martin was suspended three times from school," MSNBC.com, March 26, 2012, http://usnews.msnbc.msn.com/_news/2012/03/26/10872124-trayvon-martin-was-suspended-three-times-from-school?lite, accessed June 2012.

2. David Martosko, "The Daily Caller obtains Trayvon Martin's tweets," March 26, 2012, http://dailycaller.com/2012/03/26/the-daily-caller-obtains-trayvon-martins-tweets/, accessed June 2012.

3. David Jackson, "Obama says his son would look like Trayvon," *USA Today*, March 23, 2012, http://content.usatoday.com/communities/theoval/post/2012/03/obama-my-son-would-look-like-trayvon/1#.T9gMvGBsg1c, accessed June 2012.

4. Devin Dwyer, "Why Did Obama Speak Out on Trayvon?," ABCNews.com, March 23, 2012, http://abcnews.go.com/blogs/politics/2012/03/why-did-obama-speak-out-on-trayvon/, accessed June 2012.

5. Chris Francescani, "George Zimmerman: Prelude to a shooting," Reuters.com, April 25, 2012, http://www.reuters.com/article/2012/04/25/us-usa-florida-shooting-zimmerman-idUSBRE83O18H20120425, accessed June 2012.

6. William Deutsch, "A Transcript of the George Zimmerman Police Call," About.com, http://bizsecurity.about.com/od/creatingpolicies/a/A-Transcript-Of-The-George-Zimmerman-Police-Call.htm, accessed June 2012.

7. William Bigelow, "Witness: Trayvon Martin Attacked George Zimmerman 'MMA Style,'" Breitbart News, May 18, 2012, http://www.breitbart.com/Big-Government/2012/05/18/Trayvon-MMA-style-attack, accessed June 2012.

8. "Autopsy results reportedly indicate Trayvon Martin suffered injuries to knuckles," FoxNews.com, May 16, 2012, http://www.foxnews.com/us/2012/05/16/autopsy-results-reportedly-indicate-trayvon-martin-suffered-injuries-to/, accessed June 2012.

9. "Trayvon Martin: police sought arrest warrant against George Zimmerman," *Telegraph* (UK), March 29, 2012, http://www.telegraph.co.uk/news/worldnews/northamerica/usa/9172831/Trayvon-Martin-police-sought-arrest-warrant-against-George-Zimmerman.html, accessed June 2012.

10. Mike Schneider, "Family wants answers in Fla. teen's death," Yahoo.com, March 8, 2012, http://news.yahoo.com/family-wants-answers-fla-teens-death-162019527.html, accessed June 2012.

11. "Statement By Reverend Al Sharpton and National Action Network Regarding The Shooting of Trayvon Martin," NationalActionNetwork.net, March 12, 2012, http://nationalactionnetwork.net/press/statement-by-reverend-al-sharpton-and-national-action-network-regarding-the-shooting-of-trayvon-martin/, accessed June 2012.

12. Charles M. Blow, "The Curious Case of Trayvon Martin," *New York Times*, March 16, 2012, http://www.nytimes.com/2012/03/17/opinion/blow-the-curious-case-of-trayvon-martin.html?_r=2&ref=charlesmblow, accessed June 2012.

13. Dylan Stableford, "Trayvon Martin shooting: Debate over photos escalates," The Cutline, March 28, 2012, http://news.yahoo.com/blogs/cutline/trayvon-martin-shooting-debate-over-photos-escalates-155103512.html, accessed June 2012.

14. Joel Pollak, "The Trayvon Timeline: How Local Crime Story Became National Racial Outrage," Breitbart News, March 29, 2012, http://www.breitbart.com/Big-Journalism/2012/03/29/The-Trayvon-Timeline-How-a-Local-Crime-Story-Became-a-National-Racial-Outrage, accessed June 2012.

15. Bianca Prieto, "Trayvon Martin: 'We are gathered here today to demand justice' in teen's fatal shooting," *Orlando Sentinel*, March 14, 2012, http://articles.orlandosentinel.com/2012-03-14/news/os-trayvon-martin-shooting-death-rally-20120314_1_shooting-death-bryant-chief-bill-lee, accessed June 2012.

16. Arelis R. Hernandez, "Trayvon Martin: New Black Panthers offer $10,000 bounty for capture of shooter George Zimmerman," *Orlando Sentinel*, March 24, 2012, http://articles.orlandosentinel.com/2012-03-24/news/os-trayvon-martin-new-black-panthers-protest-20120324_1_sanford-vigilante-justice-black-men, accessed June 2012.

17. Jeff Kunerth, "Trayvon Martin death could be turning point, says the Rev. Jesse Jackson," *Orlando Sentinel*, March 25, 2012, http://articles.orlandosentinel.com/2012-03-25/news/os-trayvon-martin-jesse-jackson-20120325_1_hoodie-civil-rights-voter-registration, accessed June 2012.

18. Ben Shapiro, "Local FOX Insider: Martin Shot In Back of Head," Breitbart News, March 26, 2012, http://www.breitbart.com/Big-Government/2012/03/26/Martin-Back-Head, accessed June 2012.

19. Paul Bond, "NBC News Accused of Editing 911 Call in Trayvon Martin Controversy," HollywoodReporter.com, March 30, 2012, http://www.hollywoodreporter.com/news/trayvon-martin-nbc-news-editing-911-call-306359, accessed June 2012.

20. Tommy Christopher, "CNN Isolates Audio On Alleged 'F*cking C**ns' Trayvon Martin 911 Call," Mediaite.com, March 22, 2012, http://www.mediaite.com/tv/cnn-isolates-audio-on-alleged-%E2%80%98fcking-cns%E2%80%99-trayvon-martin-911-call/, accessed June 2012.

21. Tim Graham, "CNN Walks It Back: Oops, Zimmerman Didn't Say 'Coon,' He Said It was 'Cold'!," Newsbusters.org, April 6, 2012, http://newsbusters.org/blogs/tim-graham/2012/04/06/cnn-walks-it-back-oops-zimmerman-didnt-say-coon-he-said-it-was-cold, accessed June 2012.

22. Matt Gutman, "Trayvon Martin Case: Exclusive Surveillance Video of George Zimmerman," ABCNews.com, March 28, 2012, http://abcnews.go.com/US/trayvon-martin-case-exclusive-surveillance-video-george-zimmerman/story?id=16022897#.T9qxdGCo44Q, accessed June 2012.

23. Steve Frank, "Video reveals no blood or bruises on Trayvon Martin shooter George Zimmerman," MSNBC.com, March 28, 2012, http://ed.msnbc.msn.com/_news/2012/03/28/10909685-video-reveals-no-blood-or-bruises-on-trayvon-martin-shooter-george-zimmerman?lite, accessed June 2012.

24. Rich Abdill, "Frederica Wilson on Trayvon Martin: 'I Am Tired of Burying Young Black Boys,'" BrowardPalmBeach.com, March 21, 2012, http://blogs.browardpalmbeach.com/pulp/2012/03/frederica_wilson_trayvon_martin.php, accessed June 2012.

25. Alicia M. Cohn, "Rep. Maxine Waters: 'Stiff evidence' of hate crime in Trayvon Martin case," TheHill.com, March 28, 2012, http://thehill.com/video/house/218677-rep-waters-stiff-evidence-death-of-trayvon-martin-a-hate-crime-, accessed June 2012.

26. Mike Lillis, "Trayvon Martin's parents suggest racial profiling was responsible for his death," TheHill.com, March 27, 2012, http://thehill.com/homenews/house/218613-trayvon-martins-parents-suggest-racial-profiling-was-responsible-for-his-death-, accessed June 2012.

27. Rosalind S. Helderman, "Rep. Bobby Rush chided for wearing hoodie on House floor for Trayvon Martin," *Washington Post*, March 28, 2012, http://www.washingtonpost.com/blogs/2chambers/post/rep-bobby-rush-wears-hoodie-on-house-floor-for-trayvon-martin/2012/03/28/gIQAlf8WgS_blog.html, accessed June 2012.

28. Dan Riehl, "Hoodie-Wearing Gunmen Kill 1, Wound 5 in Bobby Rush's Chicago District," Breitbart News, March 30, 2012, http://www.breitbart.com/Big-Government/2012/03/30/Hoodie-Wearing-Gunmen-Kill-1-Wound-5-in-Rushs-Chicago-District, accessed June 2012.

29. Richard Winton, "LAPD: In stores, keep hoodie on, but lower the hood," LATimes.com, March 30, 2012, http://latimesblogs.latimes.com/lanow/2012/03/lapd-hoodie-law.html, accessed June 2012.

30. Ben Shapiro, "Twitter Buzzes With Talk of Zimmerman Riots," Breitbart News, April 23, 2012, http://www.breitbart.com/Big-Government/2012/04/23/Zimmerman-riots-Trayvon-Twitter, accessed June 2012.

31. Mytheos Holt, "Al Sharpton Threatens Civil Disobedience if George Zimmerman Not Arrested," TheBlaze.com, March 30, 2012, http://www.theblaze.com/stories/al-sharpton-threatens-civil-disobedience-if-george-zimmerman-not-arrested/, accessed June 2012.

32. Alyssa Newcomb, "Spike Lee Incorrectly Tweets Address of George Zimmerman," ABCNews.com, March 28, 2012, http://abcnews.go.com/blogs/headlines/2012/03/spike-lee-incorrectly-tweets-address-of-george-zimmerman/, accessed June 2012.

33. James Taranto, "'Riot Is the Voice of the Unheard,'" *Wall Street Journal*, April 6, 2010, http://online.wsj.com/article/SB10001424052702303411604575168041790910582.html, accessed June 2012.

34. Ben Shapiro, "Media Ignores Occupy's Violent Hijacking of Trayvon Martin," Breitbart News, March 23, 2012, http://www.breitbart.com/Big-Journalism/2012/03/23/Media-Ignore-Occupy-Violence, accessed June 2012.

35. Nancy Pfotenhauer, "The Real Reason the Left Is Attacking ALEC," USNews.com, April 23, 2012, http://www.usnews.com/opinion/blogs/nancy-pfotenhauer/2012/04/23/the-real-reason-the-left-is-attacking-alec, accessed June 2012.

36. 2011 Florida Statutes, Chapter 776, Justifiable Use of Force.

37. Jonathan Capehart, "Stand Your Ground hearing: The risk for George Zimmerman and the prosecution," *Washington Post*, June 12, 2012, http://www.washingtonpost.com/blogs/post-partisan/post/stand-your-ground-hearing-the-risk-for-george-zimmerman-and-the-prosecution/2012/06/12/gJQAzx58WV_blog.html, accessed June 2012.

38. Eugene Robinson, "Repeal the 'Stand Your Ground' law," *Washington Post*, March 26, 2012, http://www.washingtonpost.com/opinions/repeal-the-stand-your-ground-law/2012/03/26/gIQAptsvcS_story.html, accessed June 2012.

39. "Lawyer: Family of Trayvon Martin to pursue civil case," CNN.com, March 24, 2012, http://www.cnn.com/2012/03/24/justice/florida-teen-shooting/index.html, accessed June 2012.

40. "Rally for Trayvon Martin in Front of ALEC Headquarters," PRWatch.org, March 28, 2012, http://www.prwatch.org/news/2012/03/11390/rally-trayvon-martin-front-alec-headquarters, accessed June 2012.

41. Corey Dade, "The Fight Over Voter ID Laws Goes To The United Nations," NPR.org, March 9, 2012, http://www.npr.org/blogs/itsallpolitics/2012/03/09/148291825/the-fight-over-voter-id-laws-goes-to-the-united-nations, accessed June 2012.

42. Paul Bedard, "Coke caves in face of Democratic boycott threats," WashingtonExaminer.com, April 4, 2012, http://washingtonexaminer.com/politics/washington-secrets/2012/04/coke-caves-face-democratic-boycott-threat/444346, accessed June 2012.

43. Peter Overby, "Boycotts Hitting Group Behind 'Stand Your Ground,'" NPR .org, April 5, 2012, http://www.npr.org/2012/04/05/150013705/boycotts-hitting-group-behind-stand-your-ground, accessed June 2012.

44. Rebekah Wilce, "Breaking News: Coca-Cola Dumps ALEC," PRWatch.org, April 5, 2012, http://www.prwatch.org/news/2012/04/11413/breaking-news-coca-cola-dumps-alec, accessed June 2012.

45. Bedard, "Coke caves in face of Democratic boycott threats."

46. Eric Lichtblau, "ALEC Halts Advocacy of Laws Like Stand Your Ground," *New York Times*, April 18, 2012, http://www.nytimes.com/2012/04/18/us/trayvon-martin-death-spurs-group-to-readjust-policy-focus.html, accessed June 2012.

47. Ben Smith, "Obama on small-town Pa.: Clinging to religion, guns, xenophobia," Politico.com, April 11, 2008, http://www.politico.com/blogs/bensmith/0408/Obama_on_smalltown_PA_Clinging_religion_guns_xenophobia.html, accessed June 2012.

48. "NPR chief ousted after exec's racism remarks," MSNBC.com, http://www.msnbc.msn.com/id/41986715/ns/politics-more_politics/t/npr-chief-ousted-after-execs-racism-remarks/, accessed June 2012.

49. Kyle Drennen, "MSNBC: ObamaCare Protesters 'Racist,' Including Black Gun-Owner," Newsbusters.org, August 18, 2009, http://newsbusters.org/blogs/kyle-drennen/2009/08/18/msnbc-no-mention-black-gun-owner-among-racist-protesters, accessed June 2012.

50. Noel Sheppard, "Morgan Freeman: Obama Made Racism Worse, Tea Party Will Do 'Whatever [It] Can To Get This Black Man Outta Here,'" Newsbusters .org, September 23, 2011, http://newsbusters.org/blogs/noel-sheppard/2011/09/23/morgan-freeman-obama-has-made-racism-worse-tea-party-will-do-whatever, accessed June 2012.

51. Matt Kibbe, "Another actor, another baseless tea party racist claim," DailyCaller .com, October 18, 2011, http://dailycaller.com/2011/10/18/another-actor-another-baseless-tea-party-racism-claim/, accessed June 2012.

52. Ibid.

53. Kenneth T. Walsh, "Obama Says Race a Key Component in Tea Party Protests," USNews.com, March 2, 2011, http://www.usnews.com/news/articles/2011/03/02/obama-says-race-a-key-component-in-tea-party-protests_print.html, accessed June 2012. The article is an excerpt from Walsh's *Family of Freedom: Presidents and African Americans in the White House* (Boulder, CO: Paradigm, 2010).

54. Jim Hoft, "Racist Leftist Infiltrators Driven From Tea Party Rallies," TheGatewayPundit.com, April 16, 2010, http://www.thegatewaypundit.com/2010/04/racist-leftist-infiltrators-driven-from-tea-party-rallies-video/, accessed June 2012.

55. Jim Galloway, "Breitbart offers $10k reward for proof that n-word was hurled at John Lewis," *Atlanta Journal-Constitution*, March 26, 2010, http://blogs.ajc

.com/political-insider-jim-galloway/2010/03/26/breitbart-offers-10k-reward-for-proof-that-n-word-was-hurled-at-john-lewis/, accessed June 2012.

56. Touré, "The Racial Cold War Is Heating Up," Time.com, April 11, 2012, http://ideas.time.com/2012/04/11/the-racial-cold-war-is-heating-up/, accessed June 2012.

57. Jonah Goldberg, "Playing the race card again," *Los Angeles Times*, March 27, 2012, http://articles.latimes.com/2012/mar/27/opinion/la-oe-goldberg-trayvon-martin-race-20120327, accessed June 2012.

58. Heather Horn, "Europe Sees History of American Racism in Trayvon Martin Killing," TheAtlantic.com, April 3, 2012, http://www.theatlantic.com/international/archive/2012/04/europe-sees-history-of-american-racism-in-trayvon-martin-killing/255362/, accessed June 2012.

59. "MSNBC's Michael Eric Dyson Smears Conservatives as Racists: View Obama Like 'He's a Moron, He's An Orangutan, He's An Animal,'" Weasel Zippers, April 16, 2012, http://weaselzippers.us/2012/04/16/msnbcs-michael-eric-dyson-smears-conservatives-as-racists-view-obama-like-hes-a-moron-hes-an-orangutan-hes-an-animal/, accessed June 2012.

60. Brian Stelter, "Reporter Interrupts Obama During Statement on Immigration," *New York Times*, June 15, 2012, http://mediadecoder.blogs.nytimes.com/2012/06/15/reporter-interrupts-obama-during-statement-on-immigration/, accessed June 2012.

61. Noel Sheppard, "MSNBC's Touré: Obama Being Interrupted 'Cannot Be Disconnected From The Fact That He's Black'," Newsbusters.org, June 15, 2012, http://newsbusters.org/blogs/noel-sheppard/2012/06/15/msnbc-s-tour-obama-being-interrupted-cannot-be-disconnected-fact-he-s#ixzz1xv9SfTbO, accessed June 2012.

62. Michael Calderone, "Sam Donaldson Rejects Comparison To Reporter Who Interrupted Obama," HuffingtonPost.com, June 16, 2012, http://www.huffingtonpost.com/2012/06/16/sam-donaldson-tucker-carlson-daily-caller-obama-interrupted_n_1602526.html, accessed June 2012.

63. Joe Newby, "MSNBC, Politico suggest racism behind reporter's questioning of Obama," Examiner.com, June 16, 2012, http://www.examiner.com/article/msnbc-politico-suggest-racism-behind-reporter-s-questioning-of-obama, accessed June 2012.

64. *Brown v. Board of Education of Topeka*, 349 U.S. 294 (1955).

65. *Regents of the University of California v. Bakke*, 438 U.S. 265 (1978).

66. Malcolm X, *The Autobiography of Malcolm X* (New York: Ballantine Books, 1999), 208.

67. Tom Wolfe, "These Radical Chic Evenings," in Wolfe, *The Purple Decades: A Reader* (New York: Farrar, Straus & Giroux, 1982), 183–84. The essay originally appeared in *New York* magazine on June 8, 1970, as "Radical Chic: That Party at Lenny's."

68. Cardinal Lawyer, "Critical Race Theory: Of the Racists, By the Racists, and For the Racists," Breitbart News, April 2, 2012, http://www.breitbart.com/Big-Government/2012/04/02/Critical-Race-Theory-Of-the-Racists-By-the-Racists-and-For-the-Racists, accessed June 2012.

69. Richard Delgado and Jean Stefancic, *Critical Race Theory: An Introduction* (New York: New York University Press, 2012), 7–8.

70. Krissah Thompson, "2008 voter-intimidation case against New Black Panthers riles the right," *Washington Post*, July 15, 2010, http://www.washingtonpost.com/wp-dyn/content/article/2010/07/14/AR2010071405880.html, accessed June 2012.

71. James Taranto, "Majorities Say the Darnedest Things," *Wall Street Journal*, July 12, 2010, http://online.wsj.com/article/SB10001424052748704288204575363012084806400.html, accessed June 2012.

72. Benny Johnson, "Don't Miss The Connection: Obama 'Delivered' to Office By Black Panthers, Holder 'Owes Them Some Favors,'" TheBlaze.com, May 22, 2012, http://www.theblaze.com/stories/dont-miss-the-connection-obama-and-holder-delivered-to-office-by-black-panthers-owe-them-some-favors/, accessed June 2012.

73. Massimo Calabresi, "Is Racism Fueling the Immigration Debate?," *Time*, May 17, 2006, http://www.time.com/time/nation/article/0,8599,1195250,00.html, accessed June 2012.

74. JJ Hensley, Sadi Jo Smokey, and Weston Phippen, "Arizona immigration law: Al Sharpton vows civil disobedience," AZCentral.com, May 6, 2010, http://www.azcentral.com/arizonarepublic/local/articles/2010/05/06/20100506arizona-immigration-law-al-sharpton.html, accessed June 2012.

75. Kristina Wong, "President Obama Says Arizona's 'Poorly-Conceived' Immigration Law Could Mean Hispanic-Americans Are Harassed," ABCNews.com, April 27, 2010, http://abcnews.go.com/blogs/politics/2010/04/president-obama-says-arizonas-poorlyconceived-immigration-law-could-mean-hispanicamericans-are-haras/, accessed June 2012.

76. Howard LaFranchi, "Obama and Calderon agree: Arizona immigration law is wrong," CSMonitor.com, May 19, 2010, http://www.csmonitor.com/USA/Foreign-Policy/2010/0519/Obama-and-Calderon-agree-Arizona-immigration-law-is-wrong, accessed June 2012.

77. Randal C. Archibold, "Arizona Enacts Stringent Law on Immigration," *New York Times*, April 24, 2010, http://www.nytimes.com/2010/04/24/us/politics/24immig.html?ref=us, accessed June 2012.

78. Stephen Dinan, "Holder hasn't read Arizona law he criticized," WashingtonTimes.com, May 13, 2010, http://www.washingtontimes.com/news/2010/may/13/holder-hasnt-read-ariz-law-he-criticized/, accessed June 2012.

79. Donovan Slack, "Jan Brewer tarmac tiff touches nerve in black community, some commentators say," Politico.com, January 28, 2012, http://www.politico

.com/politico44/2012/01/jan-brewer-tarmac-tiff-touches-nerve-in-black-community-112617.html, accessed June 2012.

80. Joel Gehrke, "House Dems trained to make race the issue," WashingtonExaminer.com, May 11, 2012, http://campaign2012.washingtonexaminer.com/blogs/beltway-confidential/house-dems-trained-make-race-issue/537146, accessed June 2012.

81. Tommy Christopher, "O'Keefe Defends CNN 'Sex Boat' Caper and Racial Aspect of ACORN Pimp Costume," Mediaite.com, October 26, 2011, http://www.mediaite.com/online/james-o'keefe-defends-cnn-sex-boat-caper-and-racial-aspect-of-acorn-pimp-costume/, accessed June 2012.

82. Max Blumenthal, "James O'Keefe's race problem," Salon.com, February 3, 2010, http://www.salon.com/2010/02/03/james_okeefe_white_nationalists/, accessed June 2012.

83. "Minstrel Show," *Economist*, February 8, 2010, http://www.economist.com/blogs/democracyinamerica/2010/02/james_okeefe_acorn_and_racial_resentment, accessed June 2012.

4: CLASS BULLIES

1. Jerry Doyle, *Have You Seen My Country Lately?* (New York: Threshold Editions, 2009), 78–93.

2. Ylan Q. Mui, "Americans saw wealth plummet 40 percent from 2007 to 2010, Federal Reserve says," *Washington Post*, June 11, 2012, http://www.washingtonpost.com/business/economy/fed-americans-wealth-dropped-40-percent/2012/06/11/gJQAlIsCVV_story.html, accessed June 2012.

3. Stuart Varney, "Barack Obama Wants to Control the Banks," *Wall Street Journal*, April 4, 2009, http://online.wsj.com/article/SB123879833094588163.html, accessed June 2012.

4. Robert Schmidt and Rebecca Christie, "Geithner Says Banks May Convert Shares, Seek Private Investment," Bloomberg.com, April 22, 2009, http://www.bloomberg.com/apps/news?sid=afdcZEesYddk&pid=newsarchive, accessed June 2012.

5. Eamon Javers, "Inside Obama's bank CEOs meeting," Politico.com, April 3, 2009, http://www.politico.com/news/stories/0409/20871.html, accessed June 2012.

6. Barack Obama, "New Rules," February 4, 2009, http://www.whitehouse.gov/blog_post/new_rules, accessed June 2012.

7. "Joe the Plumber: A Transcript," TampaBay.com, October 19, 2008, http://www.tampabay.com/news/perspective/article858299.ece, accessed June 2012.

8. Randy Ludlow, "Checks on 'Joe' more extensive than first acknowledged," *Columbus Post-Dispatch*, October 29, 2008, http://www.dispatch.com/content/stories/local/2008/10/30/joe30.html, accessed June 2012.

9. Theodore Roosevelt, "New Nationalism Speech," TeachingAmericanHistory.org, http://teachingamericanhistory.org/library/index.asp?document=501, accessed June 2012.
10. Lawrence W. Reed, "Letter to the Editor," *Wall Street Journal*, March 8, 2006, http://www.mackinac.org/archives/2006/030806WSJ-meatpacking.pdf, accessed August 2012.
11. Russell S. Sobel, "Public Health and the Placebo: The Legacy of the 1906 Pure Food and Drugs Act," *Cato Journal*, Vo. 21, No. 3 (Winter 2002), http://www.cato.org/pubs/journal/cj21n3/cj21n3-7.pdf, accessed August 2012.
12. Judson MacLaury, "A Brief History: The U.S. Department of Labor," DOL.gov, http://www.dol.gov/oasam/programs/history/dolhistoxford.htm, accessed June 2012.
13. Todd DePastino, *Citizen Hobo: How a Century of Homelessness Shaped America* (Chicago: University of Chicago Press, 2003), 197–99.
14. Ibid.
15. "Excerpt from John T. Pace's testimony given before the Committee on Un-American Activities of the House of Representatives, July 13, 1951," http://historyproject.ucdavis.edu/lessons/view_lesson.php?id=45, accessed June 2012.
16. Dale C. Meyer, *Lou Henry Hoover: A Prototype for First Ladies* (Hauppauge, NY: Nova History Publications, 2004), 293–95.
17. DePastino, *Citizen Hobo*, 199.
18. Franklin D. Roosevelt, "The Forgotten Man," April 7, 1932.
19. Jonah Goldberg, *Liberal Fascism* (New York: Broadway Books, 2009), 150.
20. DePastino, *Citizen Hobo*, 199.
21. Carlo D'Este, *Eisenhower: A Soldier's Life* (New York: Henry Holt, 2002), 222–23.
22. "The Bonus March: Herbert Hoover's View," *American History*, June 12, 2006, http://www.historynet.com/the-bonus-march-herbert-hoovers-view.htm, accessed June 2012.
23. Franklin D. Roosevelt, "Campaign Address," October 14, 1936, http://teachingamericanhistory.org/library/index.asp?document=2563, accessed June 2012.
24. "Charles E. Coughlin," United States Holocaust Memorial Museum, http://www.ushmm.org/wlc/en/article.php?ModuleId=10005516, accessed June 2012.
25. Goldberg, *Liberal Fascism*, 141.
26. Senator Huey P. Long, "Every Man A King," February 23, 1934, http://www.hueylong.com/programs/share-our-wealth-speech.php, accessed June 2012.
27. "2008: Unions Spent $400 Million to Elect Obama," Politifact.com, February 24, 2011, http://www.politifact.com/truth-o-meter/statements/2011/mar/15/republican-national-committee-republican/rnc-said-unions-raised-400-million-obama-2008/, accessed June 2012.

28. "Transcript: Senator Barack Obama," New Leadership on Health Care: A Presidential Forum, March 24, 2007, http://www.americanprogressaction.org/events/healthforum/fulltranscript.pdf, accessed June 2012.

29. Peter Nicholas, "Obama's curiously close labor friendship," *Los Angeles Times*, June 28, 2009, http://articles.latimes.com/2009/jun/28/nation/na-stern28, accessed June 2012.

30. "Remarks for Senator Barack Obama: AFL-CIO," AFL-CIO, April 2, 2008.

31. Daniel Stone, "What Green Jobs?," *Newsweek*, July 27, 2009, http://www.thedailybeast.com/newsweek/2009/07/27/what-green-jobs.html, accessed June 2012.

32. "Union-Controlled NLRB Approves Union Thuggery in Union Elections," RedState.com, March 13, 2011, http://www.redstate.com/laborunionreport/2011/03/13/union-controlled-nlrb-approves-union-thuggery-in-union-elections/, accessed June 2012.

33. Kris Maher, "President Tells Unions Organizing Act Will Pass," *Wall Street Journal*, March 4, 2009, http://online.wsj.com/article/SB123611995496723249.html, accessed June 2012.

34. Don Loos, "21.1 Million Reasons Big Labor Pours Money Into ObamaCare," BigGovernment.com, January 7, 2010, http://biggovernment.com/dloos/2010/01/07/21-1-million-reasons-big-labor-pours-money-into-obamacare/, accessed June 2012.

35. Newt Gingrich, "Once, We Would Have Called It a Scandal," HumanEvents.com, June 10, 2009, http://www.humanevents.com/article.php?id=32212, accessed December 2011.

36. Ashby Jones, "Product Liability Winners Made Losers by Big Auto Bailouts," *Wall Street Journal*, May 27, 2011, http://blogs.wsj.com/law/2011/05/27/product-liability-winners-made-losers-by-big-auto-bailouts/, accessed December 2011.

37. Armand Thieblot and Thomas Haggard, *Union Violence: The Record and the Response by Courts, Legislatures, and the NLRB* (Philadelphia: University of Pennsylvania Press, 1983), 125.

38. Peter Grier, "How long can Wisconsin protesters occupy the State Capitol?," *Christian Science Monitor*, February 28, 2011, http://www.csmonitor.com/USA/Politics/The-Vote/2011/0228/How-long-can-Wisconsin-protesters-occupy-the-State-Capitol, accessed June 2012.

39. "Jesse Jackson in Wisconsin: We're 'Going To Escalate The Protests,'" RealClearPolitics.com, March 10, 2011, http://www.realclearpolitics.com/video/2011/03/10/jesse_jackson_in_wisconsin_were_going_to_escalate_the_protests.html, accessed June 2012.

40. Dee Hall, "More Than 80 Threats Made Against Walker, Lawmakers and Others, Records Show," *Wisconsin State Journal*, May 13, 2011.

41. Mike Johnson and Jason Stein, "Justice Department Investigating Death Threats Against Republican Senators, Representatives," *Milwaukee Journal-Sentinel*, March 10, 2011.

42. Bill Glauber, "Woman Charged With Email Threats," *Milwaukee Journal Sentinel*, March 31, 2011.

43. Ed Treleven, "Woman placed in first-offenders program for bomb threat to GOP state senators," *Wisconsin State Journal*, December 16, 2011, http://host.madison.com/news/local/crime_and_courts/article_e8322b18-27e7-11e1-b21f-0019bb2963f4.html, accessed June 2012.

44. Richard Moore, "Union Boycotts Against Walker Supporters Sputtering, Fragmenting," *Lakeland (Wis.) Times*, April 15, 2011.

45. Mary Bruce, "Wisconsin Teachers Protest Ed Budget, Union Cuts," ABCNews.com, February 17, 2011, http://abcnews.go.com/Politics/wisconsin-protests-news-wisconsin-governor-scott-walkers-proposal/story?id=12942012, accessed June 2012.

46. Charles Krauthammer, "Union owned and operated," *Chicago Tribune*, June 20, 2011, http://articles.chicagotribune.com/2011-06-20/news/ct-oped-0620-krauthammer-20110620-8_1_president-barack-obama-exports-union-address, accessed June 2012.

47. Nina Easton, "What's really behind SEIU's Bank of America protests?," CNN.com, May 19, 2010, http://money.cnn.com/2010/05/19/news/companies/SEIU_Bank_of_America_protest.fortune/, accessed June 2012.

48. Joe Nocera, "Tea Party's War on America," *New York Times*, August 1, 2011, http://www.nytimes.com/2011/08/02/opinion/the-tea-partys-war-on-america.html?_r=2&partner=rssnyt&emc=rss, accessed June 2012.

49. "NBC News Takes on Tea Party 'Terrorists,'" FoxNews.com, July 29, 2011, http://nation.foxnews.com/nbc-news/2011/07/29/nbc-news-takes-tea-party-terrorists-theyre-strapped-dynamite-sitting-middle-time-square-rush-hour, accessed June 2012.

50. Joe Klein, "Republicans' Debt Ceiling Charade Is Downright Dangerous," Time.com, July 28, 2011, http://swampland.time.com/2011/07/28/republicans-dangerous-debt-ceiling-charade/, accessed June 2012.

51. William Yeomans, "The tea party's terrorist tactics," Politico.com, July 29, 2011, http://www.politico.com/news/stories/0711/60202.html, accessed June 2012.

52. Charlie Spiering, "Biden: Tea Party stopped us from growing economy," WashingtonExaminer.com, May 22, 2012, http://washingtonexaminer.com/article/1307066, accessed June 2012.

53. Mark Duell, "'They're giving frustration a voice': Obama says he understands anger of Occupy Wall Street protesters with banks and economy," *Daily Mail* (UK), October 6, 2011, http://www.dailymail.co.uk/news/article-2046162/Obama-says-understands-anger-Occupy-Wall-Street-protesters-banks-economy.html, accessed June 2012.

54. Ben Shapiro, "Exclusive: SEIU Helps Occupy 'Abolish Capitalism,'" Breitbart

News, March 4, 2012, http://www.breitbart.com/Big-Government/2012/03/04/SEIU-lerner-Occupy, accessed June 2012.

55. "Bored with union organizing, SEIU gears up for thuggery," Washington Examiner.com, January 16, 2012, http://washingtonexaminer.com/article/162306, accessed June 2012.

56. John Sexton, "Occupiers Self-Identify as Socialists, Revolutionaries," Breitbart News, April 30, 2012, http://www.breitbart.com/Big-Government/2012/04/30/occupiers-self-identify-as-socialists-revolutionaries, accessed June 2012.

57. Lauren Gold, "Occupy LA protesters descend on Pasadena home of Bank of America executive," SGVTribune.com, May 8, 2012, http://www.sgvtribune.com/news/ci_20578022/occupiers-protest-bank-america-foreclosures-today-pasadena, accessed June 2012.

58. Katie Feola, "Occupy Wall Street Protesters Target Rupert Murdoch's House," AdWeek.com, October 11, 2011, http://www.adweek.com/news/press/occupy-wall-street-protesters-target-rupert-murdochs-house-135727, accessed June 2012.

59. Linette Lopez, "Guess Who REALLY Planned the Occupy Wall Street Millionaires March," BusinessInsider.com, October 12, 2011, http://articles.businessinsider.com/2011-10-12/wall_street/30269544_1_advocacy-protesters-new-york-communities, accessed June 2012.

60. John Hinderaker, "Occupy Violence: It's Different, Somehow," PowerLineBlog.com, May 4, 2012, http://www.powerlineblog.com/archives/2012/05/occupy-violence-its-different-somehow.php, accessed June 2012.

61. Jason Hoppin and Stephen Baxter, "County compiles list of nearly 100 problems since Occupy Santa Cruz moved in," MercuryNews.com, November 19, 2011, http://www.mercurynews.com/breaking-news/ci_19373284, accessed June 2012.

62. Duell, "'They're giving frustration a voice.'"

63. Peter Wallsten, "Obama plans to turn anti–Wall Street anger on Mitt Romney, Republicans," *Washington Post*, October 14, 2011, http://www.washingtonpost.com/business/economy/obama-plans-to-turn-anti-wall-street-anger-on-mitt-romney-republicans/2011/10/14/gIQAZfiwkL_story.html, accessed June 2012.

64. Justin Elliott, "Obama White House parrots '99 percent' line," Salon.com, October 17, 2011, http://www.salon.com/2011/10/17/obama_white_house_parrots_99_percent_line/, accessed June 2012.

65. Lee Stranahan, "New Video Reveals: New York Times Reporter Natasha Lennard Is #OccupyWallStreet Activist, Supporter," Breitbart News, October 23, 2011, http://cdn.breitbart.com/Big-Government/2011/10/23/New-Video-Reveals-New-York-Times-Reporter-Natasha-Lennard-Is--OccupyWallStreet-Activist--Supporter, accessed June 2012.

66. Ibid.

67. Jennifer Rubin, "Occupy Wall Street: Does anyone care about the anti-Semitism?," *Washington Post*, October 17, 2011, http://www.washingtonpost.com/blogs/right-turn/post/occupy-wall-street-does-anyone-care-about-the-anti-semitism/2011/03/29/gIQA43p8rL_blog.html, accessed June 2012.

68. Ben Shapiro, "Occupy Facebook Page Touts Jew Hating Cartoon," Breitbart News, April 19, 2012, http://www.breitbart.com/Big-Government/2012/04/19/Occupy-Wall-Street-Jew-Hatred, accessed July 2012.

69. Matthew Balan, "Big Three Nets All But Ignore Occupy Oakland Violence and Arrests," Newsbusters.org, October 25, 2011, http://newsbusters.org/blogs/matthew-balan/2011/10/25/big-three-nets-all-ignore-occupy-oakland-violence-and-arrests, accessed June 2012.

70. Matthew Sheffield, "National Media Ignore Would-be Cleveland Terrorists' Occupy Connections," NewsBusters.org, May 2, 2012, http://newsbusters.org/blogs/matthew-sheffield/2012/05/02/national-media-ignore-would-be-cleveland-terrorists-occupy-connec, accessed June 2012.

71. Julia Rubin, "Kanye West Joins Occupy Wall Street In Gold Chains, Givenchy Plaid & Balmain Jeans," PrisonPlanet.com, October 11, 2011, http://www.prisonplanet.com/kanye-west-joins-occupy-wall-street-in-gold-chains-givenchy-plaid-balmain-jeans.html, accessed June 2012.

72. "Michael Moore: Occupy movement 'killed apathy,'" CBSNews.com, October 29, 2011, http://www.cbsnews.com/8301-201_162-20127435/michael-moore-occupy-movement-killed-apathy/, accessed June 2012.

73. Alex Alvarez, "Michael Moore Heckled At Occupy Protest: 'Make Way For $50 Million Michael Moore!,'" Mediaite.com, March 19, 2012, http://www.mediaite.com/online/michael-moore-heckled-at-occupy-protest-make-way-for-50-million-michael-moore/, accessed June 2012.

74. "George Clooney, Penn Badgley Support Occupy Wall Street Protests," TheHollywoodGossip.com, October 7, 2011, http://www.thehollywoodgossip.com/2011/10/george-clooney-penn-badgley-support-occupy-wall-street-protests/, accessed June 2012.

75. Sophie A. Schillaci, "Miley Cyrus Supports Occupy Movement With 'Liberty Walk' Clip," HollywoodReporter.com, November 28, 2011, http://www.hollywoodreporter.com/news/miley-cyrus-occupy-wall-street-liberty-walk-266733, accessed June 2012.

76. Rory Cooper, "President Obama's Enemies List," Heritage.org, April 20, 2012, http://blog.heritage.org/2012/04/20/president-obamas-enemies-list/, accessed June 2012.

77. Kimberly Strassel, "Trolling for Dirt on the President's List," *Wall Street Journal*, May 10, 2012, http://online.wsj.com/article/SB10001424052702304070304577396412560038208.html, accessed June 2012.

78. John McCormack, "Inspector General Will Investigate Obama Admin

for Discussing Koch Tax Status," WeeklyStandard.com, October 5, 2010, http://www.weeklystandard.com/blogs/inspector-general-will-investigate-obama-admin-discussing-koch-tax-status_500861.html, accessed June 2012.

79. Jim Messina, "They're obsessed," BarackObama.com, February 24, 2012, http://www.barackobama.com/news/entry/theyre-obsessed, accessed June 2012.

80. Phillip Ellender, "A Letter to the Obama Campaign," KochFacts.com, February 24, 2012, http://www.kochfacts.com/kf/obamaletter/, accessed June 2012.

81. "Obama Campaign Attacks Koch Brothers," RealClearPolitics.com, May 3, 2012, http://www.realclearpolitics.com/video/2012/05/03/obama_campaign_attacks_koch_brothers.html, accessed June 2012.

82. Glenn Harlan Reynolds, "Tax Audits Are No Laughing Matter," *Wall Street Journal*, May 18, 2009, http://online.wsj.com/article/SB124260113149028331.html, accessed June 2012.

83. Editorial, "What Sheldon Adelson Wants," *New York Times*, June 23, 2012, http://www.nytimes.com/2012/06/24/opinion/sunday/what-sheldon-adelson-wants.html?_r=3, accessed June 2012.

84. William Bigelow, "*New York Times* plagiarizes anti-Adelson language from Obama campaign," Breitbart News, August 17, 2012, http://www.breitbart.com/Big-Journalism/2012/08/17/New-York-Times-replicates, accessed August 2012.

85. Paul Kengor, "The Obama-Axelrod Class-Warfare Machine," Spectator.org, January 13, 2012, http://spectator.org/archives/2012/01/13/the-obama-axelrod-class-warfar, accessed June 2012.

86. Josh Margolin, "Booker's big mouth ruins relationship with Obama, Cabinet hopes," NYPost.com, June 8, 2012, http://www.nypost.com/p/news/national/bam_on_cory_he_dead_to_us_1GuWVs0Tx3HuxZ9mu5SSPJ, accessed June 2012.

87. Robert Reich, "Whose Recovery?," RobertReich.org, March 30, 2012, http://robertreich.org/post/20171217334, accessed June 2012.

88. Jerome Corsi, "Democrats' War on Poverty Has Failed," *Human Events*, September 6, 2006, http://www.humanevents.com/2006/09/06/democrats-war-on-poverty-has-failed/, accessed June 2012.

89. Danielle Kucera, "Facebook Co-Founder Saverin Gives Up U.S. Citizenship Before IPO," Bloomberg.com, May 11, 2012, http://www.bloomberg.com/news/2012-05-11/facebook-co-founder-saverin-gives-up-u-s-citizenship-before-ipo.html, accessed June 2012.

90. Kevin Drawbaugh, "Facebook's Saverin fires back at tax-dodge critics," Reuters, May 17, 2012, http://www.reuters.com/article/2012/05/17/us-facebook-taxes-idUSBRE84G11A20120517, accessed June 2012.

91. A. G. Sulzberger, "Obama Strikes Populist Chord With Speech in Kansas," *New York Times*, December 7, 2011, http://www.nytimes.com/2011/12/07/us/politics/obama-strikes-populist-chord-with-speech-in-heartland.html, accessed June 2012.

5: SEX BULLIES

1. Andrew Sullivan, "A Paper On The Press And Trig," DailyBeast.com, April 12, 2011, http://andrewsullivan.thedailybeast.com/2011/04/a-paper-on-the-press-and-trig.html, accessed June 2012.

2. Ben Shapiro, "Obama Praises Trig-Truther Andrew Sullivan," Breitbart News, April 25, 2012, http://www.breitbart.com/Big-Journalism/2012/04/25/Obama-Andrew-Sullivan-Rolling-Stone, accessed June 2012.

3. Jonathan Capehart, "Same-sex marriage, the state dinner and the president's table," *Washington Post*, March 15, 2012, http://www.washingtonpost.com/blogs/post-partisan/post/same-sex-marriage-the-state-dinner-and-the-presidents-table/2011/03/04/gIQAqyHxES_blog.html, accessed June 2012.

4. Ben Shapiro, "Did Louis 'C*nt' C.K. Visit White House Along With Whoopi 'Rape Rape' Goldberg and Joy 'Bitch' Behar?," Breitbart News, March 14, 2012, http://www.breitbart.com/Big-Hollywood/2012/03/14/CK-White-House, accessed June 2012.

5. Perez Hilton, "Betty White: Sarah Palin is 'One crazy bitch!,'" PerezHilton.com, October 10, 2008, http://perezhilton.com/2008-10-10-betty-white-sarah-palin-is-one-crazy-bitch, accessed June 2012.

6. Marisa Guthrie, "Keith Olbermann Slams 'Very Stupid' Sarah Palin, Jokes About Anthony Weiner," *Hollywood Reporter*, June 7, 2011, http://www.hollywoodreporter.com/news/keith-olbermann-slams-very-stupid-195588, accessed June 2012.

7. Michael Goodwin, "Palin Derangement Syndrome Strikes The New York Times . . . Again," FoxNews.com, June 22, 2011, http://www.foxnews.com/opinion/2011/06/22/palin-derangement-syndrome-strikes-new-york-times-again/, accessed June 2012.

8. Jonathan Strong, "When McCain picked Palin, liberal journalists coordinated the best line of attack," DailyCaller.com, July 22, 2010, http://dailycaller.com/2010/07/22/when-mccain-picked-palin-liberal-journalists-coordinated-the-best-line-of-attack/, accessed June 2012.

9. Jim Newell, "Hey Kids, Check Out Lil' Trigger In His Elephant Costume," Wonkette.com, October 31, 2008, http://wonkette.com/404013/hey-kids-check-out-lil-trigger-in-his-elephant-costume, accessed June 2012.

10. Michael Saul, "Sarah Palin attacks David Letterman over 'sexually-perverted' joke," *New York Daily News*, June 10, 2009, http://articles.nydailynews.com/2009-06-10/news/17926196_1_bristol-palin-todd-palin-sarah-palin, accessed June 2012.

11. Matt Philbin, "Hate and Bile: Left-Wing Attacks on Women Get Little Press," MRC.org, March 5, 2012, http://www.mrc.org/node/39334, accessed June 2012.

12. Ibid.

13. Michelle Malkin, "Hate-a-rama: The vulgar, racist, sexist, homophobic rage of the Left," Creators Syndicate, February 25, 2011, available at http://michellemalkin.com/2011/02/25/hate-a-rama-the-vulgar-racist-sexist-homophobic-rage-of-the-left/, accessed June 2012.

14. Jane Weaver, "Cheating hearts: Who's doing it and why," MSNBC.com, April 16, 2007, http://www.msnbc.msn.com/id/17951664/ns/health-sexual_health/t/many-cheat-thrill-more-stay-true-love/#.T-kZjWCo44Q, accessed June 2012.

15. Bret Schulte, "How Common Are Cheating Spouses?," USNews.com, March 27, 2008, http://www.usnews.com/news/national/articles/2008/03/27/how-common-are-cheating-spouses, accessed June 2012.

16. Weaver, "Cheating hearts: Who's doing it and why."

17. P. Bracy Bersnak, "The Book on Phyllis Schlafly," Spectator.org, November 17, 2005, http://spectator.org/archives/2005/11/17/the-book-on-phyllis-schlafly/print, accessed June 2012.

18. William Saletan, "Don't Worry Your Pretty Little Head," Slate.com, January 21, 2005, http://www.slate.com/articles/health_and_science/human_nature/2005/01/dont_worry_your_pretty_little_head.html, accessed June 2012.

19. "Jane Fonda, Stalin, Hitler, and Ceausescu," AmericanVision.com, November 16, 2009, http://americanvision.org/1597/jane-fonda-stalin-hitler-ceausescu/#.T-k3XWCo44Q, accessed June 2012.

20. Alex Fitzsimmons, "CBS's Katie Couric Fawns Over Left-Wing Feminist and Her Outrageous Claims," Newsbusters.org, June 23, 2010, http://newsbusters.org/blogs/alex-fitzsimmons/2010/06/23/cbss-katie-couric-fawns-over-left-wing-feminist-and-her-outrageous, accessed June 2012.

21. Charles Thompson, "Pennsylvania representative asks if female co-sponsors of state ultrasound bill are 'men with breasts,'" PennLive.com, March 26, 2012, http://www.pennlive.com/midstate/index.ssf/2012/03/pennsylvania_state_rep_babette.html, accessed June 2012.

22. Steven Ertelt, "New Planned Parenthood Report: Record Abortions Done in 2009," LifeNews.com, February 23, 2011, http://www.lifenews.com/2011/02/23/new-planned-parenthood-report-record-abortions-done-in-2009/, accessed June 2012.

23. John McCormack, "After Lying About Providing Mammograms, Planned Parenthood Outraged That Breast Cancer Charity Cuts Off Grants," WeeklyStandard.com, February 2, 2012, http://www.weeklystandard.com/blogs/after-lying-about-providing-mammograms-planned-parenthood-outraged-breast-cancer-charity-cuts-grants_620875.html, accessed June 2012.

24. Jonathan Easley, "Romney: The war on women has been waged by Obama's economic policies," TheHill.com, April 10, 2012, http://thehill.com/video/campaign/220843-romney-obama-war-on-women-economy-santorum, accessed June 2012.

25. Jill Stanke, "Planned Parenthood CEO a Top White House Mandate Advisor," LifeNews.com, February 14, 2012, http://www.lifenews.com/2012/02/14/planned-parenthood-ceo-a-top-white-house-mandate-advisor/, accessed June 2012.

26. Lauren Peterson, "Why Cecile Richards has President Obama's back," BarackObama.com, May 17, 2012, http://www.barackobama.com/news/entry/why-cecile-richards-has-president-obamas-back, accessed June 2012.

27. Steven Ertelt, "Obama Promotes Planned Parenthood in Speech to Students," LifeNews.com, June 26, 2012, http://www.lifenews.com/2012/06/26/obama-promotes-planned-parenthood-in-speech-to-students/, accessed June 2012.

28. J. Lester Feder, "How Susan G. Komen may have helped Obama on contraception fight," Politico.com, February 3, 2012, http://www.politico.com/news/stories/0212/72426.html, accessed June 2012.

29. Laura Bassett, "Komen Cuts Planned Parenthood Grants Months After Arrival Of New VP, Who Is Abortion Foe," HuffingtonPost.com, January 31, 2012, http://www.huffingtonpost.com/2012/01/komen-planned-parenthood-cuts-karen-handel_n_1245568.html?, accessed June 2012.

30. David Crary, "Planned Parenthood loses Komen funds," Associated Press, February 1, 2012, http://www.usatoday.com/USCP/PNI/Nation/World/2012-02-01-APUSPlannedParenthoodKomen_ST_U.htm, accessed June 2012.

31. Jeffrey Goldberg, "Susan G. Komen Official Resigned Over Planned Parenthood Cave-In," *Atlantic*, February 2, 2012, http://www.theatlantic.com/health/archive/2012/02/top-susan-g-komen-official-resigned-over-planned-parenthood-cave-in/252405/, accessed June 2012.

32. Steven Ertelt, "Planned Parenthood: Komen Stopped $ Because Pro-Lifers Hate Women," LifeNews.com, January 31, 2012, http://www.lifenews.com/2012/01/planned-parenthood-komen-stopped-because-pro-lifers-hate-women/, accessed June 2012.

33. "Senators urge Komen to reconsider funding decision," Reuters, February 2, 2012, http://www.reuters.com/article/2012/02/02/us-usa-healthcare-komen-senate-idUSTRE81124K20120202, accessed June 2012.

34. "Andrea Mitchell interviews Susan G. Komen's Nancy Brinker," MSNBC.com, February 2, 2012, http://firstread.msnbc.msn.com/_news/2012/02/02/10303379-andrea-mitchell-interviews-susan-g-komens-nancy-brinker?lite, accessed June 2012.

35. Mike Lillis, "Pelosi: Komen reversal a 'big victory' for women's health," TheHill.com, February 3, 2012, http://thehill.com/blogs/healthwatch/abortion/208581-pelosi-komen-reversal-is-big-victory-for-womens-health, accessed June 2012.

36. "Sex-Selective Abortion Thrives in America, Courtesy Planned Parenthood," LiveAction.org, May 29, 2012, http://liveaction.org/blog/sex-selective-abortion-thrives-in-america-courtesy-planned-parenthood/, accessed June 2012.

37. Monica Langley, "Combative Top Democrat Gains Clout in Campaign," *Wall Street Journal*, February 16, 2012, http://online.wsj.com/article/SB1000142405 2970204642604577213173081025252.html, accessed June 2012.

38. Jackie Kucinich and Martha T. Moore, "Hilary Rosen says Ann Romney never worked 'day in her life,'" USAToday.com, April 12, 2012, http://www.usatoday .com/news/politics/story/2012-04-12/ann-romney-hilary-rosen-work /54235706/1, accessed June 2012.

39. David Jackson, "Obama: 'No tougher job than being mom,'" USAToday.com, April 12, 2012, http://content.usatoday.com/communities/theoval/post/2012 /04/m-obama-every-mother-works-hard/1#.T-pHWmCo44R, accessed June 2012.

40. Greg Pollowitz, "Hilary Rosen Doubles Down and then Apologizes (Not Really)," NationalReview.com, April 12, 12012, http://www.nationalreview .com/media-blog/295884/hilary-rosen-doubles-down-and-then-apologizes-not-really-greg-pollowitz, accessed June 2012.

41. "Rosen Doubles Down: 'It's Not About Ann Romney,'" RealClearPolitics.com, April 12, 2012, http://www.realclearpolitics.com/video/2012/04/12/rosen_ doubles_down_its_not_about_ann_romney.html, accessed June 2012.

42. Kirsten Swinth, "Hillary Clinton, cookies and the rise of working families," CNN.com, March 16, 2012, http://www.cnn.com/2012/03/16/opinion/ swinth-hillary-clinton/index.html, accessed June 2012.

43. Susan Donaldson James, "Sarah Palin's Parenting Choices Under Fire," ABCNews.com, September 3, 2008, http://abcnews.go.com/Business/ story?id=5710888&page=1#.T-pQJmCo44R, accessed June 2012.

44. Michelle Malkin, "The Left's war on conservative women: We're damned if we do stay home, and damned if we don't," MichelleMalkin.com, April 12, 2012, http://michellemalkin.com/2012/04/12/the-lefts-war-on-conservative women-were-damned-if-we-do-stay-home-and-damned-if-we-dont/, accessed June 2012.

45. Christina Hoff Sommers, "The War Against Boys," *Atlantic*, May 2000, http:// www.theatlantic.com/magazine/archive/2000/05/the-war-against-boys/4659 /?single_page=true, accessed June 2012.

46. "Learning About Diversity," SesameStreet.org, http://www.sesamestreet.org /parents/topics/getalong/getalong06?p_p_id=56_INSTANCE_F8vf&p_p_ lifecycle=0&p_p_state=pop_up&p_p_mode=view&p_p_col_id=column 2&p_p_col_count=1&_56_INSTANCE_F8vf_struts_action=/journal_content /view&_56_INSTANCE_F8vf_groupId=10171&_56_INSTANCE_F8vf_ articleId=21935&_56_INSTANCE_F8vf_viewMode=print, accessed June 2012.

47. "Expose Your Child to a World of Diversity," SesameStreet.org, http://www.sesamestreet.org/parents/topics/getalong/getalong03, accessed June 2012.

48. "Men who hold open doors for women are SEXIST not chivalrous, feminists claim," *Daily Mail* (UK), June 15, 2011, http://www.dailymail.co.uk/news/article-2003821/Feminists-claim-men-hold-open-doors-women-SEXIST-chivalrous.html#ixzz1Q7gpsMgF%20http://www.dailymail.co, accessed June 2012.

49. Andrea Dworkin, *Intercourse* (N.p.: Read How You Want, 1988), 163–68.

50. "Obama Says He Is Against Same-Sex Marriage But Also Against Ending Its Practice In Calif.," ABCNews.com, November 2, 2008, http://abcnews.go.com/blogs/politics/2008/11/obama-on-mtv-i/, accessed June 2012.

51. "Transcript: Robin Roberts ABC News Interview With President Obama," ABCNews.com, May 9, 2012, http://abcnews.go.com/Politics/transcript-robin-roberts-abc-news-interview-president-obama/story?id=16316043&singlePage=true, accessed June 2012.

52. "Mitt Romney: Backwards On Equality," http://www.youtube.com/watch?v=vwJJm-we-vs&feature=player_embedded, May 10, 2012.

53. "'God was testing my faith,' says Miss California after Perez Hilton calls her a 'dumb bitch' in gay marriage row," *Daily Mail* (UK), April 21, 2009, http://www.dailymail.co.uk/news/article-1172123/God-testing-faith-says-Miss-California-Perez-Hilton-calls-dumb-bitch-gay-marriage-row.html, accessed June 2012.

54. "Prop 8—The Musical," http://www.youtube.com/watch?v=B_hyT7_Bx9o, October 31, 2009

55. Jesse McKinley, "Theater Director Resigns Amid Gay-Rights Ire," *New York Times*, November 12, 2008, http://www.nytimes.com/2008/11/13/theater/13thea.html, accessed June 2012.

56. Dave Itzkoff, "Marc Shaiman on 'Prop 8—The Musical,'" NYTimes.com, December 4, 2008, http://artsbeat.blogs.nytimes.com/2008/12/04/marc-shaiman-on-prop-8-the-musical/, accessed June 2012.

57. Tami Abdollah, "A small move to counter boycott," *Los Angeles Times*, November 15, 2008, http://articles.latimes.com/2008/nov/15/local/me-elcoyote15, accessed June 2012.

58. Ian Lovett, "California to Require Gay History in Schools," *New York Times*, July 14, 2011, http://www.nytimes.com/2011/07/15/us/15gay.html, accessed June 2012.

59. Thaddeus Baklinski, "California passes bill mandating pro-gay teaching in schools, no parent opt-out," LifeSiteNews.com, July 6, 2011, http://www.lifesitenews.com/news/california-passes-bill-mandating-pro-gay-teaching-in-schools-no-parent-opt/, accessed June 2012.

60. "The 'Fistgate' conference," MassResistance.org, December 7, 2009, http://www.massresistance.org/docs/issues/fistgate/index.html, accessed June 2012.

61. Michelle Malkin, "Eastman Kodak stands by GLSEN," MichelleMalkin.com, December 8, 2009, http://michellemalkin.com/2009/12/08/eastman-kodak-stands-by-glsen/, accessed June 2012.

62. Michelle Malkin, "Explosive: The not-safe-for-school reading list of the safe schools czar," MichelleMalkin.com, December 4, 2009, http://michellemalkin.com/2009/12/04/explosive-the-not-safe-for-school-reading-list-of-the-safe-schools-czar/, accessed June 2012.

63. Michelle Malkin, "Now it's 'anti-gay' to describe safe school czar's failures," MichelleMalkin.com, October 1, 2009, http://michellemalkin.com/2009/10/01/now-its-anti-gay-to-describe-safe-school-czars-failures/, accessed June 2012.

64. Andrew Jones, "DOJ accepts ruling that transgender bias is illegal," Rawstory.com, May 22, 2012, http://www.rawstory.com/rs/2012/05/22/doj-accepts-ruling-that-transgender-bias-is-illegal/, accessed June 2012.

65. Ben Shapiro, "Obama DOJ Forces University To Allow Biological Male Into Female Restrooms," Breitbart News, May 24, 2012, http://www.breitbart.com/Big-Government/2012/05/24/Obama-DOJ-transgender-bathroom, accessed June 2012.

66. Jason Horowitz, "Mitt Romney's prep school classmates recall pranks, but also troubling incidents," *Washington Post*, May 10, 2012, http://www.washingtonpost.com/politics/mitt-romneys-prep-school-classmates-recall-pranks-but-also-troubling-incidents/2012/05/10/gIQA3WOKFU_story.html, accessed June 2012.

67. Matthew Jaffe, "Sister of Alleged Romney Target Has 'No Knowledge' of Any Bullying Incident," ABCNews.com, May 10, 2012, http://abcnews.go.com/blogs/politics/2012/05/sister-of-alleged-romney-target-has-no-knowledge-of-any-bullying-incident/, accessed June 2012.

68. John Hayward, "The Washington Post's Romney Hit Piece Comes Apart," HumanEvents.com, May 11, 2012, http://www.humanevents.com/2012/05/11/the-washington-posts-romney-hit-piece-comes-apart/, accessed June 2012.

69. Brad Wilmouth, "Donny Deutsch Lauds Obama on Gay Marriage Vs. Romney 'Bullying,'" NewsBusters.org, May 15, 2012, http://newsbusters.org/blogs/brad-wilmouth/2012/05/15/donny-deutsch-lauds-obama-gay-marriage-vs-romney-bullying, accessed June 2012.

70. Barack Obama, *Dreams from My Father* (New York: Three Rivers Press, 2004), 61.

71. Dr. Peggy Drexler, "Obama and the Bully: The Cornering of Mitt Romney," HuffingtonPost.com, May 15, 2012, http://www.huffingtonpost.com/peggy-drexler/obama-and-the-bully-the-c_b_1519373.html, accessed June 2012.

72. Rosie Gray, "Village Voice Writer: Gay Republicans Like 'Jewish Nazis,'" BuzzFeed.com, June 25, 2012, http://www.buzzfeed.com/rosiegray/village-voice-writer-goproud-are-like-jewish-naz, accessed June 2012.

73. Caroline May, "GLAAD honors biased gay blogger after applauding $100k fine for Kobe Bryant," DailyCaller.com, May 27, 2011, http://dailycaller.com/2011/05/27/glaad-honors-biased-gay-blogger-after-applauding-100k-fine-for-kobe-bryant/, accessed June 2012.

74. Gray, "Village Voice Writer: Gay Republicans Like 'Jewish Nazis.'"

75. Michelangelo Signorile, *Queer in America: Sex, the Media, and the Closets of Power* (Madison: University of Wisconsin Press, 2003), 152–53.

76. Randy Shilts, "Is 'Outing' Gays Ethical?," *New York Times*, April 12, 1990.

6: GREEN BULLIES

1. *Sackett v. Environmental Protection Agency* (2012), 132 S.Ct. 1367.

2. Abby W. Schachter, "Supremes 'Sackett' to EPA bullies," *New York Post*, March 22, 2012, http://www.nypost.com/p/blogs/capitol/supremes_slap_down_epa_bullies_SA2P8NjsPgSMQp7hiAdTcN, accessed June 2012.

3. *Sackett v. Environmental Protection Agency* (2012), 132 S.Ct. 1367.

4. Robert Knight, "Taming the EPA Monster," *Washington Times*, March 23, 2012, http://www.washingtontimes.com/news/2012/mar/23/taming-the-epa-monster/print/, accessed June 2012.

5. Speech, June 4, 2008.

6. Doug Powers, "Obama: Republican Plan Means Dirty Air, Dirty Water, and Fewer People with Health Insurance," MichelleMalkin.com, October 17, 2011, http://michellemalkin.com/2011/10/17/obama-republican-plan/, accessed June 2012.

7. Rheana Murray, "Organic food might make you a jerk: Study," *New York Daily News*, May 21, 2012, http://articles.nydailynews.com/2012-05-21/news/31804190_1_organic-food-researchers-study-author, accessed June 2012.

8. Kate Connolly, "How going green may make you mean," *Guardian* (UK), March 15, 2010, http://www.guardian.co.uk/environment/2010/mar/15/green-consumers-more-likely-steal, accessed June 2012.

9. "Prius Popularity Powered by Vanity," HybridCars.com, July 5, 2007, http://www.hybridcars.com/hybrid-drivers/prius-popularity-vanity.html, accessed June 2012.

10. Bruce McCall, "Living Up To Your Prius," *New Yorker*, April 19, 2010, http://www.newyorker.com/humor/2010/04/19/100419sh_shouts_mccall, accessed June 2012.

11. Paul Ehrlich, *The Population Bomb* (New York: Sierra Club–Ballantine, 1968), 66–67.

12. Ibid., 132–33.

13. Glenn Kessler, "U.S. oil resources: President Obama's 'non sequitur facts,'"

Washington Post, March 15, 2012, http://www.washingtonpost.com/blogs/fact-checker/post/us-oil-resources-president-obamas-non-sequitur-facts/2012/03/14/gIQApP14CS_blog.html, accessed June 2012.

14. Ehrlich, *The Population Bomb*, 135–37.

15. David Rose, "Forget global warming—it's Cycle 25 we need to worry about," *Daily Mail* (UK), January 29, 2012, http://www.dailymail.co.uk/sciencetech/article-2093264/Forget-global-warming--Cycle-25-need-worry-NASA-scientists-right-Thames-freezing-again.html, accessed June 2012.

16. James Delingpole, "Climategate: The final nail in the coffin of 'Anthropogenic Global Warming'?," *Telegraph* (UK), November 20, 2009, http://blogs.telegraph.co.uk/news/jamesdelingpole/100017393/climategate-the-final-nail-in-the-coffin-of-anthropogenic-global-warming/, accessed June 2012.

17. Suzanne Goldenberg, "Leak exposes how Heartland Institute works to undermine climate science," *Guardian* (UK), February 14, 2012, http://www.guardian.co.uk/environment/2012/feb/15/leak-exposes-heartland-institute-climate, accessed June 2012.

18. Richard Schiffman, "The Heartland Institute Self-Destructs," HuffingtonPost.com, May 4, 2012, http://www.huffingtonpost.com/richard-schiffman/heartland-institute-billboards_b_1477499.html, accessed June 2012.

19. Ben Johnson and Slave V Staff, "Heartland Institute's Leaked Documents Show Funding for Discouraging Science Education," Slate.com, February 16, 2012, http://www.slate.com/blogs/trending/2012/02/16/heartland_institute_s_leaked_documents_show_funding_for_discouraging_science_education.html, accessed June 2012.

20. Ben Shapiro, "New York Times Uses False Data To Smear Koch Brothers," Breitbart News, February 28, 2012, http://www.breitbart.com/Big-Journalism/2012/02/28/New%20York%20Times%20Uses%20False%20Data%20To%20Smear%20Koch%20Brothers, accessed June 2012.

21. "Al Gore's New Campaign," CBSNews.com, February 11, 2009, http://www.cbsnews.com/2100-18560_162-3974389.html, accessed June 2012.

22. Gabriel Perna, "Al Gore Likens Global Warming Doubters To Racists," IBTimes.com, August 29, 2011, http://www.ibtimes.com/articles/205336/20110829/al-gore-global-warming-climate-change.htm, accessed June 2012.

23. Bill Blakemore, "Global Warming Denialism 'Just Foolishness,' Scientist Peter Raven Says," ABCNews.com, April 1, 2012, http://abcnews.go.com/blogs/technology/2012/04/global-warming-denialism-just-foolishness-scientist-peter-raven-says/, accessed June 2012.

24. "Gore Implores Congress To Save The Planet," CBSNews.com, March 21, 2007, http://www.cbsnews.com/stories/2007/03/21/politics/main2591104.shtml?source=RSSattr=HOME_2591104, accessed June 2012.

25. Micah White, "An alternative to the new wave of ecofascism," *Guardian* (UK), September 16, 2010, http://www.guardian.co.uk/commentisfree/cif-green/2010/sep/16/authoritarianism-ecofascism-alternative, accessed June 2012.

26. Ian Johnston, "'Gaia' scientist James Lovelock: I was 'alarmist' about climate change," MSNBC.com, April 23, 2012, http://worldnews.msnbc.msn.com/_news/2012/04/23/11144098-gaia-scientist-james-lovelock-i-was-alarmist-about-climate-change?lite, accessed June 2012.

27. "Climate Alarmist Calls For Burning Down Skeptics' Homes," EducationViews.org, April 20, 2010, http://educationviews.org/2012/04/20/climate-alarmist-calls-for-burning-down-skeptics-homes/, accessed June 2012.

28. Richard Glover, "The dangers of bone-headed beliefs," *Sydney Morning Herald*, June 6, 2011, http://www.smh.com.au/opinion/society-and-culture/the-dangers-of-boneheaded-beliefs-20110602-1fijg.html, accessed June 2012.

29. White, "An alternative to the new wave of ecofascism."

30. "Simultaneous action needed to break cultural inertia in climate-change response," University of Oregon Media Relations, March 26, 2012, http://uonews.uoregon.edu/archive/news-release/201/simultaneous-action-needed-break-cultural-inertia-climate-change-respons, accessed June 2012.

31. Kari Norgaard, "Dear Mr. President," Whitman College, http://www.whitman.edu/content/magazine/in-their-words/dearmrpresident/norgaard, accessed June 2012.

32. Karin McQuillan, "Scientists in Revolt against Global Warming," AmericanThinker.com, November 27, 2011, http://www.americanthinker.com/2011/11/scientists_in_revolt_against_global_warming.html, accessed June 2012.

33. Marita Noon, "Panetta Beats War Drums on Climate Change," Townhall.com, May 6, 2012, http://finance.townhall.com/columnists/maritanoon/2012/05/06/panetta_beats_war_drums_on_climate_change/page/full/, accessed June 2012.

34. Kathleen Sebelius, "Health benefits of reducing greenhouse gas emissions," Wellcome Trust, http://www.wellcome.ac.uk/stellent/groups/corporatesite/@policy_communications/documents/web_document/wtx058243.pdf, accessed June 2012.

35. "Sustainability," Department of Labor, http://www.dol.gov/open/sustainability/, accessed June 2012.

36. McQuillan, "Scientists in Revolt against Global Warming."

37. Mike Brownfield, "Morning Bell: White House Wants to Keep Gas Prices High," Heritage.org, February 29, 2012, http://blog.heritage.org/2012/02/29/morning-bell-white-house-wants-to-keep-gas-prices-high/, accessed June 2012.

38. Associated Press, "Rand Paul: Obama BP criticism 'un-American,'" MSNBC.com, May 2, 2012, http://www.msnbc.msn.com/id/37273085/ns/politics-decision_2010/t/rand-paul-obama-bp-criticism-un-american/, accessed June 2012.

39. Frank James, "BP Will Feel Either 'Boot on Throat' or 'Feet To Fire,'" NPR.org, May 3, 2010, http://www.npr.org/blogs/thetwo-way/2010/05/bp_will_feel_either_boot_on_th.html, accessed June 2012.

40. Frank James, "Obama Team's Tough BP Talk Undercut By Tougher Reality," NPR.org, May 23, 2010, http://www.npr.org/blogs/thetwo-way/2010/05/obama_teams_tough_bp_talk_unde.html, accessed June 2012.

41. Nick Assinder, "Britain to Obama: Stop Bullying Us Over BP," Time.com, June 11, 2010, http://www.time.com/time/world/article/0,8599,1996056,00.html, accessed June 2012.

42. Noelle Straub, "Obama to Extend Deepwater Drilling Moratorium," *New York Times*, May 27, 2010, http://www.nytimes.com/gwire/2010/05/27/27greenwire-obama-to-extend-deepwater-drilling-moratorium-8011.html?pagewanted=all, accessed June 2012.

43. Mark Clayton, "Offshore drilling ban: Will revised moratorium appease courts?," *Christian Science Monitor*, July 12, 2010, http://www.csmonitor.com/Environment/2010/0712/Offshore-drilling-ban-Will-revised-moratorium-appease-courts, accessed June 2012.

44. Darren Goode, "Bill Clinton: Drilling delays 'ridiculous,'" Politico.com, March 11, 2011, http://www.politico.com/news/stories/0311/51150.html, accessed June 2012.

45. Charles Krauthammer, "The Pipeline Sellout," NationalReview.com, November 18, 2011, http://www.nationalreview.com/articles/283442/pipeline-sellout-charles-krauthammer, accessed June 2012.

46. David Jackson, "Obama attacks 'manipulation' of oil markets," USAToday.com, April 17, 2012, http://content.usatoday.com/communities/theoval/post/2012/04/obama-to-announce-plan-on-manipulation-of-oil-markets/1#.T-5k6WCo44Q, accessed June 2012.

47. Susan Crabtree, "Critics rip Obama claim that drilling in U.S. won't drop gas prices," WashingtonTimes.com, March 22, 2012, http://www.washingtontimes.com/news/2012/mar/22/obama-drilling-every-inch-us-would-not-cut-gas-pri/, accessed June 2012.

48. Charles Krauthammer, "Obama oil antipathy hurts U.S.," *Quad-City Times*, March 17, 2012, http://qctimes.com/news/opinion/editorial/columnists/charles-krauthammer/obama-oil-antipathy-hurts-u-s/article_5219e8ae-6f28-11e1-8281-001871e3ce6c.html, accessed June 2012.

49. Alana Goodman, "Did Oil Production Increase Under Obama?," Commentary.com, March 22, 2012, http://www.commentarymagazine.com/2012/03/22/did-oil-production-increase-under-obama/, accessed June 2012.

50. Allahpundit, "Obama: Let's eat less so that we can lead by example on climate change," HotAir.com, May 19, 2008, http://hotair.com/archives/2008/05/19/obama-lets-eat-less-so-that-we-can-lead-by-example-on-climate-change-by-eating-less/, accessed June 2012.

51. Sheryl Gay Stolberg, "White House Unbuttons Formal Dress Code," *New York Times*, January 28, 2009, http://www.nytimes.com/2009/01/29/us/politics/29whitehouse.html?_r=1&partner=rss&emc=rss&pagewanted=all, accessed June 2012.

52. John Cote, "S.F. OKs toughest recycling law in U.S.," SFGate.com, June 10, 2009, http://www.sfgate.com/green/article/S-F-OKs-toughest-recycling-law-in-U-S-3295664.php, accessed June 2012.

53. Joel Millman, "Portland Puts New Twist on Trash Pickup," *Wall Street Journal*, June 27, 2012, http://online.wsj.com/article/SB10001424052702304458604577490532687633866.html?mod=WSJ_WSJ_US_News_6, accessed June 2012.

54. Richard Black, "Gear change on road to Rio?," BBC News, March 15, 2012, http://www.bbc.co.uk/news/science-environment-17381730, accessed June 2012.

55. "Al Gore could become world's first carbon billionaire," *Telegraph* (UK), November 3, 2009, http://www.telegraph.co.uk/earth/energy/6491195/Al-Gore-could-become-worlds-first-carbon-billionaire.html, accessed June 2012.

7: SECULAR BULLIES

1. Jon Street, "Michelle Obama: There is 'No Place Better' Than Church to Talk About Political Issues," CNSNews.com, July 2, 2012, http://cnsnews.com/news/article/michelle-obama-there-no-place-better-church-talk-about-political-issues, accessed July 2012.

2. "Obama's 2006 Speech on Faith and Politics," *New York Times*, June 28, 2006, http://www.nytimes.com/2006/06/28/us/politics/2006obamaspeech.html?pagewanted=all, accessed July 2012.

3. "A statement by U.S. Department of Health and Human Services Secretary Kathleen Sebelius," HHS.gov, January 20, 2012, http://www.hhs.gov/news/press/2012pres/01/20120120a.html/, accessed July 2012.

4. "Romney: 'We Found Out' Why Stephanopoulos Asked About Contraception," RealClearPolitics.com, February 22, 2012, http://www.realclearpolitics.com/video/2012/02/22/romney_we_found_out_why_stephanopoulos_asked_about_contraception.html, accessed July 2012.

5. Matt Negrin and Sunlen Miller, "Senate Blocks Blunt's Repeal of Contraception Mandate," ABCNews.com, March 1, 2012, http://abcnews.go.com/blogs/politics/2012/03/contraception-mandate-goes-up-for-a-vote/, accessed July 2012.

6. John Parkinson, "Women's Health vs. Religious Freedom: House Leaders Debate Birth Control Mandate," ABCNews.com, March 1, 2012, http://abcnews.go.com/blogs/politics/2012/03/womens-health-vs-religious-freedom-house-leaders-debate-birth-control-mandate/, accessed July 2012.

7. Phyllis Schlafly, "Obama's War on Religious Liberty," Townhall.com, February 20, 2012, http://townhall.com/columnists/phyllisschlafly/2012/02/20/phyllis_schlafly, accessed July 2012.

8. Sandra Fluke, "Law Students for Reproductive Justice: Statement Before Congress," ABCNews.com, February 16, 2012, http://abcnews.go.com/images/Politics/statement-Congress-letterhead-2nd%20hearing.pdf, accessed July 2012.

9. Felicia Sonmez, "Obama calls Sandra Fluke, Georgetown law student assailed by Rush Limbaugh," *Washington Post*, March 2, 2012, http://www.washingtonpost.com/blogs/election-2012/post/obama-calls-sandra-fluke-georgetown-law-student-assailed-by-rush-limbaugh/2012/03/02/gIQAIoW0mR_blog.html, accessed July 2012.

10. William A. Jacobson, "Media Matters astroturfed the Limbaugh secondary boycott," LegalInsurrection.com, March 15, 2012, http://legalinsurrection.com/2012/03/media-matters-astroturfed-the-limbaugh-secondary-boycott/, accessed July 2012.

11. Michelle Malkin, "Sandra Fluke is not a 'slut.' She's a femme-agogue tool; DCCC, Emily's list fund-raise off of Rush," MichelleMalkin.com, March 2, 2012, http://michellemalkin.com/2012/03/02/sandra-fluke-is-not-a-slut-shes-a-femme-agogue-tool/, accessed July 2012.

12. Ken Klukowski, "Kagan balks at Obama EEOC claim of authority over churches," *Washington Examiner*, October 11, 2011, http://www.frc.org/op-eds/kagan-balks-at-obama-eeoc-claim-of-authority-over-churches, accessed July 2012.

13. Senator Orrin Hatch, "Protecting charities, churches and others' charitable donations," DeseretNews.com, November 6, 2011, http://www.deseretnews.com/article/700194797/Protecting-charities-churches-and-others-charitable-donations.html?pg=all, accessed July 2012.

14. Arthur Delaney, "Obama: U.S. 'Not A Christian Nation Or A Jewish Nation Or A Muslim Nation,'" HuffingtonPost.com, May 7, 2009, http://www.huffingtonpost.com/2009/04/06/obama-us-not-a-christian_n_183772.html accessed July 2012.

15. Noam Chomsky, University of Houston, Texas, October 18, 2002.

16. "Pakistani Muslims Want to Ban the Bible," FoxNews.com, June 1, 2011, http://nation.foxnews.com/culture/2011/06/01/pakistani-muslims-want-ban-bible, accessed July 2012.

17. Outofstepper, "Taliban or Religious Right?," DailyKos.com, September 21, 2010, http://www.dailykos.com/story/2010/09/21/903429/-Taliban-or-Religious-Right, accessed July 2012.

18. Josh Feldman, "Bill Maher: Taliban Wants To Go Back To 8th Century, Christian Right Wants To Go Further Back," Mediaite.com, March 9, 2012, http://www.mediaite.com/tv/bill-maher-taliban-wants-to-go-back-to-8th-century-christian-right-wants-to-go-further-back/, accessed July 2012.

19. Noel Sheppard, "Chris Matthews: Religious Right In America Resembles The Taliban," Newsbusters.org, October 22, 2009, http://newsbusters.org/blogs/noel-sheppard/2009/10/22/chris-matthews-religious-right-america-resembles-taliban, accessed July 2012.

20. Interview with Susan Harris, May 4, 2009.

21. Nina Mandell, "Dan Savage accused of bullying," *New York Daily News*, May 2, 2012, http://articles.nydailynews.com/2012-05-02/news/31543321_1_anti-bullying-pansy-bible, accessed July 2012.

22. Neetzan Zimmerman, "Dan Savage Sorry About 'Pansy-Ass' Comment, But Bashing Gay People with Bible Quotes Is Still Bullshit," Gawker.com, http://gawker.com/5906289/dan-savage-sorry-about-pansy+ass-comment-but-bible+thumping-gay-people-is-still-bullshit, accessed July 2012.

23. Charles Krauthammer, "President Obama and Stem Cells—Science Fiction," *Washington Post*, March 13, 2009, http://www.washingtonpost.com/wp-dyn/content/article/2009/03/12/AR2009031202764.html, accessed July 2012.

24. "Full Text: President Obama Speech on Stem Cell Policy Change," White House Press Office, March 9, 2009, http://www.clipsandcomment.com/2009/03/09/full-text-president-obama-speech-on-stem-cell-policy-change/, accessed July 2012.

25. Katrina vanden Heuvel, "The Republicans' war on science and reason," *Washington Post*, October 24, 2011, http://www.washingtonpost.com/opinions/the-republicans-war-on-science-and-reason/2011/10/24/gIQALl3BEM_story.html, accessed July 2012.

26. Kevin Canfield, "The Republican war on science is un-American," Salon.com, October 15, 2011, http://www.salon.com/2011/10/15/the_republican_war_on_science_is_un_american/, accessed July 2012.

27. Michael Gerson, "A Phony 'War on Science,'" *Washington Post*, May 7, 2008, http://www.washingtonpost.com/wp-dyn/content/article/2008/05/06/AR2008050602446.html, accessed July 2012.

28. Ned Potter, "Are Some Sheep Gay?," ABCNews.com, January 26, 2007, http://abcnews.go.com/Technology/story?id=2823706&page=1, accessed July 2012.

29. Max Blumenthal, "Giulio Meotti: Serial Plagiarist or Common Hasbarist," MaxBlumenthal.com, May 18, 2012, http://maxblumenthal.com/tag/pinkwashing/, accessed July 2012.

30. John Podhoretz, "Derrick Bell in 1994: 'Jewish Neoconservative Racists,'" Commentarymagazine.com, March 9, 2012, http://www.commentarymagazine.com/2012/03/09/derrick-bell-jewish-neoconservative-racists/, accessed July 2012.

31. Aaron Klein, "Obama Raised Funds For Islamic Causes," WorldNetDaily.com, February 25, 2008, http://www.wnd.com/2008/02/57341/, accessed July 2012.

32. Peter Wallsten, "Allies of Palestinians see a friend in Obama," *Los Angeles Times*, April 10, 2008, http://articles.latimes.com/2008/apr/10/nation/na-obamamideast10, accessed July 2012.

33. Michael Goldfarb, "Obama Campaign 'Flattered' by Hamas Endorsement," WeeklyStandard.com, April 17, 2008, http://www.weeklystandard.com/weblogs/TWSFP/2008/04/obama_campaign_flattered_by_ha.asp, accessed July 2012.

34. Pamela Geller, "Obama's Foreign Donors: The media averts its eyes," AmericanThinker.com, August 14, 2008, http://www.americanthinker.com/2008/08/obamas_donor_contributions_sil.html, accessed July 2012.

35. Ben Shapiro, "Media Matters' Eric Boehlert Downplayed Genocidal Anti-Semitism," Breitbart News, April 18, 2012, http://www.breitbart.com/Big-Journalism/2012/04/18/Media-Matters-Boehlert-Anti-Semitism, accessed July 2012.

36. Ben Shapiro, "Media Matters' Oliver Willis Wants Pro-Israel Liberals 'Marginalized,'" Breitbart News, April 19, 2012, http://www.breitbart.com/Big-Journalism/2012/04/19/Media-Matters-Oliver-Willis, accessed July 2012.

37. Andrew C. McCarthy, "Triple Play! Obama Blows Off Congress, Funds Palestinians, Lies About PA Stance on Israel," NationalReview.com, April 28, 2012, http://www.nationalreview.com/corner/297202/triple-play-obama-blows-congress-funds-palestinians-lies-about-pa-stance-israel-andrew, accessed July 2012.

38. "Reports: Netanyahu 'Humiliated' by Obama Snub," FoxNews.com, March 26, 2010, http://www.foxnews.com/politics/2010/03/25/president-allegedly-dumps-israeli-prime-minister-dinner/, accessed July 2012.

39. Hana Levi Julian, "Arab Anger Forces Obama to Backtrack on Jerusalem," IsraelNationalNews.com, June 6, 2008, http://www.israelnationalnews.com/News/News.aspx/126429#.T_YI3mCo44Q, accessed July 2012.

40. Omri Ceren, "Palestinians Set Obama's 1967 Border Guidelines as Precondition to Talks," Commentarymagazine.com, May 22, 2011, http://www.commentarymagazine.com/2011/05/22/palestinians-set-obamas-1967-border-guidelines-as-precondition-to-talks/, accessed July 2012.

41. "Obama State Department Won't Say If Jerusalem Is The Capital Of Israel," RealClearPolitics.com, March 29, 2012, http://www.realclearpolitics.com/video/2012/03/29/obama_state_department_wont_say_if_jerusalem_is_the_capital_of_israel.html, accessed July 2012.

42. Arnaud De Borchgrave, "King Abdullah: Create Palestinian State or Risk War," Newsmax.com, May 12, 2009, http://www.newsmax.com/deBorchgrave/Palestinian-West-Bank/2009/05/12/id/330049, accessed July 2012.

43. Jerusalem Post staff, "Saudi airspace open for Iran attack," *Jerusalem Post*, June 7, 2012, http://www.jpost.com/LandedPages/PrintArticle.aspx?id=178304, accessed July 2012.

44. David Ignatius, "Is Israel preparing to attack Iran?," WashingtonPost.com, February 2, 2012, http://www.washingtonpost.com/opinions/is-israel-preparing-to-attack-iran/2012/02/02/gIQANjfTkQ_print.html, accessed July 2012.

45. Patrick Brennan, "Israeli-Azerbaijan Deal Leaked, Bolton Blames Obama," NationalReview.com, March 29, 2012, http://www.nationalreview.com/corner/294856/israeli-azerbaijan-deal-leaked-bolton-blames-obama-patrick-brennan, accessed July 2012.

46. Ellen Nakashima, Greg Miller, and Julie Tate, "US, Israel developed Flame computer virus to slow Iranian nuclear efforts, officials say," *Washington Post*, June 19, 2012, http://www.washingtonpost.com/world/national-security/us-israel-developed-computer-virus-to-slow-iranian-nuclear-efforts-officials-say/2012/06/19/gJQA6xBPoV_print.html, accessed July 2012.

47. Dennis Prager, "George Soros and the Problem of the Radical Non-Jewish Jew," Creators Syndicate, February 27, 2007, http://townhall.com/columnists/dennisprager/2007/02/27/george_soros_and_the_problem_of_the_radical_non-jewish_jew/page/full/, accessed July 2012.

48. Alana Goodman, "Why Has J Street Defended Media Matters?," CommentaryMagazine.com, March 9, 2012, http://www.commentarymagazine.com/2012/03/09/j-street-defended-media-matters/, accessed July 2012.

49. Omri Ceren, "J Street Rolls Out the Red Carpet for BDS," CommentaryMagazine.com, March 19, 2012, http://www.commentarymagazine.com/2012/03/19/j-street-conference-red-carpet-bds/, accessed July 2012.

50. Jennifer Rubin, "Right Turn," *Washington Post*, January 18, 2011, http://voices.washingtonpost.com/right-turn/2011/01/morning_bits_40.html, accessed July 2012.

51. David Bedein, "J Street Is Anti-Israel, Not Pro-Peace," IsraelNationalNews.com, May 3, 2011, http://www.israelnationalnews.com/News/News.aspx/143869#.T_YQ6WCo44Q, accessed July 2012.

52. Barak Ravid, "J Street embraced by Obama administration, but not in Israel," Haaretz.com, October 18, 2009, http://www.haaretz.com/print-edition/news/j-street-embraced-by-obama-administration-but-not-in-israel-1.5948, accessed July 2012.

53. Devin Dwyer, "Obama: I've Proven Democrats Not 'Weak on Defense,'" ABCNews.com, March 1, 2012, http://abcnews.go.com/blogs/politics/2012/03/obama-ive-proven-democrats-not-weak-on-defense/, accessed July 2012.

54. Bridget Johnson, "Valerie Jarrett Rocks The House at J Street," PJMedia.com, March 26, 2012, http://pjmedia.com/tatler/2012/03/26/valerie-jarrett-rocks-the-house-at-j-street/, accessed July 2012.

55. Z Street, "J Street Leader: Our Job is to 'Move Jews' to Support Washington Politicians," JewishPress.com, May 17, 2012, http://www.jewishpress.com/news/israel/j-street-leader-our-job-is-to-move-jews-to-support-washington-politicians/2012/05/17/, accessed July 2012.

56. Ted Merwin and David Zax, "Out and About with Tony Kushner," GLBTJews.org, http://www.glbtjews.org/article.php3?id_article=501, accessed July 2012.

57. Frank Newport, "Democrats View Religious Groups Less Positively Than Republicans," Gallup.com, September 7, 2006, http://www.gallup.com/poll/24385/democrats-view-religious-groups-less-positively-than-republicans.aspx, accessed July 2012.

58. Mark Finkelstein, "Martin Bashir Believes Evangelicals Won't Vote For Romney Because Book of Mormon . . . Boring?," Newsbusters.org, February 9, 2012, http://newsbusters.org/blogs/mark-finkelstein/2012/02/09/bashir-slimes-mormons-evangelicals-romney, accessed July 2012.

59. Dennis Wagner, "Mormon bias still part of politics," USAToday.com, November 23, 2011, http://www.usatoday.com/USCP/PNI/NEWS/2011-11-23-PNI1123met-antimormonPNIBrd_ST_U.htm, accessed July 2012.

60. Michelangelo Signorile, "Romney's Pandering Gets Him Nowhere," HuffingtonPost.com, November 23, 2011, http://www.huffingtonpost.com/michelangelo-signorile/mitt-romney-mormon-gay-republican_b_1110108.html, accessed July 2012.

61. Alana Goodman, "4 in 10 Liberals Hold Anti-Mormon Bias," Commentary Magazine.com, June 13, 2012, http://www.commentarymagazine.com/2012/06/1¾-in-10-liberals-hold-anti-mormon-bias/, accessed July 2012.

62. Noel Sheppard, "Joy Behar Wants to See Romney's House Burn Down: 'Who's He Going to Call, the Mormon Fire Patrol?,'" Newsbusters.org, June 12, 2012, http://newsbusters.org/blogs/noel-sheppard/2012/06/12/joy-behar-wants-see-romneys-house-burn-down-it-would-be-kind-cool-mor, accessed July 2012.

63. Tina Daunt, "Cher Accused of Bigotry After 'Magic Underwear' Romney Tweet," HollywoodReporter.com, June 29, 2012, http://www.hollywoodreporter.com/news/cher-bigotry-anti-romney-magic-underwear-343651, accessed July 2012.

64. Jim Geraghty, "*New York Times* Columnist Mocks Romney's 'Magic Underwear,'" NationalReview.com, February 23, 2012, http://www.nationalreview.com/campaign-spot/291858/inew-york-timesi-columnist-mocks-romneys-magic-underwear, accessed July 2012.

CONCLUSION

1. "Convicted Bomber Brett Kimberlin, Neal Rauhauser, Ron Brynaert, and Their Campaign of Political Terrorism," Patterico.com, May 25, 2012, http://patterico.com/2012/05/25/convicted-bomber-brett-kimberlin-neal-rauhauser-ron-brynaert-and-their-campaign-of-political-terrorism/, accessed July 2012.

2. Erick Erickson, "SWATting the Ericksons," RedState.com, May 27, 2012, http://www.redstate.com/erick/2012/05/27/swatting-the-ericksons/, accessed July 2012.

3. Liberty Chick, "Flashback: Progressives Embrace Convicted Terrorist," Breitbart News, October 11, 2010, http://www.breitbart.com/Big-Journalism/2010/10/11/Progressives-Embrace-Convicted-Terrorist, accessed July 2012.

4. "Convicted Bomber Brett Kimberlin, Neal Rauhauser, Ron Brynaert, and Their Campaign of Political Terrorism."

5. Tiffany Gabbay, "Meet Soros-Funded Domestic Terrorist Brett Kimberlin Whose 'Job' Is Terrorizing Bloggers Into Silence," TheBlaze.com, May 25, 2012, http://www.theblaze.com/stories/readymeet-soros-funded-domestic-terrorist-brett-kimberlin-whose-job-is-terrorizing-bloggers-into-silence/, accessed July 2012.

6. Robert Stacy McCain, "Never Doubt That God Answers Prayers," TheOtherMcCain.com, May 21, 2012, http://theothermccain.com/2012/05/21/never-doubt-that-god-answers-prayer/, accessed July 2012.

7. Mobutu and General Ze'evi, "Andrew Breitbart: Big Deal, Big Coronary, Big Corpse," Gawker.com, March 6, 2012, http://gawker.com/5890660/andrew-breitbart-big-deal-big-coronary-big-corpse, accessed July 2012.

8. "Touré on Breitbart: What He Added To The Discourse Was Dangerous," RealClearPolitics.com, March 1, 2012, http://www.realclearpolitics.com/video/2012/03/01/toure_on_breitbart_what_he_added_to_the_public_discourse_was_dangerous.html, accessed July 2012.

9. "Andrew Breitbart's death: The 'astonishing' liberal gloating," TheWeek.com, March 2, 2012, http://theweek.com/article/index/225097/andrew-breitbarts-death-the-astonishing-liberal-gloating, accessed July 2012.

10. Charlie Spiering, "Liberals celebrate death of Andrew Breitbart," WashingtonExaminer.com, March 5, 2012, http://washingtonexaminer.com/article/1153471, accessed July 2012.

ACKNOWLEDGMENTS

In writing a book like this, there are dozens of people who aid, comfort, and inspire the author. First and foremost is my wife, Mor, who has somehow balanced her course load at UCLA Medical School with being the best wife on the planet. Having met Mor is the best thing that ever happened to me; spending each day with her is the greatest joy of my life.

My parents, David and Cindy Shapiro, are the best structure any son could ask for—they happen to be both unceasingly supportive and uncompromisingly fun. The same goes for my three younger sisters, who shall remain anonymous—they all earn a living in arenas dominated by liberal bullies. I see no reason for making those bullies' task easier—although I would not urge them to mess with my sisters.

My agent, Frank Breeden, has been a godsend. I've never met a more principled businessman, or a more honorable person.

The folks at Simon & Schuster have been terrific throughout this process. Mitchell Ivers, my editor, knows everything that needs to be done to hone a book to a razor's edge; I hope this book stands as proof of that fact. If not, the shortcoming is mine.

Larry Solov and Steve Bannon have been fantastic bosses at Breitbart News—and they've carried forward Andrew's banner as nobody else could have done. The opportunity to work with them each day to bear Andrew's torch is an honor beyond measure. My partner in crime and close friend Alex Marlow sat next to Andrew for five years—he was Andrew's first hire at Breitbart News. He embodies Andrew's vision for the site, and he imbibed Andrew's news judgment day after day. It shows. My other colleagues at Breitbart News, including but not limited to Joel Pollak, John Nolte, Larry O'Connor, Mike Flynn, Ezra Dulis, William Bigelow, Tony Lee, Michael Patrick Leahy, Meredith Dake, and the rest, make each hour memorable. A more driven team you will not find.

The radio team at Salem has given me a supreme opportunity to sit behind their microphone at KRLA 870 and KTIE 590 in Los Angeles and Orange County, respectively. Ed Atsinger is a true visionary; Terry Fahy and Chuck Tyler are paragons of radio professionalism, and I couldn't go on the air every day without their guidance and advice. A special thanks, of course, to Phil Boyce, a radio genius who was both kind enough and brave enough to give a twenty-eight-year-old a shot on LA morning drive.

The David Horowitz Freedom Center is a true fighting outfit, and they take the fight to the bullies unsparingly. Thanks especially to David Horowitz, Mike Finch, Peter Collier, and Jamie Glazov for their help and input.

The folks at Creators Syndicate, particularly Rick and Jack Newcombe, who spotted me when I was a seventeen-year-old sophomore at UCLA. If it hadn't been for them, I'd probably be in the back of the first-violin section of an orchestra somewhere.

Thanks to all those in the conservative movement who continue to inspire me—the tireless guardians of conservatism who never apologize, never compromise, and never stop pushing for American renewal.

Most of all, thanks to the Americans who keep fighting the odds—who keep fighting the bullies. It's thanks to you that this country continues to move forward. And it's thanks to you that we won't lose hope for true change.

Now let's gird ourselves for battle.

INDEX

★